Publisher's Note

The book descriptions we ask book-sellers to display prominently warn that the book may have numerous typos, missing text, images and indexes.

We scanned this book using character recognition software that includes an automated spell check. Our software is 99 percent accurate if the book is in good condition. However, we do understand that even one percent can be a very annoying number of typos! And sometimes all or part of a page is missing from our copy of a book. Or the paper may be so discolored from age that you can no longer read the type. Please accept our sincere apologies.

After we re-typeset and design a book, the page numbers change so the old index and table of contents no longer work. Therefore, we often remove them.

We would like to manually proof read and fix the typos and indexes, manually scan and add any illustrations, and track down another copy of the book to add any missing text. But our books sell so few copies, you would have to pay up to a thousand dollars for the book as a result.

Therefore, whenever possible, we let our customers download a free copy of the original typo-free scanned book. Simply enter the barcode number from the back cover of the paperback in the Free Book form at www.general-books. net. You may also qualify for a free trial membership in our book club to download up to four books for free. Simply enter the barcode number from the back cover onto the membership form on the same page. The book club entitles you to select from more than a million books at no additional charge. Simply enter the title or subject onto the search form to find the books.

If you have any questions, could you please be so kind as to consult our Frequently Asked Questions page at www. general-books.net/faqs.cfm? You are also welcome to contact us there.

General Books LLC®, Memphis, USA, 2012. ISBN: 9781150183751.

⊰⋅ ⊰⋅ ⊰⋅ ⊰⋅ ⊰⋅ ⊰⋅ ⊰⋅

PREFACE.

In the year 1849 appeared "The History of Leicester from the Time of the Romans to the End of the Seventeenth Century" and in 1871 "The History of Leicester in the Eighteenth Century," but no separate work published by the Author has brought down the entire narrative to the present period, or included it in one volume. This Pocket-edition is intended to serve two purposes— to form a concise but complete History of the Town from the earliest to the latest date, and to bring it within the reach of readers of all classes; in short, to make it a household book, enabling every inhabitant to form a general idea of the origin, progress and development of this now prosperous community. It is hoped the brief Index attached will be found acceptable and useful.

Leicester, March, 1876.

THE HISTORY OF LEICESTER. THE ROMAN PERIOD.

A.d. 50 To 450.

Chapter I.

Fifty years before the Christian Era, the inhabitants of this island were almost wholly unknown to that part of the world which was then civilized. When the first of the Caesars made a partial conquest of the Britons, the record of his achievement only occupied a few lines in the memoir of one of his biographers: it was only regarded as one of the incidents of his governorship of Ancient France. But the conqueror himself gave a more detailed account of his successes, in which, in terms clear and concise, he describes what he saw after he had landed on our shores—tells of the occupations and character of the people— and pictures the aspect of the country. The inhabitants of the districts lying on the south coast of Britain were then living in buildings like those of the Gauls on the opposite coast; they were corn-growers and had abundance of cattle;

they were very numerous, and they used pieces of brass or iron instead of money. The wild tribes of the interior did not cultivate the earth; they lived on milk and flesh, and clothed themselves with skins. They stained their bodies with a blue dye made from woad, to give themselves a fierce aspect in battle. Their towns were places in the fastnesses of the woods, surrounded by a mound and trench. These were further defended by the trunks and boughs of trees cut from the neighbouring forests, which formed barricades round such settlements. They were not always places of permanent abode; but when formed on meadows, on the banks of rivers, where their cattle could be depastured, and water could be had, they would probably be habitually occupied.

Situate in the very heart of the southern division of the island, the locality now occupied by Leicester was then, it may be presumed, such a place as that above described, where a river flowed with sinuous course, and making a bend in which a tribe of Britons could pitch their group of wigwams, they had a settlement. York, Chester, and other towns of acknowledged Roman origin, supposed to have been founded on the sites of similar British settlements, have this peculiarity; and the 'Leir, which ran with unobstructed flow to the Trent, afforded where this town now stands such a spot as the aboriginal population desired for their periodical sojourn.

But in the first century of the Christian era the scene was altered. Instead of a wooded meadow, lying on a bank sloping towards a wide and shallow river, with huts scattered about among the trees—instead of circular cabins with low walls, covered with conical roofs of straw, and having a doorway which served all purposes to the inhabitants— a town grew up before the century concluded. First of all, probably, an encampment was formed by the foreigners who came here; the natives having fled on their approach to seek shelter at a distance, or in the mighty forests which then covered the centre of our island. The foreigners were Italians, who arrived in an army headed by a general named Ostorius Scapula, who is believed to have conquered the people of these inland parts some time between the years 50 and 55, in the reign of the Emperor Nero. The same reasons which induced the ancient Britons to dwell on the site prevailed with the strangers (whom we know as Romans) to continue upon it as its occupants: the river flowing by afforded them a supply of water, and interposed, on the north and west, a hindrance to attack by the people whom they had driven from their homes. Other propraetors or generals succeeded Ostorius Scapula; at last, one more able and more noted than others arrived, who effected great changes in the island. His name was Julius Agricola. It was towards the close of the summer of the year 78 he assumed the government of Britain. Whether it was Ostorius Scapula in the middle of the century, or Julius Agricola, at a somewhat later period, who laid out the encampment where Leicester now stands, cannot be definitely affirmed; but it is a matter of history that between the years 78 and 84 Agricola formed a number of settled stations in the southern part of the country. These were rectangular in shape, and surrounded by stone walls and deep fosses.

It is considered highly probable that the site of York was occupied as a military station, by the soldiers of Agricola, when the people of the district were reduced to subjection by that eminent commander in his second campaign, in the summer of the year 79. As Agricola would pass by this locality on his way to York, it may be presumed he would lay the foundations of our Roman town walls either in that or the preceding year. A high antiquarian authority (Roy), after carefully examining the camps of Agricola, found reason to conclude that the system of camp-making made use of by that personage was about the same as that described by Polybius. The outline of his camps was rectangular. This was the shape of the outer walls of Roman York, as it was of those of Leicester—and of all the great stations on the military roads laid down by Antoninus—another piece of indirect evidence of Agricola having been the general under whose authority they were both planned and completed. Moreover, the Polybian camp measured on each side 2150 Roman feet—the Roman walls of Leicester measured 2500 Roman feet long by 2000 feet broad. The Roman walls of York were of the same form and description, though not so extensive. Within the space thus enclosed a population of from 10,000 to 12,000 would find habitation.

At the commencement, these walls formed a complete oblong or square, and about the middle of each of them was a gateway. Thus, in many or most of the towns in this country, existing where Roman camps once stood, there is a North, South, East, and West Gate. As the reader is aware, Leicester still retains the names; and doubtless the gateways which were taken down about a hundred years ago, though built long after, occupied nearly the same sites as those of Roman construction.

At this point, the station becomes a town, and its history, strictly speaking, commences. In due course, buildings of a public character — the court-house, the temple, the bath, the theatre, the governor's residence; and buildings of a private nature—the mansions of the officials and the houses of the privileged inhabitants, with the huts of the lower class,—fill the space included by the stone walls which have by this time taken the place of the earthen ramparts round the station. A regular market for the sale of the produce of the neighbouring country becomes established, and artisans and traders are induced to fix their abodes within the boundaries. The Roman language becomes spoken, the Roman dress adopted, and Roman laws obeyed. We have it on the authority of Tacitus, the historian, that Julius Agricola (the governor of the islands in the reigns of Vespasian, Titus, and Domitian) in the year 79 of our era exerted himself to promote these changes. In the outset Ratæ was a stipendiary town,

paying a certain fixed sum annually to the Imperial Government, and being under the exclusive control of the military prefect or ruler.

Within thirty years after the date of the supposed formation of the encampment on the Leir, its transformation into a regularly-organized town had in all prohability been effected. The advancement of the place must have been continuous; for its name occurs in the geography of Ptolemy, published in the commencement of the second century, about forty years after the date of Agricola's governorship. At this time it is known to the Romans by the name of Ratæ.

This name is so peculiar as to invite enquiry into its origin. It is the plural form of the noun, and implies that there was more than one town included under the designation. Venonæ (now Claybrooke) had a similar signification. As, among the ancients, Athens was called Athenæ as comprehending four distinct villages, and Syracuse, Syracusæ, as made up of five, so it would seem that Ratæ was used to denominate two, or perhaps three, British settlements closely adjoining to each other. The term in the singular number would be Rath Rat—derived probably from a Celtic word signifying a place cleared for the purpose of habitation, which the Romans adopted, adding the final diphthong to express the plural number. When Ptolemy spoke of this town by the name Ratæ, it was know to all travellers through the island by the same designation; as there was then standing on one of its highways, on the road to Lindum Colonia Lincoln), a mile-stone which told the passer-by that Ratæ was three miles distant. Erected in honour of the Emperor Hadrian, while it served as a milliary it also probably commemorated his visit to this part of the dominions, or was one result of that visit. In the customary language of adulation, used at the time by Roman subjects as an evidence of their loyally, it is dedicated to " The Emperor Csesar, Trajan, Adrian Augustus, son of the Divine Trajan Parthicus, Superior Pontiff, Consul for the third time."

The survey of Ptolemy was made

known to the world about the same year as that in which this milliary was raised, namely, the year 120. The mention of Ratae in such a work, coupled with its designation on a milestone as the starting-point to another place, in the reign of Hadrian, is suggestive of the importance which the station had then obtained in the estimation of learned men and public officers. In succeeding reigns, we are told, this island enjoyed a long period of peace and prosperity. During the sway of the Antonines, the empire reposed after the troubles and turbulence of the preceding century, and the inhabitants of Britain were left to prosecute their peaceful pursuits uninterrupted, except when the Caledonians rose against the Roman authorities in the northern districts. In the reign of Commodus there was a mutiny of the British troops; but it was not attended with any aefcual collision between them and the Emperor. When Severus assumed the purple, at the close of the second century, this province had become "extremely populous and rich. Multitudes of auxiliary troops had been gradually transplanted into it, and had no doubt taken with them or been followed by colonies of their countrymen. Merchants, tradesmen, artisans, even probably artists, and men of letters, had sought their fortune where the increase of commerce and civilization opened a field for their exertions." The freedom of the city had now been bestowed on the greater proportion of the subjects of the Empire; and Caracalla 211 to 217 A. d. extended it to the whole body of the natives. Subsequent to his reign, therefore, all the British towns enjoyed the rights of Roman citizens. They had a government of their own, resembling that of the ancient constitution of Rome, and exempt from all control by its officers. Speaking generally, the Roman *municipium* established in Ratae would consist of the people, or *plebs,* and the governing body, or *euria.*

At this epoch the space within the walls was doubtless found too limited to contain the houses required for the accommodation of the inhabitants. The safest side to build on, in those times,

was the space between the western wall and the river; and that it was so appropriated the frequent discovery of Roman remains iu that quarter attests. The Jewrywall-street pavement (which was what in modern times would be called the drawing-room of the mansion) proves the use of the situation for a large house outside the Western wall; and many other remains indicate the former existence of extensive edifices between the original Western gateway and the river. The point of intersection of the two main streets was, however, a locality conspicuous for various reasons. Here, in the military camp, were originally the quarters of the General; close to it the market-place; and, around, the spots allotted for the tents of the principal officers. It is remarkable that the very site of the High Cross of Leicester, where the vegetable market is now held every Wednesday, is nearly identical with that on which the Roman-Britons would place their commodities for sale when the camp was first formed by the soldiers of Agricola. It is equally remarkable that, close to the High Cross, where the General's quarters lay, while Ratae was a Roman camp only, and where, afterwards, the Governor's residence was erected, discoveries of columns have justified the belief the Basilica or Court House once extended, with its surrounding colonnades; the laws of Rome having been administered there year after year, by the Generals, the Governors, and the Prefects of Ratae during the four hundred years in which they held possession of this country. Judging by the fragments of columns, still preserved, this structure was large and stately, standing between 30 and 40 feet above the street-level, in width between 90 and 100 feet; in depth between 40 and 50. Other remains of a similar character, but varying in detail and proportion, found in Blue Boar Lane, and two others at the lower end of St. Nicholas-street, indicate the existence, within the area included by Highcross-street, Blue Boar Lane, the Holy Bones, and St. Nicholas-street of at least four important public buildings; and some of these remains aie splashed with lead;

suggestive of destruction by fire, when the molten fluid from the roof and gutters flowed down upon the standing columns.

The inhabitants of Roman Leicester, like their contemporaries in the other towns of Britain, had their temples, where their gods were worshipped by incantations, and sacrifices of animals were offered. The two places in Ratae, where temples reared their porticoes and pediments, are now occupied by the churches of St. Martin and St. Nicholas. The latter-named of the two temples probably rose on the conversion of the Western gateway to a new purpose, and was attached to it; the former was traced by the uncovering of the foundation walls, on the reerection of the tower of St. Martin's, a few years ago. It was not large; but the ground plan was in part made out, and the bases of columns of the Ionic order were met with in their original position, the line of frontage being carried in the direction of Highcross-street.

In the neighbourhood of temples, it is said, the bones of the animals sacrificed in Pagan rites were buried. In the Holy Bones (the name given to the street passing by the east end of Saint Nicholas' Church), such bones have been dug up in large quantities; as also beneath the steeple of Saint Martin's. In the latter case the bones lay in all directions, in large numbers, as if cast in without care or order. They were much decayed, and apparently thrown into the earth at a remote date. Of the pictures formed by these heathen temples, only conjecture can be hazarded. That which preceded the Church of St. Martin was an oblong; having a portico, with overhanging pediment in front, sheltering the raised platform on which the priests officiated and despatched the animals they offered up to their imaginary deities. Whether the temple on the site of St. Nicholas was of the same description, it is impossible to say with certainty; but the likelihood is that it would be, as it was the usual style of the heathen places of worship. Besides the public buildings already named, there were in the Roman-British towns theatres and amphitheatres. No fragment of these has yet been turned up in Leicester. A slight relic (believed by antiquaries of repute to be genuine) lying in one of the cases in the Town Museum tells a story of its own. It purports, by the letters scratched upon it, to have been presented by a gladiator named Lucius to a female named Verecunda Lydia, his sweet-heart. Should this rude and simple relic have really been what it appears to have been, the love-token of a gladiator, then it implies the presence of a class of men in Ratae whose avocation it was to slaughter each other, in the presence of the people, for their amusement on holiday occasions.

Passing from the public buildings to the streets and private dwellings, it is to be noticed that the latter were usually of one storey only, and of slighter construction than our modern houses. Of the number of these mansions, the frequent discovery of tesselated pavements, all over the area of the central part of modern Leicester, bears testimony too impressive to be questioned, and too instructive to be neglected in any estimate of the ancient state of the town. The streets seem to have been narrow in Roman-British towns generally, and Roman Leicester would not prove in this respect exceptional.

With regard to the sanitary arrangements of the place, testimony is producible from the fact of the disdiscovery of the main sewer of the Roman town, eighty years ago. The culvert had doubtless been carried along the main street from East to West, and received from the house-drains on both sides the refuse of the dwellings. Roman sewers (similar in shape to that just named) have been found in Lincoln, made of excellent masonry, and in a good state of preservation. In connection with the Roman sewer in Leicester, a branch was observed, which ran in a north-easterly direction to the town: it was made of large blocks of freestone hewn in the centre. In connection with the sewers, it may be noticed that public *latrina* seem to have been provided outside the gateways. Deep wells or pits were dug beneath them, which have occasionally been found, full of relics of the Roman inhabitants. The pit discovered in Church-gate, not many years since, close to the conjectured site of the Eastern gateway, was in connection with one of these places. For their daily supplies of water the people were dependent to a great extent on public arrangements; private wells being scarce. Troughs or tanks were set up in central or conspicuous situations, to which the inhabitants resorted; one of these, taken out of the ground at the High Cross, the very centre of Ratae, is still preserved. Outside the South wall, on the site now occupied by Millstone-lane and adjoining streets, so many traces of human interments have been from time to time discovered as to lead to the inference that there lay the cemetery of the Rataean population; while the turning-up of human bones in glass jars, still further away from the town, in separate and different localities, has shown that there existed also private burial-grounds during the Roman epoch.

Early in the fourth century, during the rule of Constantine, an Itinerary, or road-book, was compiled. In this work Ratae appears in several places. It occurs on the sixth Iter, from London to Lincoln, between Venonae Claybrook and Vernometum Willoughby-on-the-Woulds; and in the eighth Iter, from York to Lincoln, between Vernometum and Venonae. In these instances, Ratae is represented to be twelve Roman miles from Venonae and Vernometum—a distance nearly equivalent to eleven English miles. Thus we are left to infer that about the year 320—the date of the Itinerary—by means of public highways, the station was in direct and continual communication with the other great centres of population, of commerce, and of local government in this country. In all probability it was the seat of district authority, whence emanated the laws of the empire, and to whose courts the inhabitants, alike within and without the walls, were amenable.

We do not know what part Ratae played in the history of the island at the close of the period of the Roman government. By what class of auxiliary soldiers it had been populated—of what race they were—we are left entirely ignorant. The discovery of a tile, bearing upon it the stamp of the Eighth Legion, has, however, led to the inference of that body of soldiery having been stationed in Leicester in the latter part of the third century. It appears likely that the river flowing by the town was known to the inhabitants by the name of the Leir, which in its derivation is identical with the Loire. Between the two streams there is no resemblance in respect of breadth, or length, or natural features; and therefore these could not have suggested the application of the same word to the designation of the river near Ratae; though if a body of Gaulish soldiers, draughted from the districts on the banks of the Loire, were here settled by the Roman military authorities, they might have called the river by the same name as that with which they were familiar in their native plains, and have known it as the Ligur or Leir. This may be a thread too slight to hang a conjecture upon; but where History is silent, and Archaeology incommunicative, Conjecture may be left free to exercise itself in relation to the past, and sometimes serves as a valuable pioneer to discovery.

Honorius having withdrawn his troops from Britain in 411, it is on record that in the year 441, Britain, after many bloody encounters, was reduced under the rule of the Saxons. At this time, then, Ratae passes into another stage of its history—gradually, no doubt, and by no means in that abrupt manner in which it might be supposed to do; but the empire of Rome then ceased directly to influence it in respect to law, language, policy, religion, and all those matters that constitute the sum total of social and political government. It was left to encounter whatever fate might be in store for it, without help from any foreign quarter, and with a future uncertain and unpromising.

THE SAXON AND DANISH PERIOD. A.d. 450 To 1066.

Chapter II.

On the withdrawal of the Roman garrisons from this island, immigrants of a totally different race and character began, by degrees, to settle on the eastern and in its midland districts. A people who came from the banks of the Elbe, and the district known as Angeln or Anglia, and were thence called " Angles," after subjugating the natives, selected the midlands as their future home; and they gave the name " Angle "-land or England to this country, and Mercia to the central province. For many generations they occupied the land in separate communities; but after the lapse of about one hundred and forty years subsequent to the departure of the Romans, the Mercians acknowledged one chieftain named Crida. They had not as yet recognized any form of Christianity; they were heathens —worshippers of Wodin and other fabulous deities.

About the middle of the seventh century, however 653, Peada, a descendant of the old Mercian chieftains, was baptised a Christian by Bishop Finan on his marriage with Alhflseda, the daughter of Oswy, king of Northumberland. When he returned to his home in this part of the country, he brought with him four priests, to whom he entrusted the conversion of his subjects. One of these, named Diuma, was appointed Bishop of the Middle Angles, and is supposed to have been seated at Beppington, in Derbyshire, at one period the capital of Mercia, where he died. At this time the Roman British station Ratae had become known by the Saxons as Lygeraceastre, Ligoraceastre, or Legraceastre; the word signifying the "Camp on the River Lyger" or Leir. What events had happened to its inhabitants, or what fate had befallen the place itself, history does not relate; but many of its stately stone buildings had survived the vicissitudes of a period of violent warfare and frequent struggles between the natives and the northern barbarians and invading Angles.

The early Bishops of Mercia had, it is recorded, their residence in this town. In the year 679, a quarter of a century after the conversion of Peada, Theodore, Archbishop of Canterbury, divided the kingdom of Mercia into four dioceses, of which Leicester became one; though afterwards united to Lichfield for a term of years—the town and region around not becoming an independent see until Totta or Torthelm was appointed its first regular bishop, in or about the year 731. It was in the interval intervening between the conversion of Peada, and the formation of a Diocese under Totta or Torthelm, that the first church consecrated for Christian worship was erected on the site of St. Margaret's, in this town, with a rudelyconstructed residence near it for the bishop, and that Leicester became a "city"—a designation which seems never to have been wholly abandoned, during twelve centuries, though for ages it has ceased to be the actual see of a Bishop. It is very probable the formation of parishes followed the settlement of Totta in Leicester, with the erection of churches, which in the first instance were merely chambers, with altars at one end, lighted on both sides by unglazed openings, and having seats carried round them, and a low bell-tower rising above the roof; the whole being constructed of timber framework, with mud and plaster filling in the interstices. The bishop himself was originally a humble Christian missionary, the head of a band of priests, whose labours he directed and stimulated. Their teachings were those of the Catholic Church before the introduction of the doctrine of transubstantiation, the celibacy of the priesthood, the pretension to infallibility, auricular confession, and the elevation of the host; and they enforced these doctrines upon the reluctant notice of a heathen population. The first churches were St. Margaret's, St. Martin's, and St Nicholas; the two last named (as already remarked) occupying the sites of Roman temples; and three others were built in course of time. These were All Saints, St. Peter's, and St. Michael's, the first-named only now standing.

Contemporaneous with the conversion to Christianity of the Saxons or Early English—for they were, in fact, our English forefathers, speaking what would sound in modern ears as a rude and unintelligible form of our language—was their establishment of local institutions. These were chiefly two— the Portmanmote and the Merchant Guild. The former was a court in which disputes as to right to property, actions for debt, and similar affairs were settled: the latter was constituted for purposes more strictly speaking municipal and commercial—as, for example, the defence of the town, the maintenance and repair of the walls, the raising of the taxes (general and local), the regulation of the trade of the members, and their mutual protection against the assaults of the violent and powerful nobles living outside the walls. They had a building in which they transacted their business, and occasionally feasted together, called the Guild Hall. Every member had a small plot of land on which his dwelling of one storey stood, called his burgage, the possession of which constituted him a burgess. For this he made an annual payment to the lord of the district. Within their walls, the burgesses of Leicester enjoyed a considerable amount of personal and social freedom, and the advantages of local self-government. At this time the country was almost covered with woods, which came close up to the walls of the town on tts northern and western sides, the south side alone having been cleared after the district became occupied by the Romans. When the Anglo-Saxons took possession of the country, this tract was doubtless allotted to the free classes among them; there being then a large class of the "unfree," constituted in great part, probably, of the conquered Celts, who were treated as an enslaved portion of the population. As nearly every free burgess kept a cow or a horse, the right to pasturage in the meadows on the south side of Leicester was of daily use and importance.

For some generations after the appointment of a Christian Bishop among them, the English residents in Leicester must have enjoyed comparative peace and prosperity. But towards the close of the eighth century the Saxons and Angles of the Midlands began to be harassed by the landing of strangers from

Norway and Denmark, on the eastern side of the island. Shiploads, or more properly speaking boatloads, of these unwelcome intruders were continually arriving at the Wash and at the mouth of the Humber, where they anchored their small craft while they made short and hurried incursions into this and neighbouring districts. They were mostly young men, banded in companies, each company being headed by a chief called a *viking*. Strong, active, and fearless, they carried with them battle-axes, or large swords, and bucklers, which they wielded with terrible effect in fighting. They were heathens—their pleasure being in bloody encounters, and their heaven a place where they might amuse themselves for ever in conflicts hand-tohand, and carousing afterwards, drinking mead from the skulls of their enemies. They " met death with a laugh. " Their music was the roar of the waves—their recreation a stormy voyage —and their business piracy and conquest. They despised and hated the Saxons for having become Christians—they thought they were fools because they sang psalms and believed in "White Christ," instead of glorying in the din of battle and worshipping Odin. These foreigners were not tall, but compact and strongly built; they had broad faces and rather high cheek bones; their hair was generally light, or of a deep red colour; and they were ruddy-faced men. They rowed in boats up the Humber, and the Trent, and the tributary streams; and, where possible, seized the horses of the countrypeople, and rode inland—attacking the natives right and left, setting fire to churches and monasteries, and not hesitating to murder or kidnap people, when they thought it convenient to do so. These men were known as the Northmen, or, more commonly as "The Danes."

In the year 871 Leicester and Derby were taken by the Danes. At this time, those two towns, with Nottingham, Lincoln, and Stamford, formed a Danish confederation, known as the ' Five Boroughs." The vain and insolent foreigners, the "Lord-Danes" (as the people called them), with their long locks of red hair, and their formidable battle-axes thrown over their shoulders, swaggered through the ancient streets, and insulted the women, to the great mortification of the old natives of the locality. For forty years they remained masters of Leicester; until Ethelflceda, the daughter of the noble and patriotic Alfred, provoked by the ravages committed in Oxfordshire, by the Danes from Leicester and Northampton, collected her forces together and advanced upon the latter place, which she captured, and then took Derby, with great loss of men and four of her principal commanders. In simple terms the Saxon Chronicle says, "This year 920 Ethelfloeda got into her power, with God's assistance, in the early part of the year, without loss, the town of Leicester, and the greater part of the army that belonged thereto submitted to her." Mercia was now governed by kings, of whom Athelstane was one; and when he reigned Leicester was recaptured by the Danes. A mint was established here about this period, the site of which appears to have been near the North Bridge; specimens of the coins struck in Leicester, with the names of the moneyers upon them, being still preserved in the cabinets of the antiquary and the collector. Between the years 925 and 940 the Danes remained in possession of the town. Edmund encountered near Leicester, in 941, Onlaf, King of Norway, with whom and his army, he and his forces had a deadly conflict, which continued for the greater part of a day; neither of the contending parties obtaining a decisive advantage over the other. Through the mediation of Odo, Archbishop of Canterbury, and Wulfstan, Archbishop of York, the hostile monarchs came to an agreement that Onlaf should be left in possession of the portion of the country lying north of Watling Street, and Edmund of that southward of the line thus marked out—the survivor of the two to succeed to the sovereignty of the entire kingdom. The Norwegian King dying shortly after, Edmund obtained undisputed rule over England. In the year 942 the Saxon Chronicle, already quoted, relates that Edmund the king, "Lord of the Angles, the protector of his friends, the author and framer of direful deeds," over-ran speedily the land of Mercia wherever the course of "Whitwell Spring," or the " Deep Humber," the broad stream, divided the Five Boroughs.

B

They had long "bowed their heads in thraldom to the Danes, and dragged the fetters imposed on them by the Heathens, until, to his glory, King Edmund, the heir of the great Edward, the refuge of warriors, broke their chains, and made them free." For a period of seventyone years Leicester was in the hands of the Angles or English; from the year 1013 to 1041 it fell again into those of the Danes. On the accession of Edward the Confessor, the English again resumed possession, and held it until the time arrived when the invincible William of Normandy crushed alike Angle and Dane beneath the iron heel of conquest

In the time of the Confessor, Leicester was still called "a city." It enjoyed municipal rights; for the Merchant Guild was nearly identical with what, in more modern days, is called the "Corporation." The inhabitants yearly paid to the king thirty pounds of silver by tale, or number, and twenty to the ora, a Danish coin, with twenty-two and a half pounds of honey; and when the royal army was called out, twelve burgesses were bound to accompany it in the campaign. Should the king go beyond the sea against the enemy, the townspeople were obliged to send four horses as far as London to carry arms and baggage. The money would be equivalent to 1980 modern shillings, or £99; when the metallic currency had a much greater value than in modern days. This yearly tribute having been paid, the honey delivered, specified military services rendered, and the sumpter-horses supplied, the people of Leicester made their own laws, and governed themselves in Saxon times, according to their old customs; with little or no interference from external authority. Virtually, the town was a small and primitive republic; subject only to the incidence of the taxes and obligations already described.

THE NORMAN PERIOD.

A.d. 1066 To 1206.

Chapter III.

With the Conquest hy the Normans, a great and disastrous revolution was effected. For the mild and nominal rule of the native kings, the stern and oppressive rule of the resident Norman Barons was substituted. In the summer of 1068, two years after the battle of Hastings, William, accompanied by his army, assaulted Leicester; and he was resisted with such fierceness and desperation that the town, with the castle and adjoining church, was almost entirely destroyed. Twenty years after, when the Doomsday Survey was taken, there were 322 houses, the castle, the church within its precincts, and six churches besides, still standing. It may be assumed the six churches were St. Margaret's (without the walls), St. Martin's, St. Nicholas', All Saints', St. Peter's and St. Michael's (both since destroyed) —all once the centres of parishes. A population of about 3000 (including the burgesses and their families and dependents) was dwelling in the borough and its precincts, when the Conqueror besieged the place and made it his own. No detailed account has reached modern times of the event; but it is clear the assailants directed their principal efforts against the Castle, as that and the adjoining church were nearly destroyed in the assault; though the greater part of the houses were shattered and overturned. On the complete conquest of the inhabitants, their houses were shared up among the Conqueror's principal followers. The Norman Earl, Hugh de Grantmesnil (who had probably commanded on the occasion of the siege), obtained the larger share: to him were allotted 206 out of the 322 houses, most of them rendered tenantless by the death of their owners while engaged in defending their homes. The remainder were allotted to the king, the Bishop of Lincoln, the Archbishop of York, the Earl of Chester, Coventry Abbey, Croyland Abbey, Robert de Vecy, Geoffrey de Wirce, and the Countess Judith (the Conqueror's niece by marriage)—to the

Norman and other adventurers who accompanied William on his expedition. What remained of the townsmen who survived the slaughter became the serfs of the victors: 37 of them were subjected to de Grantmesnil; 17 to the Bishop of Lincoln; and one of the burgesses was the joint property of Henry de Ferrers and Robert, the king's steward. It hence seems that of the 322 homes devastated, only 55 retained their masters after the siege—the others having either fallen or deserted their ruined dwellings.

The condition of the surviving inhabitants, after their town had been besieged, their public buildings destroyed, their houses burnt, their goods taken away, and the heads of households killed in the struggle, may be imagined: for some years following the calamity the town would be a mere wreck, and the population reduced to a few miserable and abject serfs, with their wives and families. The self-government they had enjoyed in the days of Edward the Confessor was exchanged for dependence upon the Norman lord of the town, Hugh de Grantmesnil, who ruled the majority of the people through his agents and officials with absolute and unchecked dominion. He was in effect king over the town and district. His residence was the Castle, and he lived with a garrison continually around him and at his command. He treated the inhabitants as his slaves, and swept away all local institutions without scruple or reserve. The Merchant Guild and the Portmanmote were set aside, and the townsmen were made wholly dependent on the will of their imperious masters. Instead of carrying on their local trade with each other, and with the people of other places, with freedom and safety, as before the Conquest, under the operations of the Merchant Guild, they were now subject to irksome restrictions and to petty annoyances. Instead of settling their disputes in the Town Court or Portmanmote, before a jury of twenty-four burgesses, as they did of old, they were now compelled to settle them by the ordeal of battle. Hitherto, the right to gather wood from the groves which

grew close up to the ancient walls, for fuel to supply their hearths, for wood to build their houses, and for making fences, had been undisputed, and freely exercised; but in order to get it, the people had to cross the North and West Bridges. The Norman earl placed his men there and made the townsmen pay a tax on passing over, which he called "brigg" or "bridge silver." Up to this time, every free inhabitant had a right of commonage for his horse or cow upon the fields south of Leicester, without payment, as before noticed. The Norman earl took the land into his own hands, and made every man pay a certain sum for pasturage. Before the Conquest, in the reign of the Confessor, the burgesses knew no master, except the king, to whom they were obliged to make a yearly acknowledgment in the form already described. Now, under the tyrant Norman, they were made to sow his corn and gather his harvests, and do his field-labour, as his serfs, by the commands of his bailiffs and deputies. Such was the degradation to which the English townsmen had been brought by the overthrow of their compatriots at the battle of Hastings.

Within twelve years after the siege, the yearly levy made upon the inhabitants for the king's use was increased from thirty pounds of silver to forty-two pounds and ten shillings—the pounds being literally pounds' weight of silver; and, in addition, instead of sending the Conqueror a hawk, ten pounds of silver were raised, and instead of a sumpter horse, twenty shillings—it is supposed yearly. Of the minters in the borough he had twenty pounds, of which the earl claimed every third penny. The hurgesses were not only compelled to raise the taxes imposed upon them by their separate masters; but, it thus seems, had to furnish the royal purse with the sums mentioned.

Hugh de Grantmesnil remained Lord of Leicester (with a brief interruption) from the year 1068 to the year 1094, when he died, and his son is supposed to have succeeded him. In the course of his reign over the town, he took part with other Norman barons in attempting to place the Conqueror's eldest son, Robert, on the throne which "William Rufus had usurped. The enterprize failed; but Rufus ordered an army to assault the town, and particularly to fall upon that portion where the Castle and the houses belonging to the earl were situate, and the Church of St. Mary again suffered much injury in consequence. The town was taken and the townspeople plundered. On this occasion the troops were commanded by Robert, Earl of Meulan or Mellent, who afterwards became Earl of Leicester. As a young man he had acquired distinction among the companions of the Conqueror by having been the commander of the right wing of the Norman army, at the battle of Hastings, when he broke in upon the opposing division of the English army; thus leading the onslaught in that memorable engagement. Sixteen lordships in Leicestershire were granted to him by William as the reward of his services on that occasion, and his adherence to the cause of William Rufus was followed by his promotion in due course to the earldom of Leicester. He became the first of a line of resident barons who occupied the Castle as their stronghold for several generations.

In this edifice, therefore, much historic interest centres. What were the size, outlines, and nature of the construction of the former building, erected by the Saxons, no existing remains and no historical references enable us to conceive; though it is undoubted that the site on which the present building called the Castle stands was the fortress of the rulers of the place from the earliest date subsequent to the settlement of the Saxons—whether it was so even in the early British and Roman-British periods is a subject left open to conjecture. The Mount adjoining may have been the citadel of the town in primitive times. It was originally between twenty and thirty feet higher than it is at present, and the discovery of skeletons, on the removal of the earth shortly after the commencement of this century, suggests the possibility of its having been at first a burialmound, which was utilized for the purposes of fortification

by the Romans, or their successors. At the time of the Norman Conquest it was surmounted by a rudely-fashioned keep, built of stone, or by a stockaded enclosure. Coexistent with it, to the northward, would be a mansion for the use of the Mercian earls; while, on the western side of the area was probably standing a wooden structure for the accommodation of the garrison, supplanted in aftertimes by the Court House; and on the eastern side rose the chapel designed exclusively for the lords of the Castle and their retainers; the whole of these buildings being engirdled by a wall of defence, the line of which may be traced in the present day.

After the siege by King William, the damage done to the Castle House, the keep, and the church of St. Mary would be repaired, and those edifices were necessarily restored. But they were not destined to remain long unassailed; as, twenty years after, when (as already related) Hugh de Grantmesnil took part with other nobles in the attempted dethronement of William Rufus, they were greatly damaged. When Robert de Beaumont succeeded de Grantmesnil, in the year 1107, he doubtless repaired the damage which his predecessor had done to the Church, and would at the same time restore (if it had not previously been restored) the Castle residence, and reconstruct a stone keep on the Mount. From remains of similar structures still extant, the modern reader may be enabled to form an idea of that erected for his dwelling, by Rohert de Beaumont, when he occasionally stayed in Leicester; for he was by birth a Frenchman, and naturally preferred his native country to his subsequently-adopted home in Leicester. The Castle House of the Norman Earl probably consisted of only a ground floor with a first floor above; the walls being immensely thick, and the doors and windows narrow, and roundarched; the whole being covered in with a high-pitched roof. The rooms would be lighted by windows small towards the exterior, but enlarging inwards. A staircase in the thickness of the wall led up to the upper chamber; and even its ascent was barred by strong

doors secured by bolts. The fabric, indeed, constituted in its way a domestic fortress.

While dwelling here Robert de Beaumont also repaired the Church of St. Mary's, which his troops had damaged on the occasion before mentioned. He placed in it a dean and twelve secular canons, and gave them lands and houses for their support; and appropriated to them all the Churches in Leicester and its suburbs, St. Margaret's excepted. Having been a young man at the Battle of Hastings, he was advancing in years when he was made Earl of Leicester, and his conduct in connection with his burgesses, more particularly in relation to the abolition of the brutal usage of ordeal by battle, may be ascribed to the improved feeling and more humane policy superinduced by reflection as he felt his life was drawing to a close.

It may be inferred that the English burgesses besought him, very soon after his accession to the earldom in 1107, to restore their Guild Merchant, in order that they might once again enjoy the advantages of their old institution which had been withheld from them when the town fell into the hands of the Conqueror. They no doubt offered to the Earl a sum of money, raised from their hard-earned resources, sufficient to secure his compliance with their petition. When the bargain was concluded, the Earl conceded that the burgesses should have his permission to exercise, as privileges, powers which had formerly been their hereditary and unquestioned rights. The concession was committed to writing, inscribed upon a small piece of parchment, and called a " Charter." In order that it might take effect, it was addressed to the Earl's principal steward, or minister, called the Primate, and to all his chief vassals living on his English estates; and was executed in the presence of some distinguished personage. Translated from the Latin in which it was couched, it would read thus in modern English:— "Robert, Earl of Leicester, to R. Ralph, the Primate, and all his barons, French-born as well as English, on all his lands in England— greeting! Know that I have granted to my merchants of Leioester their Guild Merchant, with all their customs which they held in the time of King William, and now hold in the time of Henry the King. Witness: R, the son of Alcitill. '' This charter raised the townspeople once again into comparative freedom; though they were still fettered by many galling regulations. They could meet once more in their old Guild Hall and take council together in respect to their common concerns, and combine together to procure exemption from those regulations and the restrictions imposed upon them by the Earl's myrmidons. A second charter given to them by Robert de Beaumont allowed them to collect wood, as of old, in the adjoining forest, on payment of tolls in crossing the west and north bridges: for a man's burden weekly a farthing, a horse's load weekly a penny, and for six cart loads 7Jd. A third charter was equally important with that which revived the Guild Merchant: it was that which warranted the re-institution of the Portmanmote, and consequently abolished the ordeal by battle

The way in which this was effected, as told in an ancient record, reveals a picture of the state of society in towns, at the commencement of the twelfth century, possessing a wider than local interest. It is therefore here introduced in detail, assisted by the light thrown upon it by general historical knowledge.

Two kinsmen, named respectively Nicholas, the son of Aeon or Hakon, and Geoffrey, the son of Nicholas—Nicholas Akonson and Geoffrey Nicholson as they would now be called — had an irreconcilable dispute, in respect to the right to a piece of land, probably a burgage tenure. As neither would surrender his claim, and there was no court to which to appeal to settle the difference between them, they weℸe obliged to decide the issue by personal combat, as required by their Norman masters. The day was fixed, and the arena would naturally be the Court-yard of the Castle. On one side frowned the donjon-keep from the Mount, on another stood the Church of St. Mary, on the opposite quarter was the Great Hall, and on the fourth side was the house of the Norman

baron. At six o'clock in the morning, apparently in summer, the Usts having been staked out, the soldiery of the Earl, intermingled with the townspeople who had been admitted within the precincts of the fortress, were gathered round in a crowd to be spectators of the duel. In one part of the area a grave had been dug, where the body of the man vanquished in the mortal combat was to be thrown. In another sat the judges who presided over the struggle. The two men dressed in rude armour, wearing red sandals, and bare-legged from the knees downwards, bare-headed, and with arms bare to the elbows, and furnished with staves and bucklers, then entered the arena, and having made oath they had neither eaten nor drunk that day, nor had recourse to sorcery, fell upon each other in deadly conflict. They continued hour after hour giving and receiving blows, neither combatant gaining any decided advantage over his antagonist, until about two o'clock in the afternoon. Eventually, however, one pressed the other to the verge of the open grave, and he was about to fall into it, but was warned by his relenting kinsman, in a moment of compassion, of his immediate danger.

Stirred up by this exhibition of forbearance and the excitement which the prolonged combat had created, the multitude raised a loud shout, which reached Eobert de Beaumont in his house adjoining. He enquired the cause of the clamour, when some of his attendants explained it to him. This led to an interview between him and some of the leading townsmen, in which they made an agreement to pay him a tax of three-pence yearly for every gable in the main street of the borough (then known as the High Street), if he would, by his Charter, restore the operation of the Portmanmote, before which all pleas they might have among themselves might be thereafter discussed and decided. The Earl consented, and the Charter once more brought into force the trial by twenty-four jurors, as it had been in former days.

Eobert de Beaumont married, when in the decline of life, a lady of great

beauty, still young; and she had the reputation of being unfaithful to her lord. He who in worldly affairs was said to have been the wisest man of his time between England and Jerusalem, contracted this unfortunate marriage, which hastened the hour of his decease. The character of the man gleamed out in his last moments, as the dying embers flicker out *di* the flame of the expiring fire; he had entered the fraternity of monks in the abbey at Preaux, in France, and his confessor, as he lay in his chamber, called upon him to make restitution of the possessions he had recovered by evil means, and to repent in tears of his wickedness. The Norman greed and the Norman cunning ruled him in death, as his reply testifies. Instead of being impressed with, a sense of his wrong-doing, in dispossessing the Saxons of their houses and estates, he thought only of maintaining his family. He answered, " If I do so, what shall I leave my sons *t"* The confessor rejoined, "Let them be content with their ancient and just inheritance, and what you have lawfully gotten for them; and do you restore the rest—*or your soul will go to hell."* Evasive, the dying baron again replied, "Nay, I will rather *give all to my sons, and they shall do works of mercy for the health of my soul."* Thus perished Robert de Beaumont, on the 5th of June, 1118.

Robert " The Hunchbacked," known to his French contemporaries as "Le Bossu," from his personal deformity, succeeded his father in the earldom. He had been educated in the palace of Henry I., and had been knighted by him. No sooner had he ascended the canopied chair of his father in the Castle than he would be applied to by the burgesses to grant them the Charters, without obtaining which they felt every local custom was insecure; for no Charter seems to have been binding beyond the lifetime of the grantor. They would have to pay a considerable sum on the renewal of his permission to continue their Guild Merchant as before. This being agreed upon, the Earl addressed his Charter to all his faithful men of France and England, informing them of the fact, and commanding that the burgesses should hold their Guild and all the customs they had enjoyed in the time of his father and his ancestors as well, as honourably, and as peaceably as ever, and even better; thus indicating there was room for improvement in the treatment manifested to them by his officers. By another Charter executed at the same period at Breteuil, in Picardy, directed to all his foresters and servants of the Forest of Leicester, the Earl granted to the townsmen quiet roads for themselves and their deputies, both in wood and in plain, without any dues, to their houses,from whatever part of either forest they might come, as fully or even more so than they had them in the time of his father; forbidding his men to molest the burgesses or their assistants when in the exercise of this usage. His Primate, Ralph, was the witness to this document. By another Charter, dated at Breteuil, the Earl formally notified to his under-sheriff, his justices, and ministers of Leicester, French and English, that he had conceded to his burgesses, of Leicester, and to all who might hold themselves in their company, that they were free from all payments pertaining to hundreds and heriots, in consequence of their accustomed payments, and through an increase of £8 yearly; so that neither on account of any plea, nor any other usage, they should be required to go out of Leicester for their settlement, but only to their Portmanmote, as "of old time was accustomed." When the Earl made this grant, Ralph the Primate, Richard the Master, Baldwin de Granville, and Bernard the Primate, were present. In fact the Earl was surrounded by his Council as witnesses, when the Charter was executed and handed over to the burgesses.

Secure in the possession of their old institutions the burgesses, at the commencement of the rule of Robert le Bossu, were obviously in a better position than when his father began his sway over them. Half a century after the Conquest, they found the restitution of their ancient liberties assured to them, and their lives made happier in consquence. Before his decease, le Bossu remitted the claim to the gavel-pennies which his father had imposed as before mentioned, and for ever quitted all claim to them. This he did for the health or salvation of his father's soul

Robert le Bossu had time to devote to local works in which he took interest, which rendered him necessarily an habitual resident in his Castle of Leicester: he founded the Abbey, and he built the edifice of which the present . County Assize Court shows the remains. To the Abbot and Convent he transferred all the property his father had given to St. Mary of the Castle. Of the Abbey not a fragment has been left above ground. Built in the Transitional Period prevalent in the time of King Stephen, it was a massive structure, having probably a transept, surmounted by a low square tower.

As the evening of life drew near, the Earl did as his father had done—he retired into the shelter of a monastery; it is believed that within the walls of that fabric which once stood near this town, of which he had laid the foundations, he sought the repose he needed, and it is recorded that as he paced the cloisters the aged Hunchback customarily recited verses in praise of holy monks. He died in the year 1168 or 1169, and was buried on the south side of the choir of Leicester Abbey—the first of his family who there found a sepulchre.

This earl was succeeded by his only son, who, from the peculiarly white colour of his hands, was designated in Norman-French Robert Blanchmains. As it is the purpose of these chapters to present merely a summary of the earlier History of the borough, a bare outline of the lives of these once-famous earls must suffice. Blanchmains doubtless gave confirmatory charters to the burgesses as his predecessors had done; but none are specially attributed to him. The principal event of Blanchmains' life by which the townsmen of Leicester were affected was his hostile position to Henry the Second. There was a family feud between the king on the one hand, and his wife and sons on the other, in respect of which Robert Blanchmains took part with the latter. In conse-quence, the king despatched to Leicester his High Justiciary, Richard de Lucy, who besieged the place, while the earl was absent, being then in Normandy. A fire broke out, and compelled the inhabitants to surrender. The town was destroyed and depopulated; the people being obliged to purchase, with three hundred pounds of silver, their lives and liberty to settle in other places. They left in a mass, and sought refuge on the church lands—some went to St. Alban's and someto the borough of St. Edmunds. This took place in the summer of the year 1173; only four or five years after the death of Robert the Hunchback. In the succeeding seventeen years of his life, Robert Whitehands was involved in all the troubles of that period of English history, arising out of the dissensions existing between Henry II. and his unruly sons. In the year 1190, he made preparations for a pilgrimage to Jerusalem. Before going he arranged his affairs, and, among other things, confirmed his various grants to monasteries, but he does not appear to have added any "privileges" to those possessed by his burgesses in this town— probably after the siege by De Lucy there were few townsmen living in the borough, which for twenty years, it would seem, was in ruins and deserted by its former inhabitants. The earl was not destined to reach the walls of the Holy City; for while making the passage across the Mediterranean, he was taken unwell, and died at Duras in Greece, in the month of September, 1190.

The wife of the earl survived him. She was a descendant of Hugh Grantniesnil, named Petronilla; but was popularly known as Parnel. She had four sons and two daughters. Her second son, Robert, known as Fitz Parnel among the Normans, but as Parnel's-son among the English, succeeded his father in the earldom. The Countess Parnel was a considerable benefactress to the Abbey, the nave of which she built at her own cost; and she gave a plait formed out of her own hair to serve for the suspension and elevation of the lamp kept constantly burning in the choir of the Abbey. Her mortal remains were deposited in the ground before its high altar.

Robert Fitz Parnel was the fourth and last Norman earl of Leicester of the line of the lords of Beaumont. He was a man of short stature, but brave enough to be a constant companion of Richard Cceur de Lion in the desperate contests of the Crusades. It was while engaged in this campaign he used on his shield the armorial bearings which his vassals of Leicester adopted on their town banner. A cinquefoil of ermine on a red ground distinguished the flag of Robert Fitz-Parnel from those of his contemporaries on the tented plains of Palestine, and has ever since been retained as a historical memorial and authoritative symbol by the local authorities. He gave the burgesses two charters. By one, he abandoned the right to take from them the pennies customarily levied on them in lieu of reaping his corn on the land round Leicester— or from the owners of cows which strayed out of bounds — or upon carts which carried com to be ground at any other than the Castle Mill. By the other charter the earl merely confirmed to the inhabitants their ancient rights of pasture. In both cases he was paid a considerable sum for his concessions.

The revival of the town seems to have taken place on the lapse of a quarter of a century from its destruction by Richard de Lucy. In 1197 the Merchant Guild had been re-established (as its rolls, still extant, bear witness), and King John, in a year or two afterwards, granted charters to the burgesses, which were evidently intended to inspire confidence in them, and to induce them to settle permanently within the walls. The people who had deserted the place after the siege probably never returned, and therefore the new-comers were strangers— burgesses from neighbouring boroughs, or labouring men who had immigrated from adjoining villages; tempted by the prospect of the greater freedom of town-life and emancipation from rural thraldom. The enrolment of one hundred and eleven men in the Merchant Guild, in the year 1199, betokened the progress of the re-pop-

ulation of the borough under the rule of Robert Fitz-Parnel; whose charters furnished additional inducements to the residents to make Leicester their future home.

Robert Fitz-Parnel died in the year 1204, and was buried near the high altar of Leicester Abbey, between the bodies of his mother and grandfather. With him ceased the sway over Leicester of the representatives of the warriors of Normandy whose right was gained by the sword. He left no issue, and therefore in the male line his race became extinct. It is worthy of remark that the above brief epitome shows, that in the course of the century over which the descendants of Robert de Beaumont ruled Leicester, the townsmen had succeeded in making steady progress in emancipating themselves from baronial absolutism and oppression. At the commencement of the twelfth century they were a mere grade above bondsmen and serfs, compelled to labour in the fields about the town for their lordly masters, and to take their corn to be ground at the mill belonging to their petty sovereign and to submit to degrading customs; at the conclusion of the century they had freed themselves from the obligations of servitude, and were apparently some stages nearer to a state of individual independence and civilized usage.

THE EARLY ENGLISH PERIOD. From A.d. 1204 To 1265.

Chapter IV.

A few years before the decease of Robert Fitz-Parnel, the earldom of Leicester was put in possession of Simon de Montfort (as in the year 1200), when he is said to have recovered it, having already held it; but inthe year following he was again dispossessed of it, for

reasons not stated on the ancient guild-rolls, which merely mention the facts. Simon de Montfort (otherwise Simon the Bald) was a descendant of the ancient monarchs of France, through an illegitimate son of King Robert. He was a man of unusual force of character, and celebrated for his personal beauty as well as for the good fortune which attended him in his undertakings. He married Amicia, one of the two daughters

of Robert Blanchmains, and sister of Robert Fitz-Parnel. In consequence of his royal descent and his alliance with the Earls of Leicester, he held a high position at the English Court and among the English aristocracy. When King John ascended the throne and gave offence to his barons of Anglo-Norman descent, by the preference he showed for the French nobles who came over from Anjou and Poitiers, Simon de Montfort was found on the side of the former; and they assembled in his town of Leicester, instead of accompanying the King to France, refusing to serve him unless he reinstated them in their ancient rights and privileges. King John, however, awed them into obedience, by appearing in Leicestershire with an army; and then it was that Simon de Montfort was dispossessed of the earldom. Robert Fitz-Parnel dying without issue in 1204, de Montfort, being again received into the favour of John, in right of Amicia, his wife, succeeded in the year 1207 to her "purparty" of her late brother's honours and possessions, which were the Earldom of Leicester, the Stewardship of England, and the Honour of Hinckley; while Margaret, the other sister of Fitz-Parnel, obtained her share of his possessions, and conveyed them to her husband, Saher de Quincy, Earl of Winchester. Simon's successor in the Earldom of Leicester was his son, Simon, who married Alice, a daughter of Bouchard, Count of Montmorency. This Earl was the bloody persecutor of the Albigenses, the early Protestants of France, and he fell under the walls of Toulouse, in the year 1218. His presence in Leicester at any time is doubtful, and no Charters are alleged to have been granted by him.

During the first quarter of the thirteenth century the advancement of the burgesses was considerable and manifest. Within fifty years after Richard de Lucy's demolition of the place, the population had greatly increased, and the Merchant's Guild was their stronghold. United in its friendly circle they were benefitted in their individual capacity, their social position, and their corporate movements; they constituted a phalanx destined eventually to succeed in their endeavours to liberate themselves entirely from feudal oppression and irksome bondage. In their trade operations, they were especially indebted to their organization for their success. As already stated, the Guild was governed by the Alderman (afterwards called Mayor) and a Council composed of twenty-four of its members, who were bound, under a penalty of sixpence, to attend upon the Alderman in the Guild Hall, when he summoned them by the ringing of the bell, and to constitute his assistants in transacting town business.

It may be here observed, this district has always been adapted to the feeding of sheep and cattle. Its meadows and pastures have ever been productive of rich grass and herbage, supplying flocks and herds with the nutriment fitted to sustain and fatten them. In the nature of things, therefore, this has heen a wool-growing region ever since it has been the residence of a civilized and settled population. The townsmen, by collecting the wool from their neighbours in the villages, or inviting them to sell it in the town markets, have obtained the raw material of manufactures, which they have worked up into fabrics of rude fashion and homely use, suited for clothing and covering. Early in the thirteenth century, in Leicester, the wool was spun in the household, and then taken to the weaver, in whose loom it was made into blankets, or a coarse scarlet cloth (called russets-), which were sold here, and elsewhere, as at Stamford and Boston. Woolfells and wool were also taken there, and sold to tradesmen coming from other parts of the country, on certain days every year. To foster this trade—to make regulations for the guidance and advantage of those who were concerned in it— seems to have heen thus early an important part of the business of the Guild Merchant. A fair was held yearly in Jure, the day of keeping which the King (Henry III.) empowered the townspeople to change to February, by his Charter granted in 1229.

As a place of rendezvous (we have seen) the town was frequently resorted to by the insurgent barons. In the year 1224 they met again in Leicester, with an intention of seizing the person of Henry the Third, who was then at Northampton, and forwarded him thence a demand accompanied with a threat of war— the walls of our ancient Castle Hall then, as before, resounding with the threats of the angry nobles, as they had re-echoed their fathers' menaces against King John.

At this time surnames were almost unknown, and the inhabitants knew each other generally only by their Christian names; or they distinguished one from another by some accidental adjunct or circumstance, by his trade, or by the addition of his father's name. Everyone had the appellation which his parents desired to give, him when he was taken as a babe to the font in the parish church, and there baptized by the parish priest. All were Johns, Williams, Thomases, and so forth; but as there were many persons of the same name in a town containing a few thousand inhabitants, it was found necessary to add a descriptive or qualifying designation, to render certain who was intended when -each of the Johns, for example, was alluded to. In written documents these names were naturally entered with greater formality than they would he spoken. One man was known to he the son of such a one, as Aeon, the son of Simon, the son of Peter— that is, Aeon's father, Simon, was the son of Peter; another was Nicholas, the son of Martin; another man was tall — he was William the long; another was stout— he was Walter the fat; another was known better through his connection with an uncle—he was Alan, the nephew of Oliver; another had no legal father—he was Richard the son of Edeline; another man had a peculiar heard, perhaps a very large one—he was Simon with the heard; another was Thomas Beardless; another was Simon Foulbeard; another was only recognized through his master—he was William the man of Walter the Mercer; another had had a serious accident—he was Richard Brokenhead; another lived in a certain part of the town—he was Ge-

offrey of the South-gate; another was Walter Abovetown; another was Richard under the wall; another was the son of the Abbot—he was Arnold, the son of Geoffrey the Abbot, and, commonly, Arnold Abbot; another, perhaps, was light-complexioned, ruddy-faced, and good-looking —he was called the Flower, and hence Peter the Flower; while others were known by their trades, positions, and occupations, as Walter the Mercer, Roger, the Villein (the bondsman), William the Merchant, Hugh the Currier, Philip the Burgess, William the Palmer, Robert the Smith, Samson the Cellarer, Peter the Carpenter, Osborn the Farrier, William the Preacher, Gerald the Baker, Robert the Granger, Richard the Taverner, Adam the Miller, Walter the Vicar, Robert the Tailor, and Ingino the Hangman. A large number in addition derived their second names from the villages in which they had lived previous to their settlement in Leicester.

Among those who constituted the principal inhabitants in 1232 were these persons, who formed the Town Council in that year:—Simon Curlevache, alderman; John the son of Geoffrey (this, modernized, would be John Jefferson), Walter Kennett, Peter Caufoke, Walter the Vicar (that is, Walter Vicars), Henry Sanne (Henry Swann), William the Bland (or William Bland), Robert Warren, Simon Turk, Philip the son of Robert (who was probably known among his fellows as Philip Fitz-Robert or Robertson), Reginald of Wateberge (Reynold Wadborough), William Morel, Martin Cadge, Simon Keling, Simon Swann, Henry Costeyn, Richard Ratin, Willard, William of St. Lo (William Senlo), Lawrence the son of Ralph (that is Lawrence Raufson, or Rawson), Peter the son of Ralph (Peter Rawson), William Haldwin, John the son of Roger (John Rogerson) Peter Ediman, and Ralph of Swepston.

At this period the fabrics of St. Mary of the Castle, St. Martin, St. Nicholas, All Saints, and St. Margaret's, which had been erected during the rule of the Norman Earls of Leicester, were rendered still more stately by additions made in the Early English (or First Pointed) style of architecture. Other buildings intended for religious services were raised at the same time. One was the Church of the Black Friars among the ash trees, dedicated to St. Clement, which stood in that part of the town still called the Black Friars. This was under the care and control of the Dominicans. The second was the Priory of the Grey Friars, the site of which was on the south side of St. Martin's Church. Its tenants were Franciscans, who wore grey cloaks, and walked barefoot. Leicester owed the foundation of these two establishments, it is stated, to Simon de Montfort, the second Earl of Leicester of that name. Besides these, there were in existence at this date—between the year 1220 and 1230—the hospital of St. John the Baptist, the Spital, St. Peter's Church, St. Michael's, the house of the Brethren of the Sack, the Chapel of the Holy Sepulchre, and St. James's Chapel—all erected subsequent to the revival of Leicester, after the siege by de Lucy.

In the year 1231 Simon, the son of Simon de Montfort, the scourge of "heretics," did homage for the share of his grandmother's inheritance in Leicester. This was the most remarkable and illustrious man ever mentioned in our annals, and therefore the chief events of his life deserve more than passing allusion even in this brief history.

Simon de Montfort, it is believed, was born at the Castle of Montfort, the ancient seat of the family, in the neighbourhood of Chartres, about the year 1210. He was consequently a boy of eight when his father was killed at Toulouse, and of ten or eleven only when he lost his mother—a woman who possessed much force of character, and who must have exercised great influence in the formation of her son's mind and disposition. There is reason to suppose that in his boyhood he had come in contact with the celebrated Robert Grossetete, who was the Rector of St. Margaret's, Leicester, and subsequently Archdeacon of Leicester. As his intimate friend and father confessor, the learned ecclesiastic was alike beloved and revered by young Simon.

In personal appearance, the youthful noble was strikingly handsome. Descended from the monarchs of Frankish race, he had doubtless inherited the Teutonic characteristics of mind and body. He was inspired by their high and independent spirit, their inflexible courage, their rough honesty, and their cool sagacity. We may imagine him to have been above the ordinary stature of men, lighthaired, fair-complexioned, with regular and well-defined features, strong in build, and well-proportioned—a model of manly strength and beauty. But he was educated in a superstitious respect for the Mediaeval Church, and its great head, the Pope. Out of the atmosphere of prejudice he breathed from his birth he could not emancipate himself. From father and mother, in his childhood, he had been taught to look with horror on all who dared to question the authority of the Church of Rome; to him the early Protestants were as detestable as the Jews; and both alike he regarded as deserving bodily punishment and social degradation for their sinful heresy. One of his first acts, on his accession to the Earldom of Leicester, exemplifies this description of his character.

Before the Norman Conquest, it is recorded, the Jews were not permitted to live in this country; but William the Conqueror allowed them to settle in some of the towns, where they secluded themselves in localities apart from the Christians, who regarded them with extreme abhorrence. The quarter in which they dwelt was called "The Jewry." In Leicester they were allowed to shelter themselves beneath and around the ruins of the ancient western gateway of Roman times, which afterwards became known as the "Jewry Wall" They were the capitalists of the time. They had become so odious to the burgesses—the high interest they insisted on taking for loans being assigned as chief cause— that the townsmen. induced Simon de Montfort to grant a Charter for their total and perpetual exclusion from Leicester. Translated into English it was as follows:—" Simon de Montfort, son of Earl Simon de Montfort, Lord of Leicester, to all the faithful in Christ, by whom this present document

Siginam may be seen or heard. Let it be universally own that I, for the health of my soul, and the souls of my ancestors and successors, have granted, and by this my present charter confirmed, for me and my heirs in perpetuity, to my burgesses of Leicester and their heirs, that no Jew or Jewess, in my time, or in the time of my heirs, to the end of the world, shall within the liberty of the town of Leisester, inhabit, remain, or obtain any residence. I also wish and command that my heirs after me shall maintain that liberty entire, and shall guarantee it to the burgesses beforenamed in perpetuity. And in testimony of this I have appended my seal to the present charter. These being witnesses: Sir Aumery de Mitton, Sir Walter de Aquila, Sir Roger Blund, chaplain, William Bassett, William de Miravall, and others.''

This Charter was undated; but from circumstances following its operation, it was evidently executed in the year when Simon de Montfort succeeded to his inheritance in Leicester (1231), when he had just attained his majority. At this time his great-aunt, Margaret de Quincy, Countess of Winchester (who had been some few years a widow), taking compassion on the expelled Jews, found an asylum for them on her estates in this neighbourhood; and she wrote to Robert Grossetete, then the Archdeacon of Leicester, to consult him as to the proper mode of treating them, now that they were under her protection. His answer was lengthy; the substance of it being that the Jews should be kept at hard labour upon the land, and be supplied with coarse fare in return for their toils.

This deed could not have been executed before the young earl came to his inheritance, nor after Grossetete ceased to be the Archdeacon of Leicester, in 1231; so that it is necessarily assigned to that year.

Having adopted England as his home, Simon de Montfort now passed his time probably in the Castle of Leicester and in London. His high rank, his extensive possessions, his illustrious birth, and his personal advantages ensured for him a welcome at the English Court, where, when he was approaching thirty, he made the acquaintance of the King's sister, Eleanor, whom the death of the great statesman, William, Earl of Pembroke, had left a widow of sixteen. They were privately married in the Chapel at St. Stephen's, Westminster (Jan. 7, 1238), with the permission of the bride's brother, Henry III. Richard of Cornwall, her other brother, was however, bitterly opposed to the union, and the Court nobles were jealous of Simon de Montfort's elevated position, obtained in consequence of the alliance. An objection was also raised to it by the clergy, on the ground of the Princess having taken the vow of perpetual chastity. Simon felt it therefore necessary to proceed to Rome, to obtain a dispensation from the Pope, in which he succeeded; a rich burgees of Leicester having lent him 500 marks to enable him to make the journey. While in trouble in connection with this subject, his old friend Robert Grossetete, now Bishop of Lincoln, wrote him a letter, offering him all the consolation he could under the circumstances of his cruel treatment by his enemies. About this date, too, Grossetete remonstrated with the young lord of Leicester on his cruel treatment of Simon Curlevacho, one of the Aldermen, and of the burgesses generally; probably perpetrated while he was smarting under the annoyance occasioned by the discredit thrown upon his recent marriage. Towards the close of the year, the King having been reconciled to him, the Earl retired to Kenilworth, with his young wife, who there gave birth to a son about the end of November.

Early in the following year Simon was fully installed in the Earldom, being recognized among the barons of the kingdom, and taken into the councils of the Crown. One of his first local acts was to make a confirmatory grant to the burgesses of the Cow Hay, as a pasturage for their exclusive use and benefit. As illustrating the near relationship of the French-born lord with his English burgesses, it may be cited at full length. It ran thus:—" To all the faithful in Christ, who may inspect the present writing of Simon de Montfort, Earl of Leicester, health in the Lord! Let it be universally known that whereas Robert, Earl of Leicester, formerly my predecessor, has by his charter feoffed the burgesses of Leicester in a pasturewhich is called the Cow Hay, lying in the South Field of Leicester, between my pastures on either side. Let it be known that I have remitted, relaxed, and in every way from rue and my heirs for ever quit-claimed every right and claim that I have had, and that my heirs may have, in the said pasture, to my free burgesses of Leicester, who now are so and will be hereafter, that is to say, to those to whom the said pasture ought to belong; and that they shall have and hold the said pasture, with its appurtenances, of me and my heirs freely, quietly, and without waste, by paying thence yearly to me and my heirs or successors, for every beast agisted or to be agisted in the said pasture three pennies, as was accustomed to be given in the time of my predecessors. And for this remission, release, and quit-claim, my burgesses aforesaid have given me beforehand a colt of the value of one hundred shillings, that neither I, the said Simon, nor my heirs nor successors, nor any one for us, nor on our part, shall be able to agist or depasture our herds in the aforesaid pasture, but shall be excluded from pasturing or agisting therein for ever. In testimony of which thing I have placed my seal to this writing of quit-claim. These being witnesses: Philip Curlewan, Richard de Harcourt, Alexander de Harcourt, Henry Costeyn, Peter Rogerson, Hugh Tasch, William Tasch, Richard the son of Gosselyn, William Wakelyn, Theobold the Clerk, and others. Dated at Leicester, on the Feast of the Invention of the Holy Cross, in the year of the reign of Henry, the son of King John, the twentythird." May 3, 1239.

It is here seen the freemen of Leicester, by the present of a colt, which they had doubtless ascertained beforehand would be acceptable to their lord, Simon de Montfort, secured his recognition of their right to their pasture called the Cow Hay. The circumstance indicates the relative footing the two parties occupied, and it may be imagined the townsmen often saw the great Earl riding,through their streets on the colt they had given to him.

By another charter, undated, which may be assumed to have been nearly contemporaneous with the foregoing, Simon de Montfort confirmed the release of the burgesses from petty payments and exactions before spoken of; receiving a gift on so doing. The document recites that he had abandoned all claim to those pennies which had been formally taken from the men of Leicester in lieu of the performance of field-labour; to those pennies which had been taken on flocks and herds straying upon his lands (but not to certain customary payments on their account); and to those pennies which had been taken upon carts and waggons carrying corn to other mills than his own, to be ground, reserving to himself the right to multure, and their coming to his mill in Leicester to find multure without impediment and delay. For this renewal of ancient exemptions, the Earl received from the burgesses fifteen marks of silver. To ensure their liability from any future revival of the claims referred to, he attested the deed by placing his seal at the end of it in presence of Sir Stephen de Seagrave, Sir Thomas de Neville, Sir Gilbert de Seagrave, Sir Nicholas de Cestres, and Sir William de St. Edmunds. This proceeding and the execution of the charter relating to the Cow Hay, probably took place in the hall of the Castle now standing.

It would seem very likely the Earl's pecuniary necessities at this time had their influence upon the formal enforcement of these charters upon the town's people. The position he held at Court being unsatisfactory and uncertain, he had recourse apparently to the expedient of exacting money from the burgesses by way of making himself ready to meet emergencies. One of these very soon occurred; for although received into his brother-in-law's favour at the end of the preceding year, and present in June at the baptism of Prince Edward, yet, when the Queen was "churched" on the ninth of August, he was publicly insulted and disgraced by King Henry, and fled hastily down the Thames to France the same evening.

The Earl remained abroad until the following spring, when he was welcomed back to England by his royal brother-in-law. In accordance with the religious notions of the age, he resolved to take the cross, and make a journey to Jerusalem, with the view of expiating the offence he had committed against ecclesiastical law in having married a woman who had taken a vow of perpetual chastity. He accordingly made preparations for the journey, and sold property to enable him to defray the expense; but he never fulfilled his intention. For some succeeding years he was engaged in the wars against Poitou and Gascony, to which province he accompanied Henry in the year 1242, though he was subjected to all the inconvenience of being exposed to the jealous temper of that sovereign. But as his military talent and force of character rendered him indispensable to Henry, he was appointed Governor of Guienne six years after. "The stern justice of his rule" here rendered him unpopular among the burgesses of Bordeaux, and the "complaints of the Gascons brought about an open breach with the king," by whom, in a dispute, he was called, "a false traitor." He was superseded in command, and forced to seek refuge in France. The importance of his position was such, however, that he was offered the regency of that kingdom, during the absence of St. Louis in the Holy Land. On his refusal to accept that post he returned to England to re-enter the service of Henry.

At this time, his character was fully developed. It is observed in an extensively popular work, recently published—the *Short History of the English People*—that "his life was pure and singularly temperate; he was noted for his scant indulgence in meat, dr̄ink, or sleep. Socially he was cheerful and pleasant in talk; but his natural temper was quick and fiery, his sense of honour keen, his speech rapid and trenchant."

While their feudal master was engaged in campaigning abroad, the burgesses were pursuing their humble labours at home—weaving cloth and blankets, night and day, in order to improve their social condition and municipal position. They had heretofore held their public meetings, to which they were summoned by the striking of a bell, in an old Moot Hall, of which the site is now unknown. As a proof of their growing prosperity, may be mentioned their purchase of another building on the eastern side of the graveyard of St. Nicholas's Church, which they converted into a Guild Hall, during the term of office of Peter Eogerson, who was the first man to whom the term "Mayor" was applied in Leicester. This was in the year 1251. The records of the Merchant Guild also attest the extensive and extending commercial operations of its members, in its notices of their periodical journeys with their saleable commodities to Stamford and Boston; their goods probably finding their way from that port to France in the course of the thirteenth century.

The townsmen had had to contend against the unprincipled rapacity of the baronial agents before Simon de Montfort came to the earldom. It has been stated how the son of Robert de Beaumont remitted the payment of certain taxes, and abandoned all claim to them for ever,-by one of his Charters. This Charter, with others, was placed in the care of Lambert, the Town Clerk. Being a rich man, his premises were broken into one night and' set fire to by burglars, who had been tempted by his wealth to commit the robbery. In the progress of the conflagration the liberating Charter and many other town documents were consumed. Not long after, one Simon Maudit (which means in English Simon the Accursed), a clerk or lawyer, had in farm the bailiwick of Leicester.

By this arrangement he paid a round sum yearly to the Earl—it would seem Robert Blanchmains—and then extorted as much as he could from the poor burgesses to reimburse himself. Knowing well enough the Charter of exemption from gavel-pennies had been burnt at Lambert's fire, and could not therefore be produced to prove the injustice of his claim, he still insisted on demanding them from the townspeople, who had no alternative but to pay them, as they could not produce the documentary proof of their abandonment by Earl Robert le Bossu. This unjust imposition continued for many years. A local exaction, equally unfair in principle, had been made in respect to bridge-money, by a man named Penbrioch, to whom one of the Norman earls had had given a piece of ground to build upon near one of the bridges—the North or West Bridge—between the town and Leicester Forest. This Penbrioch at first collected his payments at the outlet of the wood, afterwards at an intermediate point, and at last at the bridges, from the townsmen who resorted to the Forest to pick up the dead wood and boughs scattered about by the tempestuous winds. His levies became known as "pontage" or "bridge-silver." Penbrioch not only demanded money from those who took the dead wood, but from those who carried away green wood, and what was for sale—quite without right to do so —and appropriated the customs to himself.

The burgesses had no other remedy for this state of affairs than to make a bargain with Simon de Montfort to grant them a Charter, specially releasing them from the burdens inflicted on them by iniquitous tax-gatherers as here explained. They therefore raised a subscription throughout the town, dividing it into four districts, in the neighbourhood of the four gates. The highest amount individually contributed was 10s., paid by the four richest burgesses—Martin Cadge or Cagge, Robert Parser, Ralph Oliver, and Ralph of Swepstone. None gave less than 3s. The total raised was £18 7s. The gavel-pennies and the bridge-money were extorted from the ţe townsmen until March 12, 1255; the Charter of exemption having been obtained some time previously, for which the Earl received the amount already named. Not even a noble so patriotic and magnanimous as Simon de Montfort protected his burgesses from the extortionate practices of his agents and bailiffs.

The Charter translated from the orginal in Latin was as follows:—" To all the faithful in Christ by whom this writing may be seen or heard: Sir Simon de Montfort, earl of Leicester, steward of England, health in the Lord! Let it be known to all men that we have remitted and quitclaimed for ever, for us and our heirs, all those pennies which in any manner were accustomed to be exacted and taken under the name of pontage at our bridges of Leicester, which are called 'brigge silvir;' and at the same time all those pennies called 'govel pennis' which were accustomed to be exacted and taken in our town of Leicester; so that neither we nor our heirs, nor any one in our name, shall henceforth be able to take or exact anything in the name of the aforesaid pennies which are called brigg silver and govel pennies, from our burgesses of Leicester, or their heirs or successors, or any other persons from whatever place they may be; nor that the said burgesses, or their heirs or successors, shall be able to take or exact anything in any manner from any one under the name of brigg silver or govel pennies. And for this remission and quitclaiming our mayor and burgesses of the community of Leicester have given and quitclaimed from them and their heirs perpetually, to us and to our heirs or assigns, fifty-six shillings and eight pennies annual rent, to be received in our town and field of Leicester, namely, from four virgates of land in the Southfield of Leicester, which we had from Andrew Soterel, forty shillings-which Simon of the Sauce formerly was accustomed to receive annually from the said land; and in our town of Leicester, and in the suburb of the said town, sixteen shillings and eightpence, that is to say, in the parish of St. Nicholas, from certain land which belonged to Robert the brocher of Baldwin of Scbarneford, near the land which was Geoffrey of Huncote's, twenty pence; from the land which was Hugh of Stockton's, near the land which was Walter Long's, fourteen pennies; from certain land lying between that which was Walter Long's and that which was Robert the Cunver's, twenty pennies; from land in St. Martin's parish, which was Griffin the Fol's, twelve pennies and one capon; from land lying between that which was Ralph Albold's on each side, two shillings and six pennies, and two hens; from land in the east suburb which was Gamil the Waterman's, nine pennies and three hens; from land which was Richard the Breth's or Brett's, nine pennies and four hens ; from land which was Robert the Merchant's, ten pennies, one farthing, and three hens; from Elias of Burbach's land, four pennies, a farthing, and one hen; from Ivan .John of Stretton's land, four pennies, a farthing, and one hen; from Ralph Clovelec's land, six pennies; from Peter Peatling's land, twelve pennies and four hens; from Richard Caprun's land, three pennies and two hens; from William of Barkby's land, three pennies; and from certain land in the northern suburb, in All Saints' parish, lying between Walter the Wheeler's land and that of John son of the same Walter, twenty pennies and one capon: with the homages, services, reliefs, and all outgoings and liberties proceeding from the said rents. And that all these things aforesaid may obtain the strength of firmness for ever, we, and our mayor and burgesses of Leicester, have concluded this present charter in handwriting, and have corroborated this part of the same charter by the apposition of our seal. These being witnesses: Sir Ernald Dubois, Sir Ralph

D

Bassett, Sir Richard of Havering, Sir Thomas of Estley, Sir William Burdett, Sir Robert of Folville, Sir Ralph the Chamberlain, Sir Robert Motun, Henry Mallory, and others."

The condition of the burgesses had, at this period, owing to causes not now known, become much deteriorated. It may be that they were required, even more frequently than appears on the surface, to find money to fill the exchequer of their feudal lord, by methods which the obtainment of Charters only did not fully represent. The troubled state of the country also occasioned an injurious interference with their local industry. There was, however, an undisputed falling-off in the number of the population— especially of the inheritors of burgess property; the lastborn sons, not the first born, being those who succeeded to their fathers. With a view to remedy this state of affairs, Simon de Montfort, being at Westminster, executed this Charter:—" To all the faithful in Christ: Sir Simon de Montfort, earl of Leicester, seneschal of England, health! Be it known to all men that we,—for the health of our soul, and the souls of Alianor, our wife, of our boys, ancestors and successors, at the instance and supplication of the burgesses of our town of Leicester, and for the common good and amelioration of the said town, which on account of a defect of heirs and their weakness has now fallen away to destruction and ruin, with the common consent and will of all our burgesses of our afore-mentioned town of Leicester, have granted, and by this our present charter confirmed, that all the first-born of legitimate matrimony, in our before-named town of Leicester and its suburbs, shall henceforth obtain and have the paternal inheritance and habitation of their father, peacefully, quietly, and without any contradiction, and whoever may be their legitimate heirs shall succeed them: so that the last-born sons in our said town of Leicester, who succeeded as heirs to their fathers or ancestors, before the granting and executing of this our charter, shall have and possess for the entire term of life, peacefully, quietly, and without any contradiction, their inheritance and habitation, and their first-horn sons shall succeed to their inheritance according to the grant hefore-named. These being witnesses: Sir Roger de Gurney, earl of Winchester, Ralph Bassett, William Bassett, Richard of Havering, Thomas of Estley, knight, Bartholomew le Jeune, Richard Morin, Andrew de la Breche, Alexander the Clerk, and others. Given at Westminster, on the Friday next after the feast of St. Luke the Evangelist, in the thirty-ninth year of the reign of king

Henry the son of king John."

Subsequently to this time, the Earl's history became of national, if not of European, interest and importance. He now consecrated his efforts and energies to two great objects—the emancipation of the people from royal tyranny and the foundation of the representative system. For the accomplishment of these he fortified himself with the constancy and devotedness of a martyr, as he finally received a martyr's recompense. The nobility of English descent ranged themselves under his leadership, in opposition to those who had come over from Savoy and Provence under the favour and protection of the king, whose wife was a native of the latter principality. For the first time after the Norman Conquest, the barons of Anglo-Norman descent took part with the English middle class and common people against the Crown; the contemptuous violation of the Great Charter by the royal favourites having in especial exasperated the nation against the insolent and intrusive foreigners. Besides which, the folly of Henry, in proposing to plunge into a war to obtain the crown of Sicily, induced the barons to combine, and compel him to agree to the appointment of a Council for the reformation of the government. This body drew up the "Provisions of Oxford," under which the royal authority was virtually placed in commission. A war between the king and barons ensued. At the battle of Lewes, Henry surrendered, and his brother, the king of the Romans, was captured; while prince Edward was given as a hostage to the victorious party headed by Simon de Montfort. In order to strengthen himself, the earl now January 1265 founded the House of Commons, by summoning to Parliament, for the first time in our history, two citizens or burgesses from each city or borough in the kingdom.

The popularity and power of the great leader of the barons now culminated. They were the themes of poems and other pieces written in Latin by persons who had been bred at the Universities, and who led the way as bold reformers. "The refectory of the monastery not less than the baronial hall now rang frequently with the outburst of popular feeling," says Mr. Wright, in his preface to the volume of Political Songs published by the Camden Society, and "amid the Baron's wars was composed the first political song in English that has yet been found. It is remarkable that all the songs of this period which we know are on the popular side of the dispute—all with one accord agree in their praise and support of the great Simon de Montfort."

His career was, however, fast coming to a close. The great drama of his life, unparalleled probably by any which our country has witnessed, terminated in the tragedy at Evesham, where he fell overwhelmed by his enemies, who decapitated him, and, it is related, forwarded his head to his wife in their brutal triumph. The cause of the people was now for the time overthrown, and their grief for his loss universal. In their estimation he was a true saint and martyr, for long after his death they made pilgrimages to his tomb, where, it was said, miracles were wrought through the influence of the departed spirit of the murdered hero. "The career of Simon de Montfort," remarks Dr. Freeman, in his essay on the *Growth of the English Constitution,* "is the most glorious in our later history. Cold must be the heart of every Englishman who does not feel a thrill of reverence and gratitude as he utters that immortal name." THE PLANTAGENET PERIOD.

FROM A.D. 1265 TO A.D. 1399.

Chapter V.

As a consequence of Simon de Montfort's appearing in arms against the King, he forfeited his earldom of Leicester, and his family were attainted, losing all their rights of inheritance. The King then granted the earldom and honour of Leicester, with the lands of the late Earl, and other possessions, to his second son, commonly designated "Edmund Crouchback." This personage does not seem, from the records left of the period, to have been a resident at the castle, or to have shown any interest in the welfare of the burgesses; but he took the revenues of his office, and large loans from them, immediately on his appointment. He lived (as Simon de Montfort had done) very frequently at Kenilworth Castle, where workmen were sent from Leicester on numerous occasions— carpenters, smiths, and masons—to rebuild or add to that stately structure.

In one hundred years the inhabitants, by their rude manufacture of cloth and their dealings in wool, had risen much above the servile condition in which their predecessors existed under the Norman earls. They were therefore enabled to provide among themselves an annual income for town purposes much exceeding that which they had done, and to advance money for local objects. About this time a tax or talliage was paid to the king (Henry the Third), which was supposed to be equivalent to a twentieth of the movables of his subjects. In Leicester, 480 persons paid their shares, and the whole sum was £96 8s. 10d.: the movables of the town, consequently, were then not worth £2,000, in the money of that period. On an average each taxpayer paid 4s.; though some paid four times that amount, and others paid a few pennies only. Even the hangman (called in the Latin "Jngino carnifex") paid a mark. The contributions were collected by different persons resident in the north, south, east, and west quarters of the town, and in the Bishop's Fee; there being four collectors in each quarter, with a clerk or writer to help them, in one instance: for they could not write their own names, the Mayor himself keeping his accounts with a notched stick. From these tax lists are taken the names of Richard of Asfordby, Robert of Sharnford, John of Queniborough, William of Sileby, Alan the gardener, Henry the goldsmith, Simon keepguest, Thomas the blood-letter, William the parchmenter, Richard the cutler, Adam the weaver, Reginald the slater, Curtis the cordwainer, John the fisher, Richard the tanner, William Miles (the soldier), William the marshal (or farrier), Nicholas the chaloner, Hugh the comber, John the sturdy, John whiteside, Hugh the long, Roger the stooping, Margaret the greedy, Alicia the fat, Henry brownman, John fullgood, Henry above-town, William under-the-wall, John of the hall, William ace, William sixand-twenty, Simon careless, Maria widow of John Crace, William pick, Robert the may, Bertram Caprun, Adam cockney bred, Geoffrey the mouse, and many others, equally graphic but sometimes less fit to mention to modern ears. Their trades were as various—there being among them vintners, parchmenters, gardeners, fishers, cutlers, weavers, butchers, cordwainers, bridle-makers, slaters, masons, coiners, carpenters, linen-drapers, mercers, dyers, homers, leadbeaters, packmen, armour polishers, riders, a summoner, and a fere or leman, with others.

As one means of obtaining the advantages of the Guild protection, sometimes traders or workmen settled in the Bishop's Fee (now occupying the space of St. Margaret's parish) outside the town walls, and thus tried to evade the payment of contributions to the Guild. The Bishop's Fee was, in fact, anciently a jurisdiction distinct from the borough, under the authority of the Bishops of Lincoln and their bailiffs, in whose courts its inhabitants did "suit and service;" and this state of things frequently led to disputes. In the year 1272, Richard of Bromley and Thomas of Bruntingthorpe, on their admission into the Guild, pledged themselves not to remain in the Bishop's Fee: and two years afterwards William Rogerson of Knighton was admitted, on condition that he would be obedient to his companions of the Guild in lot and scot, and in all other respects, whether he lived in the fee of the Lord Bishop of Lincoln or elsewhere.

It was a great advance in the mode of administering justice when, in the year 1285, judges of assize were appointed to go into every shire two or three times every year, in the intervals of the vacations of the courts at Westminster. In this way, the arbitrary authority of the barons over the towns was curtailed, very advantageously to the liberty of the subject; the decisions of comparatively impartial and learned men being thus substituted for those of feudal nobles, or

their stewards, who were too often men of violent and unscrupulous character. In the great hall of Leicester Castle, sitting on raised seats under their canopies of state, surrounded by their retainers, they dispensed the laws too often in accordance with their own cruel and angry passions; but when the judges appointed bythe king came, they shared few or none of these feelings, their only object being to administer the law, except, perhaps, where barons on the spot possessed an undue influence. It seems that judges had visited the town at an earlier date than that of the appointment of justices of assize by Edward the First. Sir Gilbert of Preston, judge, was supplied with bread and wine on coming to Leicester in the year 1258, and Sir Robert Walrond, the king's justice, was in the town in the same year—a payment being made to William, the bailiffs clerk, for writing an account of an inquisition taken in his presence. And they are distinctly mentioned as holding their sittings in the hall of the castle in the year 1274—eleven years before the justices of assize are recognized in history. They were usually accompanied by their own clerks and doorkeepers, to whom the burgesses made customary presents; of which regular records are made on the Guild Rolls.

In the year 1290 the town was rich enough either to re-build or greatly repair the West Bridge, at an outlay of £28 0s. 5d. The stone was brought from a quarry near at hand, and the wood used was purchased in the Saturday market. The common workmen were paid Id. and 2d. each per day: the masons and carpenters 4d. each—Id. per day more than they were paid in 1265. The money required to pay for the work done was raised in various ways: a great proportion was received at St. Martin's Church (then called the Holy Cross) in oblations or offerings, another considerable sum was the proceed of a kind of borough-rate paid over by John Alsy the Mayor, another by a separate collection made in the town, another by a second and separate collection—the priests, the borough, and private individuals unitedly assisting in the task of obtaining the

money.

Although Simon de Montfort had summoned burgesses from boroughs to appear in Parliament thirty years before, for the first time burgesses were sent to Parliament from Leicester in the year 1294. The names of the two were Ralph Norman and Robert of Sharnford. They were members of the Guild, chosen by members of the Guild— the political progenitors of the modern freemen. They were paid 2s. each per day, from the town purse, for their services; which (it will be seen) was about six times more than the masons who built the West Bridge received. When they entered the apartment in which the nobles and knights sat, they were not expected to speak, but to sit while the taxes were levied, and merely to give their assent to the motions—they were considered very "low fellows" by the aristocratic portion of the assembly. Some of them were drapers, some keepers of taverns, and some dealers in cloth. When they returned home, a few of the leading townsmen met them at the taverns—sometimes at that kept by the member himself—and there heard his account of the business done, while drinking their representative's and host's wine and beer. The burgesses did not value the privilege of parliamentary representation: they would in truth have been much obliged to the sheriff had he sent them no writ to elect members.

In the year 1299, the Earl of Leicester died at Bayonne. The successor of Edmund Crouchback in the earldom of Leicester was his eldest son, Thomas, who is known equally well in history, or perhaps more commonly, as the Earl of Lancaster. He was the nephew of the reigning monarch, Edward the First; and this connection with royalty was attended with misfortune to himself and his burgesses of Leicester. His succession to the earldom was signalized by the levying of a heavy tax upon the inhabitants for his benefit; the sum of £48 10s. Id. having been raised on the occasion. This proceeding created great and general dissatisfaction. One of the people showed his anger in presence of the Mayor; another cursed the jury who assessed the tax, and assaulted the collector-; and a third broke the seal of the document under authority of which the levy had been imposed. In the year following, the inhabitants were again subjected to this process of what may be termed extortion; a "gift" being then made to the earl's royal uncle, when he came to Leicester (probably on his way to Scotland, on his third expedition against the people of that country), and to the earl himself. About 286 persons contributed to the amount; the greater number paying twelve pennies each— a sum equivalent to a day labourer's weekly wages —and a few other townsmen ten times as much each person. Again, in the thirty-fourth year of Edward's reign, a "gift" was raised for the earl, on the coming of the king's justice. There were 325 contributors. Four townsmen gave 16s. each. Two or three years after, a fourth tax was levied for the earl, to which there were 385 contributors.

It may be inferred from the increase in the number of tax-payers, and from their ability to raise these repeated levies, that the inhabitants were becoming yearly more numerous and prosperous; and this supposition is confirmed by an historian, writing of this period (Thierry), who says that the richer inhabitants of the great towns now endeavoured to imitate the nobles in their habits and by speaking French, and adopted the custom of addressing each other by the title of "sir" or "sire." At this time, there was a marked prevalence of crime in the town. There were two local officers named "coroners," who were appointed by the king, whose duty it was, in conjunction with two officers called the town bailiffs, to take cognizance of all crimes committed in the place. The bailiffs corresponded to the police officers of the present day their duty being to apprehend and to keep in custody (temporarily at least) all offenders against the law. The coroners were virtually magistrates, with limited power, whose business it was to examine evidence, and to commit to prison persons charged with crime, there to await their trial by the judge of assize.

Up to a certain period, prisoners were sent to Warwick gaol; but Edward the Second ordered a prison to be provided in Leicester, which was not completed until the year 1309, though some place of detention—probably a dungeon in the Castle—had been used before that period. The king's coroners kept records of their acts; and these, known as the "pleas of the Crown," written upon ancient rolls of parchment, still exist, to attest the criminal condition of Leicester in the reigns of Edward the First and Edward the Second.

In one particular there was a remarkable difference between the medieval and the modern town—in the middle ages the walls surrounded it, completely separating the inhabitants from their neighbours in the county. Entered by low gateways, which were opened in the morning and closed at night, the town was shut up completely, when necessary; all escape from it being prevented when the warders closed the gates. The townsmen might be said to be thus enclosed in a large prison; but they were in this way protected from the incursions of formidable bands of robbers and marauders who roamed about the open country, to the terror of the peaceably-disposed. At the same time, an offender against the law was in consequence unable to avoid capture, unless he could rush through one of the gates before the town bailiff could seize him and take him into custody. To prevent the criminal fiom escaping, on the instant of his detection the townsmen gave an alarm by shouting, and by calling aloud "hue! hue!" which was "raising the hue and cry;" and then some person ran to the town gate or gates, and saw that they were quickly closed. Perhaps one cause of the frequent occurrence of violent crimes and deeds of bloodshed, was the general custom of carrying arms—many men wearing their swords regularly, others frequently carrying pole-axes and bows and arrows, and every townsman wearing at his girdle the knife with which he cut up his bread and cheese or his meat at his meals. Passionate and impulsive, but not deliberately cruel, the townsman,

when provoked by insult or injury, real or supposed, found his pointed meat-knife ready at his belt, and often committed a crime in a moment for which he atoned in the Castle-yard; and which he might have refrained from, had not the knife been constantly at his fingers' ends promptly to do his bidding. But the deed being done, he had to evade the officers of justice by getting outside the walls before the gate was shut; while his wounded victim, stricken to death, lay weltering in his gore, listening to the priest who was administering to the dying man the last rites of the Church— administering to him extreme unction, hearing a hurried confession gasped out, and putting to the lips of the penitent the sacred wafer. One other chance had the criminal to save himself—he might seek the church of St. Mary, or All Saints, or some other church, and within its walls claim sanctuary, and thus obtain a temporary refuge from the town bailiffs. Scarcely had a year passed in which some deed of blood was not committed—the knife being the weapon with which the wound was in most cases inflicted.

The yearly routine of town life, in other respects, seems to have varied very little. The burgesses found it expedient customarily to fee the earl's steward; they regularly made allowances to the clerks, the crier, and the attendants of the Judges; and they gave presents to the earl's minstrels, the earl's treasurer, and the earl's treasurer's attendants. Before the close of Edward the First's reign, the town had a sergeant and a clerk; the former, probably, carried the Mayor's mace—the latter was a secretary in regular attendance on his worship. He was generally called the Mayor's clerk.

It was the fate of the Earls of Leicester to be in almost constant antagonism to the crown. Thomas of Lancaster followed in this respect in the track of Simon de Montfort; as he headed the barons in their insurrection against Edward the Second, when that sovereign had incurred their displeasure by acts of favouritism to Piers Gaveston, and he remained out of favour for some years.

In the month of March 1322 the earl and his forces were defeated. He was taken prisoner unresistingly, and in a few days after beheaded on an eminence near his own castle of Pomfret.

Henry, the brother of Thomas, Earl of Lancaster and Leicester, was his successor. He was allowed by the king his cousin (Edward the Second) to enter upon the title, possessions, and honour of the earldom of Leicester in the year 1324. On his accession, he was presented by the people of Leicester with presents, and the Mayor (John Norton) proceeded to Earl Shilton, where the earl had a castle, and was then staying, to present his duty to his superior. The Mayor had a conversation with the earl— or, as the ancient roll says, had "a colloquy" with him—at Earl Shilton; and there was much feasting and drinking of wine on the occasion; for half the town receipts of the year were expended on the journey.

The earl had in early life been a warrior, having served in Flanders and in Scotland; being in middle age when his connection with Leicester commenced. In the first year of Edward the Third's reign, he procured a reversal of the act of attainder passed against his brother, and thus secured for himself the vast possessions which had been his brother's.

Earl Henry (unlike some of his predecessors) was a regular resident in Leicester. The Castle, then rendered habitable by the addition of domestic edifices standing on the site of the Castle House, became his accustomed dwellingplace. Here he was visited by his young relative, Edward the Third, with his Queen, in the year 1327. Six years afterwards, the king was again in Leicester, at the house of his kinsman, the earl; and, in fact, the ancient town records abound in mentions of these visits, when the royal attendants, the minstrels, and the servants of the king and queen were entertained and presented with gifts by the Mayor and Town Council. To send casks of wine to the Castle, with bread and poultry, was now indeed the yearly custom.; and its great hall was often the scene of those princely festivities where

the king, the queen, the nobles, the knights, and the ladies, habited in the picturesque costume of the Middle Ages, sat at the board in the presence of the people, and were feasted with all the luxuries and delicacies which the bounteous hospitality of the age provided, while the troubadors sang and recited their romances of love and chivalry, and the waits played to the assembled throng their ancient melodies.

The Earl of Leicester became attached to this locality, and appears not to have taxed his burgesses so heavily as his unfortunate brother. To his permanent residence in the place two public measures, which have left their impress on the town of Leicester, are attributable: he added the Newarke to the Castle, and he erected the building known as Trinity Hospital.

Before the Teign of Edward the Third that suburb of Leicester now known as the Newarke had no existence as a separate district. It was in all probability a level meadow, and used for the grazing of cattle—the ancient stone-wall of the Castle precincts then bounding it from the South Gate to the river; its continuity being broken by the Turret Gateway, which (now a ruin) was then guarded with heavy gates and portcullis, and formed the only entrance to the bailey of the Castle from the south side of the fortifications. Earl Henry enclosed the area lying just outside the Castle in this direction with a strong wall, which he supplied with towers and gateways for entrance to it and for its greater security. One of them, now called "the Magazine," was at the same time a barrack for armed men; a second, in the south wall, perhaps served the same purpose; and a tower near Swan's Mill probably commanded the approach in that direction. When this outer defence to the Castle was completed, it was simply distinguished from the older fortifications by the name of the New Work, which term in succeeding times has been corrupted to the Newarke.

On the completion of this fortified area, the earl placed, just within its space, and close under the Castle Keep, another building devoted to a peaceful

purpose, where ample protection against the lawless depredator was insured. Here he erected A Hospital. In the year 1330 he obtained the royal letters patent, dated Woodstock, the second of April, authorizing him to found the institution in honour of God and the Virgin Mary, for the maintenance of fifty old men, and five old women as their nurses, to be under the management of a master, four chaplains, and two clerks; also for the foundation of a chapel and houses for the habitation of the master and chaplains; with liberty to endow the institution with four acres of land in Leicester and the advowson of the Church of Irchester, in Northamptonshire. To this the endowment of Duffield Church, in Derbyshire, was subsequently added. It seems to have been a few years in course of erection, and when completed was known as the New Hospital; Trinity Hospital being its comparatively modern designation. In an account (dated 1344) it is thus alluded to:—"For the expense of divers men working about the ditch against the New Hospital, for six days, 17s." Before he died, it appeared that the Earl had begun, or contemplated, the erection of another building near to the Hospital. This was the Collegiate Church Op St. Mary Op The Newarke, which was intended probably to serve as the place of worship for the earl and his domestics, and the garrison, instead of the older fabric then standing on the eastern side of the Castle courtyard; and as the mortuary chapel of the earl's family. The site selected for this church—once the most elegant ecclesiastical structure in the town—was opposite the Hospital. Not a vestige of its superstructure now remains; but its associations are still manifold and interesting.

The earl was now growing old and infirm. He lived at the Castle House, and it may he presumed his was a very familiar form to the townsmen; often seen in the streets in friendly converse with the inhabitants. To his other infirmities, blindness was added. The earl made his will, in which he directed that on his decease his body should he buried in the chapel of the hospital he had founded.

He died shortly after, in the year 1345, at the Castle House, when he was more than seventy years of age. He was not buried where he had wished to be; but in a chapel of the new church in the Newarke. The great Edward, with his queen, Philippa, and a crowd of barons and bishops, were present in the church at the funeral ceremony performed over the remains of the aged noble. A few years after a monument, representing the earl and two of his children, was raised to his memory on the north side of the altar of the Collegiate Church; but of this, or of its original site, no trace whatever now exists.

The main road through Leicester, in the reign of the Edwards, running from the South to the North Gate, was the scene of many a picturesque procession; for then the kings and their queens, attended by their richly-attired retinues and by armed escorts, were often passing from one part of the country to the other through this, the central Midland town, making their lodging for the night at the Abbey, where ample accommodation for such large parties then existed. Here, too, were the principal taverns, wine-shops, and cook shops, where the humbler class of travellers found food and shelter on passing through Leicester. And here, probably, the best houses stood, known by their wider fronts and higher gables, overhanging the causeways. Entering the low arch of the South Gate, through heavy doorways and beneath a frowning portcullis, the burly porters giving him a scrutinizing look as he passed by, the ordinary stranger found himself in the High Street. Approaching the ancient High Cross, the site of the Wednesday's Market, its gilded vane would tell him. he was in the heart of the old borough of Leicester. As he progressed, he would see on his right hand the church of St. Peter, the place of which is now occupied by the Borough Gaol; and probably nearly opposite to this church would be standing the principal inn in the town, on the spot where the Blue Boar was erected in the next century. The traveller would shortly after pass beneath the portals of the North Gate out of the ancient walls of Leicester.

It was at this period when the Mayor, with the Bailiff —then, perhaps, the Earl's representative—and the " good people of Leicester" (as the record describes them) made a number of laws or regulations for the government of the town. John Levirich was Mayor. They ordained first, that the king's peace should be kept in Leicester, and that no person, no matter what his condition, should be allowed to go about the streets armed in a coat of mail, Or any other armour, either by night or by day—a precaution probably rendered necesary by the frequent personal conflicts in the streets to which the carrying of weapons gave occasion. The bread of the people being then, as ever, the staple article of subsistence; ale being the common beverage; and French wine, from the vineyards of Gascony, procured by way of Boston, being the luxurious drink of the rich inhabitants; the Mayor and his associates made strict regulations concerning their supply and quality. It was ordained that no baker should bake fewer than four loaves for a penny, to be well made and well baked, as long as the wheat was 4s. the quarter. The brewers were not to brew less than a gallon of the best at a penny, and of other beer a gallon at a farthing; so long as the quarter of barley was at 4s. The vintners (who then kept shops, at the counters of which wine was sold in small measures) were bound to sell Gascony at 6d. the gallon, and they were prohibited from keeping the

E dregs to mix with the good wine. A custom then prevailed among a certain class of inhabitants, called "forestallers," of intercepting the country people on the mornings of market-days, as they were coming into the town, and buying up their eggs and poultry, in order, by getting the whole supply into their hands, to sell them again to the townspeople at the highest prices they could obtain. This was called "regrating." The Mayor and his colleagues ordained that no poulterer, regrater, nor cook, should purchase any kind of victuals before six o'clock in the morning; and that forestalled should not be al-

lowed to go to the end of the town to purchase any kind of provisions coming into it. The cooks, like the vintners, were independent of the innkeepers, and their shops were much more frequented than the taverns, which were generally more in use as lodgings for travellers than as places of resort for occasional refreshment. The cooks had a careless and uncleanly habit of throwing all their refuse into the streets, before their doors, thus creating very unsavoury smells. To remedy this, the Mayor and his colleagues threatened the offenders with a "grievous" penalty, if they continued the practice. In this age of insanitary customs, the townspeople kept pigs on their premises very commonly, and, not content with that, they let them loose in the streets; so that herds of those animals ran about the place, feeding probably upon the garbage thrown in the middle of the ways by the thoughtless and careless portion of the inhabitants. To mitigate the nuisance, the local authorities required that no pigs should be allowed (unless they were *rung*) to go loose in the High Street, and that line of street which connected St. Nicholas' Street with the East Gates. In the back streets, it is to be supposed, the pigs, unrung, wandered and rooted up the pavement as they pleased. On market-days, when provisions were high, strangers would sometimes mount the waggons of the country people, and harangue them, with threats of popular violence, to put lower prices on their provisions than they intended to do. This and some other practices met the disapproval of the Mayor and Town Council, and were duly interdicted.

In a town where the refuse of its dwellings was thrown into the streets, and swine were generally kept and ran unchecked in the highways, the free ventilation of the air being neither cared for nor studied, epidemics necessarily inflicted extensive mortality. In 1340 a strange kind of sickness was generally prevalent throughout the country, and was fearfully operative in this town in particular. Those who were seized with it were severely afflicted with pain, and in their paroxysms made a noise resembling that of dogs barking.

The successor of Earl Henry was his oldest and only son, Henry, who was created Earl of Derby in the year 1337. He was almost continually engaged in the wars of the period, either in Scotland or France, and was distinguished by his knightly courage and prowess. The burgesses of Leicester made him gifts before he became their lord; on one occasion presenting him £20, when he returned from Scotland, and on another sending to him bread and wine when he was hunting at the Frith, in the forest near Leicester. When he succeeded to his father in the year 1346-47, the townsmen signalized the opportunity by special gifts, among which were lampreys procured from Gloucester, and fish from the Soar.

A still more terrible plague raged through England in the year 1349 than that which has just been noticed. Its ravages in Leicester were appalling. The people were carried off by hundreds, if not thousands. The number of deaths in St. Leonard's parish was 380; in St. Martin's above 400; and in St. Margaret's 700; the mortality in other parishes being after the same proportion. These particulars are supplied by a writer who, living then in Leicester Abbey, was an eye-witness to the dreadful effects of the plague. At the time when the dead lay on every side, the things of this life had little or no value in the estimation of survivors, who did not know what a day might hring forth in relation to themselves. Henry of Knighton tells us that a horse, which in ordinary times would be worth 40s. , would now sell for 6s. 8d., a fat ox for 4s., and a cow for Is., and other things after the same rate. It was observed that the pestilence was most destructive among the poor and therefore ill-fed portion of the inhabitants.

In the year following, an adjourned meeting of Parliament was held in this town; being the first occasion on which such an assembly was seen in Leicester. The effects of the plague do not seem to have deterred the Lords and Commons from holding their session in this locality. It was at this meeting that the Commons manifested their opposition to the Duke of Sussex, which was followed by his banishment by the royal order. The two houses met, in all probability, in the Hall of the Castle and in St. Mary's Church.

The lord of the town, already Earl of Lancaster, Leicester, Ferrers, Grismond, and Derby, was in the year 1349 created Earl of Lincoln; and with this accumulation of honours was associated an accumulation of responsibilities, as there was scarcely an embassy or campaign with the conduct of which he was not at this period entrusted; but the greatest of his honours was his elevation to the Dukedom Of Lancaster, which took place on the 6th of March, 1351. This was conferred on the earl by the special charter of Edward the Third, and, being girded by a sword, he was formerly invested for life with the title and dignity by the consent of all the prelates and peers sitting at Westminster. By this act he was endowed with a princely authority, acquiring power to have a chancery or court in the county of Lancaster, and to issue writs from that court under his own seal; not only such as related to crown pleas, but those connected with the common law of the kingdom. All the liberties and regalities pertaining to a County Palatine were, in fact, granted to him—the Duke being within his palatinate a sovereign, equal to any of the Dukes or Grand Dukes of modern Germany, in the nature of his power, and superior to some in the extent of his jurisdiction. *No* subject in England had ever before attained powers and honours so extensive as this nobleman.

The Duke of Lancaster was often a resident in the Castle; and, when there, probably gave audiences to his burgesses, who, whenever they felt any local custom irksome, sought his aid to release them from its continuance, or his help at the court of the sovereign to procure a charter of privileges. The regraters (spoken of already) who purchased provisions wholesale, and sold them retail, were subjected as hucksters to a payment called "huckster-moll," which was first levied upon them in the time of Earl Edmund, the duke's grandfather, more than fifty years before. When the duke was at the Castle of Leicester, in the feast of the Magdalen, in the year 1353, he gave the inhabitants a release from the payment in question. The duke reserved to himself in this charter the right of panishing offenders against the assize of bread and beer, and all offenders against common or special law. With the superstition so characteristic of the age in which he lived, the duke assigned as his reason for abandoning the "huckster-moll" his desire in this way— by performing a work of charity—to promote "above all things the salvation of his own soul and those of his ancestors."

When the middle classes of the towns began to grow comparatively rich (as they did in Edward the Third's reign) they founded associations called Guilds, having a similar object in view. They were also accompanied by public processions, in which the host (the consecrated wafer) was borne in procession through the principal streets, on a certain day every year, carried by a priest under a canopy; of which the Mayor and chief men of the town were proud to be the bearers. From the fronts of the houses tapestries were hung, and the day was one of general rejoicing. The Guild of this kind best known and earliest established in Leicester was called the Guild of Corpus Christi, and was constituted in the year 1349-50. On the Thursday after Trinity Sunday, in every year, the procession of Corpus Christi took place in this town, and was the principal holiday of the people.

Henry, Duke of Lancaster, enlarged the foundation of the Hospital in the Newarke begun by his father, and completed the Collegiate Church of "the Annunciation of the Blessed Virgin," in the year 1354, and it became a place to which pilgrims thronged from all quarters. He provided for a dean, twelve prebendaries, thirteen vicars choral, three clerks, six choristers, and a verger, who constituted the college. On the day when the regulations were adopted (in April 1355) the hearts of all reverent believers were made glad by a peculiar present. The duke made a gift to the college of a precious relic, which was no other than a thorn said to have been taken from the crown which Jesus Christ wore on his way to the crucifixion, and which the King of France, John the Good, had given to the duke as a marked act of favour, on a memorable occasion, four years previously!

The town had, at this date, besides its markets on Saturday and Wednesday, a yearly fair, noticed in a former chapter. Originally it was held in June; in the reign of Henry the Third the day of holding it was altered to the second of February. In 1351, the Duke of Lancaster obtained from the king, for the benefit of the burgesses, the grant of another market and a second fair to be held in Leicester, which, it seems, was May Fair. It was to be regulated by the Mayor and two or three of the burgesses, who were to be chosen yearly, and called the "Stewards of the Fair." In the year 1360, the fair held in May was superseded and Michaelmas Fair held in lien of it, as appears by the Charter of Edward the Third. In this document (still in existence) the king refers to the petition of "his beloved and faithful relative, Henry, Duke of Lancaster and Earl of Leicester," to change the day of holding the fair from the feast of the Invention of the Holy Cross, and fifteen days after, to three days before and three days after the feast of St. Michael; and the monarch then, "mindful of the laudable and profitable dutifulness of the said duke for a long time shown" to him, grants his request. It is provided that all persons frequenting the fairs, whether natives or foreigners (that is, visitors from other towns) shall be free of toll, of payments for their stalls, and breaking up the pavement in fixing their booths, and all other customs and payments.

From January to July 1361, a terrible pestilence swept over England and France, nearly as fatal as that which only thirteen years before had made of this town a huge charnel-house. The duke had already executed his will, which was dated at his Castle of Leicester on March 15, 1360. He would seem to have

been a little more than fifty years of age; but the wear of military life in the Scotch and French wars had perhaps prostrated him prematurely. He gave minute instructions respecting his funeral; and his affection for the memory of his father induced him to desire that he might be buried near his remains, in the Collegiate Church of the Annunciation of our Lady at Leicester, close to the high altar. He, the greatest of the king's subjects, desired no ostentatious funeral. "Let me be buried," he said, "without pomp of armed men, or horses covered, or *other vanities.*" The pestilence seized him when he was in this town, and on the 24th of March, 1361— a week more than a year after the day on which he had made his will—died the first Duke of Lancaster at Leicester Castle.

While Edward the Third was carrying on his campaigns in Flanders, his queen was residing in the city of Ghent (pronounced commonly "Gaunt"), and on Midsummer Day, in the year 1340, gave birth to a third son, John, who was always called John of Gaunt in consequence. He was trained in all the accomplishments considered in his age necessary to the prince and the soldier. When young, he had frequent opportunities of visiting the household of his kinsman, Henry, Duke of Lancaster, and of enjoying the society of his fair cousins, the ladies Maud and Blanche. Probably he was a guest at the Castle of Leicester, where the duke and his daughters lived at intervals, and where the last months and last hours of the former were passed. That he was familiar with the place there is every reason to believe; but (what is more important to history) he conceived a very ardent attachment to Blanche, his younger cousin. She was not more than sixteen years of age when this passion was first formed. When John of Gaunt was eighteen (only two years older than Lady Blanche) he was so deeply enamoured of her that he sought to express his feelings in verse. He wrote thus:—

Lord! It maketh mine heart light,
When I think on that sweet wight,
That is so seemly on to see;

And wish to Q-od it might so be,
That she would hold me for her knight—
My lady that's so fair and bright.

The royal lover, when nineteen, was married to Lady Blanche, at Reading, in Berkshire. Maud, the elder daughter of the Duke of Lancaster, had married her cousin, William, the Duke of Bavaria, who was the son of Louis the Fourth, the Emperor of Germany.

When Henry, the first Duke of Lancaster, died, he left behind him, as his only successors, these two daughters. The elder inherited the castle, manor, and other possessions appertaining to the earldom of Leicester, and her husband was designated Earl of Leicester and Steward of England (by courtesy). But she enjoyed them only a brief period; her decease, without issue, taking place in the year following that in which her father's occurred. The Lady Blanche succeeded to her share of her father's possessions, which lay chiefly in the counties of York, Lancaster, Chester, and Warwick. Her husband, on the decease of the Duchess of Bavaria (by virtue of Blanche's right to inherit what had belonged to her sister), laid claim to the whole of the titles, rights, and privileges, which had been the Duchess's, and thus succeeded in obtaining the vast heritage and apanage of the late Duke of Lancaster. A few months after, he was advanced in parliament to the dukedom himself. The king completed the investiture by girding him with a sword, and placing upon his head a cap of fur surmounted by a circlet of gold adorned with pearls. For a few years only, after this accession of honour, had John of Gaunt the happiness to possess his young wife. Like her sister, she seems to have been of frail constitution. She died in 1369, when only in her twentyseventh year. For three years the duke mourned her loss; but in the year 1372 he took a second wife, espousing Constance, the elder of the two daughters of the King of Castille and Leon. On making this marriage (the king being dead), he assumed the title ot King of Castille, and impaled the royal arms upon his shield; though he was not successful in maintaining his claim.

In its corporate capacity, the town possessed property to a very limited extent, and collected but a very small income, in the middle of the thirteenth century. At first, its accounts were so unimportant that the items were loosely entered upon a Guild roll by the Mayor's clerk, the Mayor keeping the purse or bag, which literally held all that was received from all sources. In the year 1257, this total was derived from the payments of new members entering the Guild, and from the rental of one house which belonged to the borough: the items being, respectively, 31s. 8d. and 19d., altogether 33s. 3d. Between forty and fifty years after, the person (not the Mayor) to whom the treasurership was entrusted gave aD account of his receipts and expenses: they were, for the year 1297, respectively, £7 16s. 7d. and £8 10s. 8d. In the year 1318, the expenses had increased to £31 11s. 5d,, exceeding the receipts by 4s. 11d. At this time, Hugh the town sergeant and the Mayor's clerk received each half a mark (6s. 8d.) yearly for their services. When, however, the town income improved (as it did in the reigns of Edward the Second and Edward the Third) the Mayor was allowed to hold an annual feast, which generally followed upon the presentation of the Mayor in the Earl's court, held in the Castle, in recognition of the Earl's feudal authority over the townsmen. At this feast the Earl's steward was entertained as the principal guest. An additional cause of augmented income, probably, was a fresh arrangement entered into by the burgesses with the Duke of Lancaster in relation to the town-tolls. It seems that in the year of his decease, the burgesses made a contract with him to convey to him and his heirs the manor of Wrangle, in Lincolnshire, upon condition that he should release the inhabitants of the town, and strangers visiting its markets and fairs, from tolls, stallages, and pickage.

The property of the town in the middle of the fourteenth century consisted of a tenement at the West Gate, a chamber over the East Gate, and a place near the South Gate— the gates being, in truth, in the possession of the Mayor and burgesses; but in the last quarter of the century they acquired property at Whetstone, which raised the amount of rental from about 9s. yearly to 27s. 3d. yearly. In Eichard the Second's reign the yearly receipts had grown under these heads to nearly £6, namely, 36s. from the rents in Leicester, and £i 1s. from rents in Whetstone. In addition to this, about the same time the Duke of Lancaster made a transfer of nearly all the payments he levied by his bailiffs upon the townsmen, and all the sums they collected usually under the names of ancient customs, to the Mayor and burgesses, for a yearly payment to him in gross of £20. In this way the townspeople were relieved of the exactions and always officious interference of the Earl's bailiffs, and probably realised by the contract a considerable surplus for the common advantage; while the ancient baronial connection of the lords with the townspeople was thus reduced to a mere shadow.

But another consequence was, that the Mayor and Town Council and townspeople felt it necessary formally to institute a new class of borough functionaries, named Town Chamberlains, upon whom devolved veiy important duties. First, the Mayor was not in future to be held accountable for the town moneys: he was to be paid ten pounds of silver yearly, on tbres days stated, of which 40s. was to be allowed for his feast, 40s. for the wages of his sergeant, 20s. for his clerk, and the remainder for his own charges and expenses. Secondly, it was ordained that if any costs should be incurred "on account of our lord the King, the lord of the town, or any other lord or lady whatsover, or any other man, in the name of the said town, that the said expenses should be ordered by the Mayor for the time being, the Mayor with the jurors and twenty-four of the commons, or by the whole of the community." Thirdly, it was ordained that the two Chamberlains, annually chosen, should repair, maintain and mend, the gates, walls, ditches, pavements, and houses belonging to the town, on view of the Mayor for the time being, and at the expense of the whole community. Fourthly, it was ordained that the two Chamberlains should annually collect all rents and other payments belonging to the community and to the Merchant Guild, and render their accounts yearly before the Mayor and certain auditors, to be chosen by the Town Council and community. And, fifthly, it was ordained that the Chamberlains should receive yearly 40s. of silver from the town, to be paid to them on three certain days, every year for their services.

In the month of September 1392, William Mercer and William Spencer gave to the Mayor and burgesses lands and tenements in Leicester, Whetstone, and Great Glen, towards the amendment and reparation of the six bridges within the town of Leicester, and for other charges within the said town arising. Before this donation became valid, however, an inquiry took place to ascertain how far the interests of the Crown would be affected by the transfer; and the result was, that in consideration of a payment of £20 to the King he granted his license to his "beloved Mayor and Community" that William Mercer and William Spencer might assign to them, to hold for themselves and successors, the property in question.

In the latter part of the fourteenth century the town became the scene of memorable events, arising out of the intellectual and theological revolution which then commenced in this district. In 1374, John of Gaunt conferred the rectory of Lutterworth upon Wickliffe; and this Was followed by the general diffusion of the Eeformer's views in the town and county of Leicester. He organised a body of poor priests, who, in respect to their outdoor ministrations, like the Primitive Methodists of a later age, went from town to town, and village to village, in defiance of bishops and clergy. They inveighed everywhere against the corruption, the venality, and the hypocrisy of the established priesthood. In Leicester the cause was taken up by a poor little, inconsiderable townsman named Smith, and a priest named Wagstaffe, and these two men used to resort to the end of the town, near the Horse Water on the Belgrave Road, and there expounded the principles which they had learnt, doubtless, from Wickliffe. At first, the poor only went to hear them—then the rich; and, at last, they made so many converts, that the authorities expelled them from the society to which they belonged, and banished them altogether from the town. They especially provoked the wrath of the ecclesiastical authorities by ridiculing the saints and burning an image of St. Catherine. But the movement in Leicester was not stopped by the expulsion of the two Wickliffites: it seems only to have derived additional-force and prevalence from the measure.

It was then attempted to put down the movement with a high hand, and accordingly the great heretic himself, Dr. Wickliffe, was summoned to appear before the Bishop of London, in St. Paul's Cathedral, to answer the charge of holding heretical doctrines. The proceedings terminated in utter confusion, amid which John of Gaunt and Wickliffe escaped from the cathedral. Five years after (1382) the ecclesiastical opponents of Wickliffe renewed their efforts to crush him and his disciples. They associated with him in their accusation Nicholas Harford, Philip Reppington, John Ashton, and Lawrence Redman, against whom they took formal proceedings. Of these men, the three first-named were bachelors of divinity. Reppington was a canon of Leicester Abbey: he afterwards recanted and was made abbot, and then he became a bitter persecutor of the Wickliffites. Of Harford's and Redman's fate little or nothing is recorded. Wickliffe was condemned by the convocation held at Oxford, deprived of his professorship of Divinity, and banished from the University. John of Gaunt either would not, or could not, defend him any longer from the persevering persecution of the bishops; and, besides, the Pope had summoned him to Borne, to answer for his heresies. Scarcely three months subsequent to this date, he was assisting his curate in the celebration of the mass, in

the church at Lutterworth, on the 29 th of December, 1382, when he was seized with paralysis. In this condition he was carried out of the chancel to the parsonage, and there, two days after, he died.

The seed sown by Wickliife and his disciples in this locality had produced an abundant harvest. It was said, not many years after, that in Leicester and Leicestershire, there was not a man or woman (except the priests and nuns) who did not openly profess their disbelief in the doctrines of the church, and. their approval of the new views of the Lollards. The place of the great man himself was also quickly and not unworthily filled: the mantle of Wickliffe fell upon the shoulders of William of Swynderby.

This was a man of remarkable character. A recluse, living in a cell he had made for himself in the woods which approached the western gateway of the town, he led a life of religious reverie and solitude. He frequently issued from his retreat and visited this town, in order to address the inhabitants. On these occasions he spared neither the vanity of the women in their fondness for showy dress, nor the covetousness of the men, who were absorbed then, as now, in money-making. Nor did he spare himself; for he refused the gifts which the townspeople continually pressed upon him, and he lived in all austerity the life of a hermit. John of Gaunt ordered that he should be provided with the necessary means of subsistence, and even the monks of the abbey esteemed him for his sanctity. Swynderby preached from the pulpits of St. Martin's and St. Margaret's Churches in this town, and in the parish churches of Melton Mowbray, Hallaton, Harborough, and Loughborough

At this time, also, among the townspeople there were some who openly and boldly avowed the Lollard doctrines— their disbelief in the real presence, their disapproval of the worship of images, the non-necessity of confession to a priest, the fitness of every good man, though unlearned, to preach the gospel, and other similar convictions. The names of these persons were Robert

Dexter, Nicholas Taylor, Michael Scrivener, John Henry, William Parchmener, and Roger Goldsmith; in addition to Smith and Wagstaffe, of whom mention has been made already.

The church of St. Peter was at this date standing in the parish to which it gave a name, near to the street still called St. Peter's-lane. In the graveyard, a female devotee had been allowed to seclude herself in a hut with which she had provided herself, and was called an "anchoress." She was known by the townspeople simply as "Matilda." In her quiet and solitary cell, the roar of the waves of controversy reached her ears, and she, too, caught the enthusiasm of her neighbours in respect to the prevailing teachings of the Lollards. Impelled by her zeal, she emerged from her retreat and often spoke in the churchyard of St. Peter's to crowds of eager listeners. While she was thus holding forth, Swynderby was sometimes preaching on the same spot as that on which Smith and Wagstaffe had so often addressed the people, on the Belgrave Road, near the chapel of St. John the Baptist. Two millstones were left there for sale: the bystanders placed one upon the other, and from this elevation the forest hermit poured forth his exhortations and warnings to the listening throng of sympathising townspeople.

For seven years subsequent to the death of Wickliffe, these proceedings were carried on with great fervour and popular approval. The hermit, the anchoress, the converted priests, and the zealous laymen, all laboured together in the dissemination of the new views. The ecclesiastical authorities were for some time apparently passive; but they were all the while secretly active and incessantly watchful. They commissioned spies to go among the Reformers, to take notice of their proceedings. These men were friars, named Frisby, Hinceley, and Blaxton. The second was an Augustine, and the third a Dominican. When all was ready for the attempt to suppress the "heretical" movement, in the year 1382, the wellconcerted measures of the church dignitaries were successively carried out. Swynderby was cited to appear at Lincoln; to which city he went, accompanied by many of the most considerable of the inhabitants of Leicester. The accusation of heresy was preferred against him before John, Bishop of Lincoln; and so certain were his accusers of convicting him, that it is related that they carried wood with them to that city, to supply the necessary materials for burning him at the stake. But Swynderby shrank from martyrdom: he recanted, and promised never more, either secretly or openly, to teach his doctrines to the people, and he undertook to read his recantation in those pulpits in which he had preached his so-called "heresies." Yet he afterwards violated his promises, and pursued his mission of propagandism in the west of England; and it is supposed that he was at last burnt to death in Smithfield, early in the reign of Henry the Fourth.

It was towards the close of the same year as that in which Swynderby was taken to Lincoln that Courtney, Archbishop of Canterbury, made an official visit to this town, taking up his residence at the Abbey. The hierarch was evidently resolved on crushing the Reform party with all the weight of the Church, and, if need be, to destroy itwith flames and to drown it in blood. He summoned before him Dexter, Taylor, Wagstaffe, Scrivener, Smith, Henry, Parchmener, and Goldsmith. They were to appear at the Abbey on the 1st of November; but when that day arrived, none of them were present. "Whether they were obstinate or terrified, does not appear. The primate was not, however, to be thus easily baffled: his next step was to excommunicate the offenders amid all the thunders of the church's anathemas delivered from the high altar of Leicester Abbey. On the following day (Nov. 2) he laid the whole town under interdict; so to remain as long as any of the excommunicated persons should be sheltered within its walls, and until they should abjure their heresies, and seek at his hands the requisite absolution. By this measure the archbishop suspended all the operations of social and commercial life in the place; paralyzing every movement of the inhabitants. On the 6th of November, he issued his order to the Mayor and Bailiffs to arrest the recusants; and before the 17th Smith and Dexter were in the hands of the authorities, with Dexter's wife, Alice, who, it seems, had shared her husband's convictions. These three persons recanted, and were then compelled to do penance. The other heretics—Taylor, Wagstaffe, Scrivener, Henry,, and Parchmener— probably fled from the locality, and sought concealment elsewhere.

William Smith and Roger and Alice Dexter, were compelled to do penance on the Sunday next after the 17th of November in this manner: all being in their shirts, with no other garments upon them, were compelled to hold images of the crucifix in their right hands, and in their left hands tapers of wax, and in this condition to go before the cross three times during the procession of "the cathedral church of our lady of Leicester"—in the beginning, middle, and end of the procession—and when before the cross they were devoutly to bend their knees and kneel, and kiss the crucifixes in their hands. They were then to stand, during mass, before the cross, with the images and tapers in their hands; and at the conclusion to make offerings to the priest who had celebrated the mass. This was not all: on the Saturday following, the three persons were to stand in the same almost unclothed state in the full and public market, holding the crosses in their right hands, which they were devoutly to kiss three times—at the beginning, middle, and end of the market. William Smith, being some what acquainted with the Latin tongue, was required to say an anthem with a collect (Sancta Katherina), and Roger and Alice being unlearned were to say Ave Marias and Paternosters. A third time they were to go through a similar process in their own parish church; but the archbishop, out of compassion for the penitents, thinking that they "might take some bodily hurt, standing so long naked," mercifully allowed them to be covered with necessary garments while hearing the masses, though they were to remain bareheaded and barefooted. Still, in his benignity to the souls of the penitents, the archbishop thought it necessary they should remain for some hours uncovered in the market-place on a day in November!

Matilda, the anchoress, also retracted her statements, performed forty days' penance, and then was re-admitted to her hut in the churchyard—there to meditate for the remainder of her days on the church's tenderness in dealing with its erring children!

The space before the Great Meeting in this town was known about a century ago as "the Goldsmith's grave." In ancient days, only outcasts and lost persons were allowed to be buried in unconsecrated ground, and persons excommunicated by the church were of this class. The tradition is that one of the Wickliffites was here thrown into the earth, without ceremony. The probability is, that it was Roger Goldsmith; and that here, abandoned by every human creature, he may have perished while the town was under interdict. When these examples had been made of heretics, the townspeople seem, outwardly at least, to have returned to their ancient usages.

Although John of Gaunt was in this town and district a favourite with the populace, this was not the case in London, where he was much disliked, chiefly because he had threatened personal injury to the metropolitan bishop when Wickliffe appeared before him at St. Paul's cathedral, and because he had proposed a bill in the House of Peers to deprive the city of London of its privileges. While the duke was absent in Scotland, Jack Straw and his followers set fire to his house in London, called the Savoy Palace, and burnt his rich furniture, deeds, and valuables. One evening a messenger arrived in the town, informing the Mayor that the rioters were rapidly approaching Leicester—being then at Market Harborough—and by one o'clock next day would be at the town gates, as they intended to plunder and destroy the Castle. However, the insurgents never reached Leicester; but the circumstance served to evoke a display of attachment to the interests of the duke which proved how high he stood in the estimation of his burgesses.

John of Gaunt had castles at Lincoln, Kenilworth, Bolingbroke, and Pontefract; but his favourite place of reaidence was undoubtedly at the Castle of Leicester. In the month of August, 1390, the duke here received Richard II. and his queen, the archbishop of York, the duke of York, the duke of Gloucester, the earl of Arundel, the earl of Huntingdon, and many other lords and bishops; and for several days the duke entertained the royal party. In the year following he was almost continually dwelling in Leicester Castle, in those intervals which elapsed between the frequent visits he made to France as a negociator of international treaties. While he was absent, engaged in completing a treaty of peace with tbe Dukes of Berry and Burgundy, his Duchess Constance died, most probably at the Castle, for her interment took place in the Collegiate Church of our Lady, near the high altar, in the month of June. It is one of the blots on the character of this Duke of Lancaster that he contracted an intimacy, during the lifetime of his Duchess Constance, with Catherine Swinford. Originally in the service of John of Gaunt's first wife, she became the mother of three sons and a daughter by the Duke, all born illegitimate. At this time she was living openly with him at the Castles of Leicester and Lincoln. When in this town her influence over her protector was well understood by the burgesses, as an item in the account of the Mayor of Leicester, for the year ending Michaelmas, 1378, bears evidence. It records that the Mayor asked for an allowance for a horse and an iron platter, to be given to the Lady Catherine of Swynford, for supplicating in "influential quarters" for the expedition of business touching a tenement in Stretton and other houses.

The duke did not long survive his marriage with this lady, and within two years after appears to have had a premonition of his decease; as, early in the month of February, 1398, he made his will, which, like those of his predeces-

sors, the first duke of Lancaster and the father of that duke, was dated from the Chamber in which they died in the Castle House of Leicester. In this document John of Gaunt made the most careful disposition of all his effects. One year after the date, overwhelmed with trouble, and afflicted with disease, he died at Ely House, Holborn. He was buried, as he desired, in Old St. Paul's Cathedral, near the grave of his first wife, Richard the Second being present at the funeral, which was conducted with great pomp and solemnity.

After the decease of this nobleman, there were no longer any resident lords. For nearly 350 years had these barons exercised an authority, at one period almost supreme, by degrees diminishing to a shadow of its former greatness, in the Borough of Leicester. As the reader will have observed, they were men who had always held high positions in the state; sometimes helping to make and to unmake the kings of England. The Castle of Leicester was at once their feudal fortress and their palatial residence; but, after John of Gaunt had made his will in one of its chambers, no other personage of lordly degree seems to have dwelt within its walls. It fell gradually into disuse as a place of abode, and finally into dilapidation and decay; and there were no longer seen in the streets of Leicester the stalwart forms of its ancient barons.

THE LANCASTRIAN AND YORKTST PEEIOD. FROM A.D. 1399 TO A.D. 1485. Chapter VI.

Thfi only son of John of Gaunt, born in wedlock, was known as Henry of Bolingbroke. He married Mary de Bohun, daughter of Humphrey, Earl of Hereford, by whom he had four sons and two daughters. This lady was the mother of that "madcap" prince, whom Shakspere has associated with Sir John Falstaff. She had been dead about five years, when her husband obtained the crown, on the abdication of Richard the Second. He was thus the third Duke of Lancaster; having held that title during eight months before he was crowned Henry the Fourth of England. On his attaining the monarchy, all his lesser ti-

tles merged into it; with the rest, the earldom of Leicester, and the possessions pertaining to that earldom, including the castle and manor of Leicester, which still remain the royal property, excepting so far as any manorial rights may have been transferred to the town authorities at dates subsequent to the time of Henry the Fourth.

We have seen that in the year after the occurrence of the plague in this town, in the reign of Edward the Third, an adjourned meeting of parliament was held here. It was sixty-four years after when the legislature again assembled within the walls of Leicester. In that interval, the Wicklifntes had carried on their proceedings in this locality, as already related. Leicester was appropriately chosen, then, as the place in which Parliament could mark its high displeasure in regard to the growing heresy of the day. In the great hall of the Grey Friars Monastery, near St. Martin's Church, and another building called *le Fermerie,* near at hand, the two houses assembled on the 30th of April 1414.

The Bishop of "Winchester, who was the king's uncle, forgetful of the tolerant part played by John of Gaunt, his father, sounded the first note for the persecution of the Lollards. The two houses did the bidding of the bishop; they enacted that all public officers should assist in extirpating heresy, and that heretics should be burnt at the stake, and their lands and goods confiscated. It is illustrative of the remarkable contrasts which history presents, that in this very session, in which relgious liberty received a very severe blow civil liberty gained a great step in advance: in this session the king granted for the first time that no law should be enacted, binding the Commons, *without their assent*—the rule having been, previously, to take that for granted. This must always be known as the Fire and Faggot Parliament, and must ever be identified with the town of Leicester; where the tares of heresy having grown, the torch for their destruction was kindled.

Eleven years after the date of this meeting—when Henry the Fifth had been gathered to his fathers—and Henry the Sixth was the child-king of England, Parliament again assembled in Leicester. This time it met in the great hall of the Castle, where now the assizes are held. In the year 1425, however, the space within the boundary walls of the building formed one large apartment, and this was the scene of the legislative deliberations.-When Lords and Commons were here assembled (Monday, February 18) the Bishop of Winchester (the same pereonage as that already mentioned) taking a text from the writings of St. Paul, addressed the body at length.

At this time a bitter feud was existing between Humphrey, Duke of Gloucester (youngest brother of the deceased monarch, Henry the Fifth), and the Bishop of Winchester; in consequence of which, John, Duke of Bedford—then constable of England—prohibited the barons and their followers, on both sides, from appearing at Leicester with their weapons. But the injunction was evaded by the same persons carrying upon their shoulders clubs, which were called "bats," and hence this was called the Parliament of Bats. When the clubs were also forbidden, the hostile parties loaded the long sleeves of their coats with great stones and plummets of lead, and, aimed in this way, combatted each other. The duke and the bishop were apparently reconciled by the intervention of Parliament. The houses were prorogued from the 20th of March to the Monday next after the ftast of St. George, in Leicester, when business was resumed.

A quarter of a century elapsed before another meeting of Parliament took place in this town. It was adjourned from Westminster, owing to the insalubrity of the air in that locality. The most stirring topic of debate at this time was the conduct of the queen and the Duke of Suffolk. During the session (which began on the 29th of August, 1450) the Commons presented an indictment against the duke to his peers, and persevered so violently in their opposition to him that many of the lords would not attend in their places in Leicester. The Parliament was accordingly re-adjourned to Westminster. This was the last occasion on which this town was the temporary seat of the Legislature.

In the year following, that bloody civil strife began which has been designated the "Wars of the Roses." Pichard, Duke of York, was the representative of his grandfather, Edmond of Langley, the fifth son of Edward the Third, and of Anne, his mother, who was the heiress of Lionel, Duke of Clarence, the third son of Edward the Third. Having thus the prior claim to the crown, the Duke of York had recourse to arms in the assertion of it in the year 1451; and the battles of St. Alban's, Blore Bath, Northampton, Wakefield, Mortimer's Cross, Bernard's Heath, and Towton, followed. In these actions the burgesses of Leicester bore their part.

At Kirby Muxloe, near this town, was residing at this date a family in the condition of knights, of ancient origin, named Hastings. Sir William Hastings entered the service of Richard, Duke of York, when a young man, and thus became early known to the sons of that nobleman, of whom the eldest was Edward, Earl of March. By this local connection, it is likely Sir William Hastings acquired an influence in this town, in the absence of a resident baron of the Lancaster family, and thus carried over to the Yorkist cause the Mayor and Corporation. The people of Leicester fought under their own flag, at the bloody battle of Towton, on the side of the Yorkist monarch; and probably had on other fields also lent their aid to his cause. Other towns, too, had taken their part with Edward, led by their captains, under their ancient ensigns. As a contemporary ballad, in its quaint terms, says:—

The wolf came fro Worcester, ful sure he thought to bite,
The dragon came fro Gloucester, he bent his tayle to smyte;
The griffin cam fro Leicester, fleying in as tyte,
The G-eorge cam fro Nottingham with spere for to fyte.

With the battle of Towton, a decisive superiority was given to the Yorkists, and the House of Lancaster was dispossessed of the throne, after having occupied it about sixty-two years.

The year after, when the victorious young monarch was at Leicester Castle, the mayor and two borough members had an interview with him, on which he granted the inhabitants twenty marks yearly for twenty years, in requital of their services against his enemies. About the same period also 1462, Edward gave a charter to the inhabitants for the appointment of a mayor, four magistrates, and a recorder, to decide upon all matters of transgression, misprison, extortion, and so forth; matters of felony, and offences against the laws relative to the coinage, being excepted. At a later period of Edward's reign, after the battles of Bamet and Tewkesbury, in which the townsmen again combatted on his side, he made them a second grant of £20 yearly for the term of twenty years; which was followed in a year or two by the concession of a license to hold a fair about the time of the Feast of St. Philip and St. James—the re-institution of the well-known May Fair.

One invariable consequence of Civil War is the relaxation of the laws of the land, if not an abandonment of all respect for them; men becoming, in the constant practice of violence and by the frequent use of arms, reckless of all civil restraints. Accustomed to the license of the military campaign, and of a wandering life, they too frequently learn to despise the wholesome usages of well-ordered and settled communities; and even the members of such communities themselves become in turn infected by the contagion of disorder and lawlessness. In Leicester, it would appear, the presence of disbanded soldiery, and the repeated passage of bodies of armed men through the town, and the unsettling influence of internecine strife, produced their natural effects in the critical period intervening between the battles of Towton and those of Barnet and Tewkesbury, in the irregular proceedings of the governing body, and the turbulent conduct of the townspeople. When the Town Council met in the Guild Hall, the mass of the inhabitants, whether privileged or unprivileged, freemen or non-freemen, intruded themselves, and in an unseemly manner interrupted the business; sometimes shouting out and nominating the Mayor for the ensuing year. The Mayor and his Brethren, the chosen Council of the Guild, felt called on to provide a remedy for the confusion and hindrance to the transaction of their affairs thus occasioned. They therefore resolved, on October 18, 1467, all the "Commons" being present, to commit to prison for forty days any unfranchised person—that is, any one who was not a member of the Merchant Guild, in other-words, a freeman—who entered the hall and attempted to remain there; adding a fine of 11d., to he paid before the offender was liberated. If any person cried out or named any of the Mayor's Brethren to the office of the Mayoralty, before the preliminary proceedings had been complied with, he was liable to a certain period of imprisonment and a penalty. At this time, too, it was a common practice among men to appear in the streets in their armour; wearing their habergeons about their necks and chests, and their helmets, and carrying their bills, swords, long staffs, and daggers, and thus provoking breaches of the public peace. Ihey also met together in assemblies within the town; some of them wearing the liveries of noblemen and gentlemen, as their avowed retainers The townsmen also took different sides, identifying themselves with one or other of the conflicting parties in the State; lending the countrymen of the adjoining district who cane into the place as "sympathizers" bills, staves, pole-axes, and other weapons, to help them in the affrays which were doubtless occurring every day. The Mayor (Richard Gillot), being at the head of the town government, was at this peculiar emergency entrusted with almost despotic power. He summoned all the people to appear at the Common Hall, or at any other place he might appoint, to help him in keeping the king's peace, and if any man refused to come, the Mayor could break open the door of the recusant's house, and

drag him to the place of rendezvous. By regulations adopted at a Common Hall, held within a week or two after that at which the non-freemen were debarred from being present at the Corporation Meetings, the extraordinary authority here described was given to the Mayor, and all manner of men were forbidden to wear armour, or carry weapons in the street unless in support of the chief magistrate; but a knight or esquire might have his sword borne after him by his servant. Every person coming out of the country into the town was compelled to leave his weapons at his inn, and nobody was allowed to walk out after nine o'clock had struck, without light or without reasonable cause, on pain of imprisonment. No man living in the town was allowed to " draw to conventicles, meetings, or assemblies within the town"; "nor to take any livery, gown, or holding of any man of any estate or degree, for maintenance of any man, or of any kind of dispute "; nor to lend any kind of weapon to "any other man of the country "; nor to refuse to disobey the summons of the Mayor's officers, when required to ride on the side of the king, or to accompany the Mayor when he needed their help and presence. Three years later the battles of Barnet and Tewkesbury happened, being followed by the firm establishment of Edward the Fourth on the throne. But the fierce and terrible encounters of the partisans of the rival houses of York and Lancaster had disturbed society to its deepest foundations, in every city and borough in the island.

When Bichard the Third had succeeded his brother Edward, the "slander ran upon the town of Leicester," says an ancient record, "to the utter destruction of this great town," that it was infested with " evil-disposed persons," "vagabonds," "pettybribers,rioters," "evil-disposed women," and common scolds; and there were broken pavements and stones, timber, and filth lying about the streets in all directions. In order to remove the public reproach to which these persons, and the state of things generally had given rise, it was ordained by the Mayor, "the right hon-

ourable and worshipful John Boberds," his Brethren and the Commonalty assembled at the Common Hall, that the town should be divided into twelve wards, with an Alderman placed over each ward, on whom were conferred plenary powers to correct and punish transgressors.

The Earl of Richmond having landed at Milford Haven, on the first of August 1485, Richard made his preparations to prevent his further progress; making Nottingham the principal rallying-place for his forces before advancing to intercept the progress of his enemy. It seems probable he entered Leicester with his army on the evening of Friday or Saturday, the 19th or 20th; mustering his forces here on the Sunday after. As he rode into the town at the head of his men, his countenance was frowning with anger, and he breathed out curses against his enemies. He took up his lodging while in Leicester at the principal inn, then standing in the main thoroughfare, called the Blue Boar. Here he slept one or two nights; his eagerness to prevent Richmond's advance to London moving him to march on, without delay, towards Atherstone. IJe left Leicester on the Sunday, with the greatest pomp, wearing on his head the royal diadem. Tradition relates that when he was riding over the old Bow Bridge, an aged crone seated there, observing his armed heel came in contact with a stone, remarked that where it had struck his head would very soon strike. On the evening of Sunday the opposing armies lay within three miles of each other. In the course of the night Richard is said to have had the fearful dreams which Shakespeare describes. On the morning of Monday, the ill-fated monarch, with his 16,000 men, prepared to encounter his foe with half that number. The battle began about ten o'clock, and ended about noon; Richard being slain, and his naked corpse brought to Leicester, hacked to pieces, and thrown across the back of a horse— his head striking where his heel had struck only the day before. Alter being publicly exposed a few days, it was buried by the Franciscan Monks in their cemetery, near the

Church of St. Martin.

Chapter VII.

The occurrence of a bloody conflict near the town must have done much to brutalize the population. The streets, especially in the neighbourhood of the High Cross, often witnessed the affrays of armed men; market day being the time when they commonly happened. In the third year of Henry the Seventh, during the mayoralty of Kichard Wigston, at a Common Hall, at which the Mayor's Brethren and all the Commons attended, it was resolved that if any person made an affray at the High Cross, and drew blood, he should pay a fine of 6s. 8d., and the same amount if any offender committed the offence on the market-day, in any part of the town, without shedding blood. Were any person to draw the blood of an opponent, in any part of the town, not on the market-day, a penalty of 3s. 4d. was to be itiflicted.

On the suppression of the Civil "War, however, accompanied by the very general destruction of the aristocracy, the royal authority became consolidated and undisputed. Henry the Seventh was virtually an autocrat. In this town, we learn, at the meetings of the Corporation, the "Commonalty"—the mass of the townspeople—still insisted on being present when the Council chosen to transact the public business ordinarily assembled. By their " obstinacy and exclamations," besides "frequent breaches of the peace," the interlopers, "who contributed little or nothing to the public charges," as the old records relate, created great confusion at the assessing of the public burdens and the election of the burgesses in Parliament; indeed, they rendered such meetings little better than what, in modern phraseology, are called "bear-gardens." The King accordingly, having been duly informed of this state of affairs, forwarded his mandate to the town, requiring the the Mayor and his Brethren, and the Bailiff, thereafter to choose forty-eight of the most "wise and sad commoners" to be present at the Common Halls and other assemblies, when the Mayor, Justices, and Members of Parliament were chosen and the taxes were levied, and they together were to order and direct all matters arising among them. It was not without bitter opposition this municipal revolution was effected; but an Act of Parliament having been passed (1490), embodying its details, the new system was enforced, and regulated the proceedings of the Corporation thereafter. Before the termination of the first Tudor's reign, a royal charter conferred powers on the Corporation, which added to it their authority what the concentration of its numbers had strengthened not many years before: the Justices appointed by it being enabled to adjudicate in cases of murder, felony, and other grave offences. Besides which, the right to be taxed by themselves, independently of the county justices, was granted to the body. The borough magistrates were also at this time allowed to have "wages," as their contemporaries had in the country.

Among the families of the town who had " grown with its growth," and shared in its prosperity, on the cessation of the Civil War, was one named Wigston. Originally, perhaps, a simple peasant, living in an adjoining village, its founder had laid the basis of his descendants' ampler fortunes in the earlier part of the fifteenth century, by engaging in the wool trade. Leicester, as the centre of a grazing district, has for an unknown period been the storeplace and mart of the raw material of which one kind of clothing is manufactured. In the course of the labours of three or four generations, the Wigstons accumulated great wealth, and were enabled to purchase estates. The bulk of their property fell by inheritance to William of Wigston, who had doubtless increased it by his own industry and enterprise. This remarkable and munificent man— who stands out to all time as the town's most considerable benefactor—was approaching old age, when, being without children to inherit his possessions, he resolved on bequeathing them to purposes of charity. The only form of it which seemed open to him to adopt was the foundation of a Hospital. Associating with himself his two brothers (one of them a priest) in the year 1513, he obtained letters-patent from Henry the Eighth to found and endow such an institution, for the benefit of twelve poor men and twelve poor women; assigning, as his motive for so doing, his desire to offer "an evening sacrifice to the Most High," now that " the flower of his age had passed in earthly cares and employments." The building wherein the recipients of Wigston's bounty were to lodge, was commenced shortly after the dace of the letters-patent; but the benevolent Wigston who saw it begun did not live to see it completed. His executors finished his work about the year 1520, and for three centuries and a half it provided a place of refuge for a long list of aged persons who might, in its absence, have perished in utter destitution and hopeless misery.

At this period all England was full of the story of Cardinal Wolsey. That ambitious and haughty prelate divided the attention of the world with his royal master. By his supple and pliant manners, and his accommodating principles, he had succeeded in retaining the king's favour for many years; but ia the course of the proceedings taken by Henry to procure a divorce from Queen Katherine, Wolsey had awakened the royal suspicions that he was not faithful, and that he was deceptively seeking to promote his own personal purposes. All parties at the same time conspired to destroy him. On the 9th of October, 1529, the Attorney-General commenced a prosecution against him for procuring bulls from Eome without the king's license. Wolsey confessed the offence of which he was accused by the Attorney-General: and the effect of the sentence upon him was that the Cardinal, with all his vast possessions, fell into the king's hands. In the following February the Earl of Northumberland was chosen to apprehend him for high treason. He was carried first to Sheffield Park, the residence of the Earl of Shrewsbury, where he was lodged eighteen days; the Earl providing for him several servants among his own gentlemen, and directing that the Cardinal should be served in his own chamber at dinner and supper with as much honour and as many dainty dishes, as he was accustomed to have in his own house when at liberty. After "Wolsey had been at Sheffield Park a fortnight (during which period he declined to take part in hunting or any other sport, but gave himself to devout prayer continually), he was taken unwell after eating heartily of warden pears at dessert. On Thursday, the 25th of November, he set out southwards, in the custody of Sir William Kingston and the Guards, who, as soon as they saw their old master in such a painful condition, with tears in their eyes testified their sorrow. On Saturday they pursued their way to Leicester; on the way he became so extremely unwell, and his attacks were so frequent, that several times he was in danger of falling from his mule.

After a long ride on a dreary November day, over a desolate country, and prostrated by a severe and agonising disorder, the Cardinal reached the portals of our Abbey in the darkness of the evening. He was met at the gate by Abbot Pexall and the whole Convent, amid the glare of many torches. They received the Cardinal honourably and with great reverence. Exhausted by the fatigues of his journey, and the uninterrupted pangs of his complaint, he said to the abbot, "Father Abbot, I am come here to lay my bones among you." The attendants led his mule to the foot of the stairs conducting to his chamber, and there he alighted. Master Kingston then took him by the arm, and led him up the stairs. He lent heavily on the Constable; for that person afterwards told Cavendish he had never carried a heavier person in all his life. As soon as he was in his chamber, the Cardinal went to that bed from which he never rose again.

All Sunday he rested undisturbed; on Monday morning, about eight o'clock, when Cavendish stood by his bedside —the windows being shut close, and wax-lights burning upon the cupboard—he perceived the shadow of his attendant upon the adjoining wall, and

asked who was there. Cavendish replied that it was he; when a conversation ensued, in which the prostrate prelate enquired what it was of the clock. The reply was that it was past eight o'clock in the morning. "Eight of the clock *1*" asked the Cardinal, his mind evidently wandering as he repeated the remark interrogatively several times, "eight of the clock, eight of the clock; nay, nay, it cannot be eight of the clock; for by eight of the clock ye shall lose your master; for my time draweth near that I must depart out of the world."

An interview with Dr. Palmes, his confessor, hastened the end of the Cardinal. When it was over he seemed likely to die—he swooned several times. In his last confession, the Cardinal roused himself up for one final effort, and spoke his mind in these ever-memorable words:—

"Well, well, Master Kingston, I see the matter against me how it is framed; but if I had served God as diligently as I have done the king, he would not have given me over in my grey hairs. Howbeit this is the just reward that I must receive for my worldly diligence and pains that I have had to do him service; only to satisfy his vain pleasure, not regarding my Godly duty." He concluded, "Master Kingston, farewell. I can no more, but wish all things to have good success. My time draweth on fast I may not tarry with you. And forget not, I pray you,

Q what I have said and charged you withal: for when I am dead, ye sball peradventure remember my words much better." He then drew his speech at length—his tongue failed him—his sight failed him—his eyes were glazed in death. The persons around him put him in mind of Christ's passion, and sent for the Abbot to anoint him with the hallowed oil; and the accompanying service was ministered to him by the Abbot. But his spirit was not there. At eight o'clock on Tuesday morning it had departed; thus fulfilling his prophecy.

Sir William Kingston immediately despatched a messenger to the king, to inform him of the Cardinal's decease.

It was resolved to inter the body on the following day (Wednesday), and the Mayor and his Brethren were invited to attend at the Abbey and to look upon the last remains of Wolsey. Meanwhile, the attendants took the body out of bed and prepared it for interment. In his hairshirt was he laid in a coffin of boards; having upon him all the rich vestures and ornaments which he was professed in when consecrated bishop and archbishop. His mitre, his crosses, his ring, and his pall were placed either upon him or near him; as if he were intended to appear at the Day of Judgment still my Lord Cardinal of York in all his pomp and splendour. Lying thus all Tuesday in his coffin, open and barefaced, not yet removed from the chamber in which he died, the Mayor and his Brethren, and many other persons, saw the Cardinal's mortal remains.

About four in the morning of Wednesday, the monks sang mass; after which the coffin was lowered into the grave made in the chapel, and the earth was thrown over all that was left of the Cardinal, in the presence of Master Kingston, Master Cavendish, and the servants; and thus at six o'clock the whole ceremony was concluded.

The ancient fabric did not long outlast the mighty Cardinal. Six years after, an Act of Parliament was passed for the suppression of the lesser monasteries, and only three years later still another act was adopted, by which the surrender of the larger monasteries to the Crown was confirmed. The royal commissioner (Mr. Francis Cave) visited the Abbey in 1537, and called on the Abbot and Convent to surrender. This, in the first instance, they refused to do; but they consented before August, the date of his letter. Not long after, the plate and jewels were set aside for the king; the furniture and goods sold; the church, cloisters, and monk's apartments stripped of the lead which covered the roofs; and the whole building dismantled and left to fall into utter ruin and decay.

While all this was taking place in regard to the Abbey, the various ecclesiastical bodies in the town were dissolved, and their possessions granted to the Crown. In the year 1545 all colleges, free chapels, chantries, hospitals, and fraternities, with their lands, tenements, and other property were delivered over to Henry the Eighth. In the spring of that year a sale took place of the priests' vestments, the rich hangings of the altar, and the plate belonging to St. Martin's Church. In the following year other articles were similarly disposed of by the churchwardens. Meanwhile, the Bible was fastened to one of the pillars of the building for public perusal, and works enforcing the doctrines of the Reformed Church—as the "Paraphrase of Erasmus"—were purchased for the use of the congregation. When young Edward had succeeded his father, the stripping of the remaining ornaments from St. Martin's was continued; and, very generally in all the churches, the altars were taken down, Communion-tables being substituted. The great changes effected in the parish church of St. Martin were probably witnessed in all the other churches.

When Queen Mary followed her brother, on his decease, an attempt was made to reverse all the proceedings taken by the Reformers, by the restoration of the ornaments to the churches and of the use of the old ritual; and the infatuated revivalists persecuted a young husbandman named Thomas Moore, who was summoned to appear before the Bishop of Lincoln in the churches of St. Martin and St. Margaret, to meet various charges of heresy. In answer to questions, he boldly avowed his disbelief in the Real Presence; saying that the body of Christ was no more in the sacrament on the altar than His body within his doublet would be in a piece of bread, were he to say, "Take, eat—this is my body." He was burnt to death in this town for his so-called "heresy" in the month of June, 1556.

Two years after, the bells of the town churches rang out merrily to celebrate the proclamation of Queen Elizabeth. The introduction of new social and political influences followed. Hitherto, no law had existed for the maintenance of the destitute poor, who were left to crowd around the gateway of the Abbey, and the doors of the religious houses, there to receive the doles handed to them by the monks. A class of abject paupers must thus have been created. In this town, the first care of the authorities after the Reformation, was to find profitable industry for the poor inhabitants. The earliest endeavour in this direction was in the reign of Edward the Sixth; when it was agreed at a Common Hall that every year each of the Twenty Four (as the leading men of the municipal body were then designated) should cause two "kerseys" (a "kersey" being a piece of woollen cloth eighteen yards long), and each of the Forty Eight (as the remainder of the body was called) one "kersey," to be made. Altogether, 1,728 yards of cloth were to be woven in looms by the unemployed poor; and this was the beginning of the effort to employ the pauper population! About ten years subsequently, so ineffectual was the operation of this expedient that, over and above the collection made by virtue of Queen Elizabeth's statute, the four different classes constituting town society—the Twenty-Four, the Forty-Eight, the "best of the Commoners," and the " Second Commoners,"—paid respectively on their marriages, to the parishes in which they lived, 2s. 8d., 16d., 8d., and 4d. each, and on the "churching" of their wives the same sums; a poor man garbed in a black gown, and wearing a badge on his sleeve, being appointed to go round to the inns, and places where strangers resorted, to solicit alms for the poor. Even a lottery was had recourse to by way of eking out the funds for their relief. All these schemes, however, were only of temporary avail; the only satisfactory methods being those by which work was found in some branch of lucrative manufacture. The kersey-making does not appear to have answered long; for in 1572 a clothier named Bradgate, from Gloucester was invited to settle in the town, to set up cloth-making, at the special request of Henry, Earl of Huntingdon, then a resident in Leicester, and by the offer of a loan of 100 marks, for seven years, made by the Town Council. Thomas Bradgate came here accordingly. A member of his family, Henry Bradgate, succeeded him; but in 1584 he became embarrassed, and the Mayor and his colleagues wished to supersede him—a proposal to which the Earl would not consent. He, therefore, struggled on, though unsuccessfully; and, fifteen years after the cloth-making was altogether abandoned.

Before the Reformation, the tradesmen treated Sunday very much as they did every other day—keeping open their shop-windows for the sale of goods on that day; and the victuallers opened their doors during service-time on Sundays and Church festivals. At a Common Hall, held in February, 1562, an order for the closing of shops and public-houses on Sunday was passed, and the following year the authorities enacted that no butcher should sell meat on that day; nor was any miller to be allowed to S carry corn to, or from his mill on the same day of the week, until service was concluded in all the churches. All this time, too, compulsory attendance at week-day religious services was enforced by penalties.

Before the Reformation also, literary education was very generally neglected. Few men had been taught even its elements. It is doubtful whether the Mayors, as a rule, could even write their own names. But in the reign of Elizabeth this reproach was wiped away. Dr. Penny, Bishop of Carlisle, who had been Abbot of Leicester Abbey for thirteen years, on his decease, sometime in the early part of the sixteenth century, had given certain land to the local authorities to enable them to found a Grammar School; but in the year 1539 Mr. Beaumont, the Recorder, took the liberty of mis-appropriating the bequest. The movement was taken up again at the beginning of the reign of Elizabeth, in an earnest spirit, and a school-room was provided; but in the fifteenth year of her reign, the Church of St. Peter, then standing in a dilapidated condition, the Queen allowed the Mayor and his fellow-burgesses to take away all the lead, stone, and timber of the falling structure, and to use them up in the erection of a Free Grammar School. They had eight or nine years before granted annually a sum to be employed in the payment of the salaries of three masters. In this way the institution was established. As might have been inferred from the spirit of the times, much of the instruction was theological, a Calvinistic catechism being its basis; it was accompanied with classical teaching.

One great drawback on the happiness of the townspeople at this date was their poverty. The Mayor, in his letters addressed to the Earl of Huntingdon, customarily dated them from the "poor town of Leicester." In a report on the state of the town, drawn up in October 1587, a jury of investigation set forth that they were in " great decay" 235 houses in the town which had belonged to the dissolved colleges, hospitals, and guilds; that there were 406 bays of houses, with the timber, plaster, and slates, utterly "wasted and carried away"; and that some of these, standing in the principal streets, had fallen into ruin. Immediately consequent on the completion of this enquiry the inhabitants made an application to the Crown for a grant of the buildings enumerated; alleging that it was a "piteous thing to behold the great gaps and ruins— yea, even in the principal streets of this town.. Thirty parish churches there come to six, and four-andtwenty wards to ten"—a somewhat unveracious statement; though it would appear to have served its purpose, as the Queen, in a charter granted in the year after the date of the report, gave the Mayor and burgesses in fee-farm the week day shambles, the lands formerly belonging to the four colleges or guilds in Leicester, and the lease in reversion of the whole of the Newarke Giange.

The great acquisition of property by the burgesses, here indicated, was accompanied by the Incorporation of the Borough. The Queen, in the charter by which she conceded in fee-faim the shambles, lands, and Grange to the inhabitants, also conferred on them this position, which they had never before possessed. It is a mistake to suppose they had previously been "incorporated" in the legal sense of the term. The

term "Corporation," though used for convenience of designation, in connection with the Mayor and Aldermen and burgesses of earlier times, was not known to our civic ancestors before the reign of Elizabeth. It is, in fact, the abbreviated form of "Incorporation." But after the charter came into operation it was commonly and properly employed. The "Incorporation" of the inhabitants was rendered absolutely necessary in consequence of the transference of the property to them; as, without it, they could not thereafter sue or be sued, plead or be impleaded, legally hold or legally transfer land or houses: with the charter all these powers were conveyed from the Crown to the local community.

In the same year as that in which the borough of Leicester was incorporated, a great national event occurred: Elizabeth's Great Charter to Leicester is associated in our local annals with the Invasion of England by the Spanish Armada. At this time the arrangements for the protection ol England were such as would seem to modern readers very inadequate. In a town like Leicester only ten pikemen had been kept in readiness for some years; when, in 1583, the lords of the Privy Council charged the inhabitants with the cost of two demi-lances and four light horsemen, to be ready upon one day's warning, and in the following year the authorities were ordered to muster all the townsmen, on proper occasions, under the instructions of the Privy Council. The Mayor and his Brethren tried to escape the obligation to raise the horsemen, on the plea that it would be accomplished to their great injury or "utter undoing;" but the Government replied by requiring the borough to find twenty foot soldiers, the county meanwhile providing one hundred and thirty. These were pikemen, who were provided with iron caps for the head, and breast and back plates. In the year of the invasion the greatest efforts were made to supply soldiers to the army. Thomas Skeffington, Esq., the High Sheriff of the county (being at the time a resident at Belgrave), summoned together all males between the ages of 19 and 50, able to bear arms. Of this

class there were then 12,530 in the town and county; 2,000 of whom were despatched to the camp at Tilbury, there to be ready for service, the remainder being sent back from the place where they had assembled to their homes, furnished with various weapons, and under orders to muster as soon as they should hear news of the Spaniards having landed in England. The town was called on to supply 80 soldiers; 40 of whom were trained and despatched to Tilbury fort under command of Sir George Villiers—the other forty remaining at home as a body in reserve. Of the 40 men who were forwarded to the camp, 8 were supplied with muskets, 18 with calivers (a kind of hand gun), and 14 with pikes and corselets. By the gallant exertions of the British admirals, under the blessing of Providence, the Armada that was intended to be "Invincible," was scattered in the British Channel. On all sides there were unrestrained rejoicings: on every hill blazed a bonfire, in every hamlet a feast was made, and in every city the Corporation gave a banquet, to manifest the popular exultation and gratitude. The old Guildhall of Leicester was renovated and decorated for the occasion; and the Earl of Huntingdon, his brother, Walter Hastings, Esq., of Kirby Muxloe Castle (who had been in command of the Leicestershire men), and Thos. Skeffington, Esq., the High Sheriff, with most of the gentry of the county, and the magnates of the town, were sumptuously entertained at dinner by Mr. Geo. Noryce, the Mayor, in the ancient fabric; the bells of the adjoining tower of St. Martin's Church ringing merry peals as the guests sat at the feast.

The immediate effect of the Incorporation was not the improvement of the condition of the townspeople. Whatever amount of property the Corporation had acquired, they were in a Wretched position ten years or more after the date of the charter. This was described by the Mayor, in a letter to the Earl of Huntingdon, dated March 1599, wherein his lordship was asked to "enter into consideration of the poor estate of the Town of Leicester, being now so decayed (by reason of long and extreme famine) as the greatest part of the inhabitants are almost brought to ruin and decay, our daily charge so increasing, as well in supporting our families, as otherwise, much more than we can undergo: our gains and trades very little. The provisions for soldiers, fifteens, and subsidies; the relieving of the poor (sent to us daily that have not dwelt with us this twenty years); doth mightily deject us in such sorts as these, and greatly augment contrariety among us, and many hy these means are ready to refuse our societies. "We have no cloth-making, nor other exercises, to maintain our poor; nor are we able, by occasions aforesaid, to set up any. The town is Her Majesty's, and never so poor nor more distressed than now it may he. There is among us some few, of some wealth, but the charge of the Corporation must be supplied by the most."

In the June of the year in which this deplorable picture was drawn of the state of the town, a second or supplementary chatter was granted by the Queen. It comprised an extension of privileges; one of these being authority to hold a Wool Market on certain days, for the sale of wool, yarn, worsted, and other similar commodities—the fines, tolls, and other receipts to be applied to the use and maintenance of the poor. A Wool Hall had already been provided at the end of Causeway-lane, near All Saints' Church (a representation of which, with two towers, appears in Speed's Map of Leicester); but the difficulty was to find supplies of the article, owing to the market being little known in the district; and consequently the buyers far out-numbered the sellers. Country gentlemen were written to, soliciting them as a favour to forward their wool to the new market; among these was Sir Andrew Noel, Knight, of Brooke, who answered the Mayor very cavalierly, and finally broke off all negociatious with his worship.

The long reign of Queen Elizabeth, the last of the Tudor sovereigns, closed on the 25th of March, 1603, when she was in her seventieth year.

THE STITAET PERIOD. PROM A.D. 1603 TO A.D. 1649.

Chapter VIII.

When Queen Elizabeth died, the crown passed, without opposition from any quarter, to the Stuart family, which was then represented by James, the son of Henry Stuart, Lord Darnley, and Mary, Queen of Scots. James was the sixth monarch of that name in Scotland, and the first in England by right of descent. He was approaching forty years of age when the news of his royal kinswoman's decease was conveyed to him by Sir Robert Oirey. He left Ediuburgh for London on the 5th of April 1603, in order to take possession of the crown.

The princess Elizabeth (afterwards Queen of Bohemia) entered the town on the 23rd of June, the day before the Queen and the Prince (Henry Frederick), on their way southwards to the metropolis. They were all received with public formalities, and presents were made to them of standing cups of silver, double gilt, with wine and delicacies. Prince Charles (afterwards Charles I.) a mere infant, was brought to the town in August by Lord Fyvie.

An event happened in the town in the year 1605, which has been associated with a tradition that links the name of Richard the Third with Leicester. This was the murder of Mrs. Clarke, landlady of the Blue Boar—the inn in which that monarch slept on his resting in Leicester befoie the Battle of Bosworth. The story is that her husband had come into sudden possession of money, through accidentally finding in an old bedstead, which King Richard had left behind him, and which had remained ever after in the inn, a large quantity of concealed treasure. Succeeding to her husband's property, thus obtained, her servants conspired with confederates to murder her, and carried out their purpose. Whatever may have been the true account of the origin of the landlord's fortune, must ever be a mystery; but the facts remain that his widow was murdered, and two malefactors, a servant-girl and her paramour, were executed for the offence. Respecting the bedstead, it is known that such a piece of furniture, designated "King Richard's

bedstead," was exhibited in the town in the time of James the First, and that a bedstead alleged to have been the very same article, the oldest portion of which is apparently of contemporary date with the reign of Richard, was preserved at Beaumanor Park by the late William Perry-Herrick, Esq.

A popular insurrection took place in the year 1607, in which some of the inhabitants of Leicester were induced to take part, and which was not suppressed without much trouble and the punishment of the offenders. The malcontents had for their leader "Captain Pouch," that nickname being given to a poor man named Reynolds, in allusion to his wearing a pouch attached to his girdle. The discontent had its origin among the labourers in the villages, who had been thrown out of employment in consequence of the inclosure of the land for pasturage and the discontinuance of tillage; they met in large bodies and took down the inclosures, and filled up the dykes surrounding them. Their movement continued from the beginning of May to the beginning of July; during which interval something like martial law was in force in the town, the Earl of Huntingdon, the lord-lieutenant setting up a gibbet in the Market place, to overawe the townspeople, and placing the Mayor (Mr. Chamberlain) and Alderman Robert Heyrick, under arrest for a month, on the alleged ground of their having been compromised by the removal of the gibbet in the night, and of the Mayor's refusal to set it up again! The quarrel was, however, made up in the following August, by the Kecorder, the Mayor, and several of the Aldermen, dining with the Earl at his town-house in High-street.

In the year 1612, James the First himself visited Leicester, the ungainly monarch being met in the Frog Island by a municipal procession, and addressed by the Kecorder in a Latin oration. He was the guest of the Earl of Huntindon, in High-street; and the royal visit was long remembered—by the townspeople generally, who had to pay the heavy expenses incurred This must have been a period of trial of various kinds to the inhabitants. Poverty, heavy taxation, and royal visits combined, were enough to depress their spirits; but a calamity worse than all these periodically afflicted them—its name was the Plague. As underground drainage was comparatively unknown, all the filth that was not carted away was thrown on the surface of the streets, or in obscure places of deposit, near the houses of the people. The latter were generally small, containing narrow, low, and unventilated rooms, often over-crowded. That some disease should intensify and culminate every few years, was only to be expected; the wretched sufferers naturally gave it the name of "The Plague. " At very early dates its fearful presence was recognized by its terrific ravages; without going back further than the commencement of Queen Elizabeth's reign, these are the dates when its visitations were recorded: 1564, 1571, 1583, 1593, 1607, 1610, and 1611. In the year last named above 600 deaths, in a population not exceeding 3,000, were attributed to the epidemic!

Afflicted by plague, the townspeople were in a most pitiable condition; and they were equally sunk in ignorance and superstition. As if old age and feebleness were not disadvantages trying enough to poor women, they were then sometimes subject to the opprobrium of witchcraft. In the bright summer of 1616, on the morning of July 18, nine women were executed at the gallows on the charge of having bewitched a youth named Smith, aged 12 or 13 years, the son of Mr. Smith, of Husbands Bosworth! It was said six of these poor wretches had familiar spirits—one like a horse, another like a dog, another a cat, another a fulmart, another a fish undescribed, and another a codfish; each of which tormented its victim! When the horse possessed the boy, he would whinny; when the cat he would mew. He went into fits; Sir Henry Hastings, and even stronger persons, tried to hold the youth quiet on such occasions; but they could not. And all these strange contortions took place in the presence of the most distinguished persons of the district. So the judges of assize ordered

the poor women to be hanged, and they were hanged; as Mr. Alderman Heyrick relates at the time, in a letter written to his brother, Sir William, in London.

Poor, plague-stricken, ignorant, and held in commercial bondage, all classes had an unenviable existence. The tradesmen in 1617 could not even sell wool freely in Leicester; for it was not a staple town—being excluded from the list of privileged places. A petition being forwarded to the king at York, and presented to him by his favourite, Villiers, then Earl of Buckingham, asking for the "privilege," he granted its prayer, and thenceforward the Leicester merchants were placed in the same position as those of other towns in this respect.

In March 1625 King James died, and three days after Prince Charles was proclaimed his successor at the door of the Town Hall, at the High Cross, at Bear Hill Cross (now the Haymarket), and at the Gainsborough Chamber. Before the year was over a dark cloud hung over the inhabitants. In their consciousness of approaching danger, they sought relief in solemn fasting, and daily prayer in the churches; while on Wednesday a sermon was delivered in one church only—attendance being promoted thereat by the suspension of trading and tavern-frequenting on that day exclusively. The Plague was now raging in London. From the 29th of May until August it prevailed in this town, chiefly in Soar-lane at the North Gate, about the Red Cross, and in St. Mary's Close. No account of the extent of the mortality has reached us; though the amount of money expended on remedial and preventive measures indicates its severity and long-continuance.

Hitherto, the forest of Leicester, being close at hand, had remained in its primitive condition. To it the poor townspeople, in the absence of coal, resorted for firewood; while carts brought daily along the forest-roads to the town, pit coal and other commodities. In the year 1626 the Government resolved on converting the whole area into tillage land, and in this measure they were stimulated by the neighbouring proprietors, who were all trying to obtain

"slices" of the soil, to add to their contiguous properties. The Corporation opposed the proceeding, by the presentation of memorials to the king and his favourite, the Duke of Buckingham, but fruitlessly; as in the month of December 1627 the disafforesting was completely carried out. The poorer class of the community rose in rebellion against the proceeding, and filled up the dykes formed to divide the allotments, and in every other way endeavoured to thwart the progress of the inclosure; some of their ringleaders being tried and punished for their resistance at the summer assizes in 1628. As a compromise, the king allotted forty acres of land, near Galliard's Lodge, for the benefit of the poor inhabitants; and the annual rent is now divided among them every year, under the name of the "Wood and Coal Money." In this way they were supposed to bo compensated for the loss sustained in being deprived of opportunities of picking up sticks in Leicester Forest. To the Corporation twenty acres were awarded, in lieu of the right of common they had enjoyed in respect of the Grange lands.

Before the great event of the Seventeenth Century (the Civil War) had happened, some few incidents of local importance occurred, which may not pass entirely unnoticed in these pages. The great majority' of the Corporation were Puritans in the Church of England—the "Evangelicals" of the day—who had been indoctrinated in Calvinism, while hoys, at the Free Grammar School. The leading spirits among them were the Heyricks, with whom Sir William Herrick, of Beau Manor, sympathised and co-operated. They had appointed a Town Preacher, a Mr. Sacheverell, who once every week delivered a lecture in St. Martin's Church, wherein he expounded to them what they considered to be "the true gospel." That "godly man" dying in 1626, they had to appoint his successor. The Confrater of Wigston's Hospital at that time was a Mr. John Angel, who stood high in the estimation of all the religious ministers and schoolmasters in the town, who all, without exception, signed a testimonial in his favour. Very powerful influence was brought to bear in favour of a competitor for the office. It was, however, useless; as Mr. Angel was chosen almost unanimously. He was a man of learning—" a good scholar, and a sound divine," Sir William Herrick called him—and took great interest in the improvement and extension of the Town Library; of the origination of which a brief account may be here introduced.

About the.middle of Queen Elizabeth's reign, a few book-shelves, with books on them, were fixed in the belfry of St. Martin's Church, which was then called the Library. The Earl of Huntingdon and various pious persons made additions to these, and studious and thoughtful townsmen were allowed to peruse them at certain hours. Subsequently, a salaried keeper of the Library.was appointed by the Corporation. The literature of the time was almost exclusively theological. Twenty-four volumes of this kind were purchased by the Corporation. They were chiefly anti-Romanist in character; the Puritans evidently labouring under a constant dread of the reascendancy of Popery. The books accumulated so largely that it became necessary to remove the collection from the belfry into the chancel of St. Martin's Church, where it remained until the year 1633. Mr. John Angel having stirred in the matter, induced the Corporation to appropriate a room as a Library in the block of building which constituted the Guild Hall premises; standing opposite the western entrance of St. Martin's Church. The books were placed there, and have ever since remained in the apartment thus provided. They do not consist solely of works on divinity; there being among them histories, dictionaries, classical writings, and scientific treatises— bearing honourable testimony to the love of learning cultivated among our Puritan ancestors.

Two additional outbreaks of the Plague happened in 1636 and 1638-39. In the latter year forty-one persons died. It seems that the resolute enforcement of sanitary precautions, however imperfect, had done much to diminish the fre-

quency and malignity of these visitations after that of the year 1611.

The young king, under bad advice, began his reign with extravagant ideas of the royal power and prerogative; believing, to the fullest extent, in the "right divine." He wished to rule without the intervention of Parliament; several of the patriotic members, whom he called "common vipers," he committed to the tower; and he dissolved the House in anger. He endeavoured, by levying "shipmoney," to raise taxes without the consent of the people, as represented by the House of Commons. Then he called another Parliament together, towards the close of the year 1640; to serve in which the burgesses of Leicester elected Lord Grey, a son of the Earl of Stamford, and Mr. Thomas Coke, of Gray's Inn, London. For the two years subsequently, a succession of Parliamentary

H struggles between the partizans of the King and the champions of legislative independence followed. The aristocracy and gentry were unwilling to stand out in antagonism to the royal authority; for they were monarchists, and respected the ancient constitution; but they could not and would not tolerate a system of autocracy. The King, on the other hand, persisted in enforcing his preposterous pretensions to arbitrary rule. At last, the two parties resolved to settle their quarrel by the arbitrament of the sword. Not without much reluctance and great sorrow, did many of the leading men appeal to arms; and on both sides every effort was made to win over sympathizers and helpers.

Already, in this county, various leading men had committed themselves by adopting sides in the bitter controversy. As staunch supporters of Charles, Henry, Earl of Huntingdon, Walter Hastings, Esq., Henry Hastings, Esq. (afterwards made Lord Loughborough), Sir Richard Halford, and others, had publicly taken their stand; while, with equal alacrity, the Earl of Stamford, Lord Ruthin, Sir Arthur Hesilrige, and others, threw themselves into the arena on the part of Parliament. The first overt acts on both sides were the Earl of Stamford's summoning of the trained bands,

or Militia, to meet on the Corn Wall, in Leicester Marketplace, on the 8th of June, 1642, and the publication of the King's commission of array in Leicester, on the 16th. On the 22nd, Mr. Walter Hastings having read the royal commission at the Cross, in Loughborough, came to this town at the head of his Derbyshire colliers, whom he had armed with pikes and muskets. With banners flying and drums beating, they entered Leicester: where a great commotion was raised by their presence. The sheriff (Mr. Archdale Palmer) was lodging at the Heron Inn; prepared there to take action on behalf of the Parliament. Mr. Hastings, accompanied by Lord Lovelace and Mr. Killigrew, rode into the inn-yard, apparently to intimidate the sheriff and their opponents: vowing vengeance upon the Earl of Stamford in particular. Mr. Hastings even declared he would eat up his lordship: upon which a bystander said, "Leave one bit for me." Mr. Hastings was evidently in a highly excited state of mind, and, turning round to the crowd of townsmen standing about him, he appealed to them in a short sentence or two for their encouragement: "What my friends and townsmen," he said, "ye stand for the King and the Hastings, who have ever been true to the crown!" To this there was no response; on the contrary, the assembly shouted back they were all for the King and Parliament—meaning thereby they were opposed to the King's rash proceedings at that time. In the afternoon, Mr. "Hastings went with his party to the Horse Fair Leys, an unoccupied piece of ground close to the Old Magazine, where the trainbands were accustomed to muster, intending there to-read the royal commission of array. He had alighted from his horse, and was about to carry out his intention, when he was interrupted by the high sheriff, who directed to be read the votes of the two Houses of Parliament, affirming the illegality of the commission of array. The Parliamentary messenger (Chambers) then offered to arrest the chief " delinquents" present, Hastings, Halford, Bale, and Pate, calling on the high sheriff to assist him, and the gentlemen here named to obey. Mr, Hastings evaded a distinct refusal, by saying his party would all be found at the Angel Inn. An armed rencontre seemed then inevitable; but a shower of rain fortunately fell, and hindering the soldiers from discharging their match-locks, a collision was prevented. The cavaliers and their partizans then left the ground to proceed to the Angel—not, however, before the Parliamentary messenger had been insulted by Mr. Hastings trying to ride over him, and had been knocked over into the town ditch. Seeking shelter in their inn, the cavaliers and their men were watched by the Parliamentary officials, who intended to take them in their beds on the following morning; but the principal men quietly escaped before their intending captors were in search of them, leaving some of the private soldiers behind in their beds, in a state of helpless intoxication.

Charles himself, who knew something of the town and people of Leicester—having first seen the place as a child, and subsequently—paid a special visit to it with his Queen, in August, 1634. Bowls of silver and of gilt were presented to him on the occasion by the Corporation; and when he passed on to Bradgate, they forwarded to the Earl of Stamford a hogshead of claret. The temporary visits to the Earl and to the town were doubtless intended to conciliate favour in both quarters. Again, on the 22nd of July, 1642, the King came to Leicester with the Prince Charles, and was received with every demonstration of loyalty. The day after he met the gentlemen, freeholders, and other inhabitants at the Castle, the Assizes being in progress, and there addressed them; expressing his confident reliance on their assistance in bringing horses, men, money, and hearts worthy of his cause, and alleging his readiness to defend with his life their religion, liberties, and laws. He was at this time the guest of Christian, Countess of Devonshire, a zealous adherent, who was living at Leicester Abbey, a mansion of which the ruins now remain. The day after, the King attended St. Martin's Church, where the Countess had ordered a

throne to be erected, and the floor to be strewed with flowers. The Mayor and Corporation, wearing their robes of office, and accompanied by the symbols of authority, attended in state to pay this indirect homage to their sovereign. Again were Charles and his son, Charles, in Leicester, on the 18th of August, when the Corporation met them on their entrance into the town, and presented a "fair wrought purse, with fifty pieces of gold," to the Prince, who accepted the testimonial. Four days after, having visited Coventry, where the citizens closed their gates upon him, the King rode with some of his lords and attendants to his friend, the Countess of Devonshire, at the Abbey, being joined there by Prince Rupert. Here they dined. The king then continued his journey to Nottingham. On his arrival there, in the afternoon, he planted his standard on the hill near the Castle, and thus openly declared war against the partizans of the Parliament.

In the following fortnight the entire of the royal cavalry advanced from Nottingham in the direction of Leicester. On the 5th of September its head-quarters were at Queniborough, under the command of Prince Rupert. On the day after, that impetuous and fiery cavalier addressed a letter to the Mayor of Leicester, peremptorily demanding a loan of two thousand pounds for the king's service; and threatening to appear next morning before the walls of the town "in such a posture with horse, foot, and cannon," as should make the Mayor know that "' tis more safe to obey than resist his Majesty's commands." Six dragoons came for the money the next day, when they returned with £500, hastily raised by the local authorities. But the king having been duly apprised of this outrageous proceeding by Sir Henry Hungate, felt himself under the necessity of repudiating the act of his rash nephew; and, on the day after the money was sent to Rupert, wrote a letter to the Mayor and Aldermen of Leicester, from Nottingham, utterly disavowing the warrant requiring the loan, and expressing his strong disapproval of it; and, moreover, requiring the Prince to

revoke his missive. It must be recorded, however, that although the Prince had said that "his Majesty's gracious promise" would "seem much better security than the public faith, which is the usual assurance that the party which call themselves the Parliament do give," the amount borrowed by Eupert was never repaid to the town of Leicester.

The King opened the campaign in the year 1646, hy proceeding from Oxford, with his nephews, the Princes Rupert and Maurice, to Chester, intending to release that city from the blockade by Sir William Brereton, and to invest Leicester, with a view to divert the attention of Fairfax from Oxford. In February this town was very inadequately defended; as in that month Sir Marmaduke Langdale's dragoons entered it unopposed, its governors were divided among themselves, and there was only a small body of Parliamentary soldiers in the garrison. In April the Committee of Both Kingdoms appointed by Parliament wrote to the Town Committee, urging them to attend to the repair and strengthening of the fortifications. The latter body consisted of Thomas Haslerigge, John Browne, Francis Smalley, William Stanley, Edmund Cradock, Valentine Goodman, and John Swinfen. A.bout two years before, they had formed a line of defence round the town, and subsequently had been at great expense in the construction of outworks. They replied to the communication that they had never thought of deserting the town or any part of it, but had fortified and were proceeding with the further fortification of the outworks. They had never had any other intention in fortifying the Newarke (which, it appears, some of the principal inhabitants had done, having houses there, leaving the remainder of the inhabitants to run their risks of injury from the enemy) than as a place of resource in case of absolute necessity, and to render the Magazine safer. Their greatest want, said further the Town Committee, was of ordnance and arms, and therefore they desired that these might he sent them, under the charge of Commissioner Bluut, as speedily as possible. It is on record, notwithstanding the reply of the Town Committee, that in order to preserve a few outlying buildings, they rendered necessary an undue extension of the line of defence, and they also refused to allow the wall of the Kewarke to be fortified, because "Master Wadland, their clerk, had a piece of land there, which he was unwilling to have cut up." This state of affairs was communicated secretly to the royalist party by some traitor in the cam p. in Leicester.

In this emergency Oliver Cromwell was consulted. His reply was that he had been called off from following the King to Oxford; but he had left a considerable body of horse, under Colonel Vermuyden, to watch the movements of the enemy; he therefore advised the Town Committee to correspond with that officer in relation to their preparations for defence.

The Town Committee was now very much thrown upon its own resources. About 900 of the townsmen, between the ages of 16 and 60; about 150 men impressed from the county; 480 of the regular infantry; and 340 horse soldiers, with their officers, constituted the defensive force of the place. Sir Robert Pye rendered his assistance to Lord Grey, with Lieutenant Colonel Whitbrooke, and Major Innes, who fell back into the town with 200 cavalry soldiers on the approach of the enemy. Meanwhile, the royal army was steadily drawing near, and on the 29th of May it " pitched down" before Leicester. The King took up his temporary abode at the Vicarage House at Aylestone, where he remained to watch the progress of the siege. His army was composed of 5,520 cavalry and 5,300 infantry—altogether 10,820 men; the besieged numbering about 2,070, with the advantage of a line of defence to shield them from attack. On Thursday the 29th, the whole infantry drew near; and in the evening the enemy were observed to be planting a battery against the wall of the Newarke, on a part of the Raw Dykes, little more than half-a-mile from the town. The next day a summons to surrender was forwarded by Prince Rupert to the

soldiery, the townsmen and the countrymen, offering them quarter, and permission was given to Major Innes to march away the commanders. All the Committee (with the exception of Sir Robert Pye and Major Innes) were resolved to reject the proposal. It was thought only right the Corporation should be convened to meet in their usual place of assembly—then the Mayor's Parlour of the old Guildhall—where Prince Rupert's summons was laid before them; the Committee sitting in permanence and deciding on making attempts to gain time by parleying with the royal commander. Twice they sent messengers to him, who were twice repulsed with rude replies. In the interval a rampart in the Newarke was faced with woolpacks. A second messenger camo from the Prince demanding the final answer of the authorities to the summons to surrender. While the Corporation were considering the matter, and before more than two of its members had had time to express their opinions in favour of resistance, the thunder of the artillery playing with renewed roar upon the.Newarke wall was heard in the ancient place of assembly. This occurrence at once terminated the councils of the Corporation. At six o'clock the breach in the wall was completed. As night drew near, it was noticed that the enemy had prepared to storm the works at numerous points, by cutting down bushes and boughs of trees with which to fill up the ditch of the line of defence, and make a pathway over it, in various places. The assault was made simultaneously in several parts of the line, with a view to deceive the garrison as to the precise locality where the main attack would be ofiered. The principal struggle was at the breach, where the enemy came to direct encounter with the long pike. Four times they assailed the besieged, and four times they were resolutely repulsed by death-dealing volleys of musketry. Two of their colours were wrested from them, and many of their pikes were snatched out of their hands. Every time they fell back the cavalry forced them to renew the attack. At last the assailants effected an entrance at the

breach; a reinforcement of horse having arrived at the Newarke, who dismounted, and, being fresh in the conflict, fought probably with greater energy than the townspeople. The garrison and townspeople fled backwards, fighting through the Newarke, up the Highcross-street, to the Wednesday Market, where the enemy followed them, received by volleys of musketry from the house windows and of missiles from the house-tops. The town soldiery on the east side fought the ground step by step up to the present High-street, and in St. Martin's Church and Churchyard, whence they fired on their assailants. They were met by two bodies of the enemy up the streets leading from the Eastgates. The other party of the besieged made a bold stand for upwards of an hour near the High Cross, where they drew up their artillery, and the cavalry for a time sustained the attacks of the royal soldiery. The townspeople being dislodged from St. Martin's Church, and driven towards the Cross, the victorious Cavaliers fell on the two bodies of the town's defenders, there collected, who, with the foe before and behind them, had no other alternative than to throw down their arms and beg for quarter. At first this was refused, some defenceless soldiers being killed in the heat of the moment. In one house, which appeared to be better "manned" than others, where a portion of the Committee was sitting, and some Scotch soldiers had retreated, in order to fire on the besiegers, the whole of the inmates were put to the sword without mercy. It is said that while the King's soldiers were stripping and maiming some of their prisoners, near the High Cross, and were being expostulated with for so doing, by their own officers, Charles (being clothed in bright armour) rode up and said, " I do not care if they cut them more for they are mine enemies." The number of the slain was estimated by the Committee at 709, besides those who died of their wounds afterwards. By other parties the number was calculated to be much less. An eyewitness (Quartermaster Simmonds) observed that more dead bodies lay just within the line of defence than without—that thirty or more were at the breach—and that every street presented some sight of this kind.

As if to add to their disasters, on the day after the capture (Sunday), King Charles ordered the Mayor, Aldermen, and Burgesses of the town of Leicester to levy upon the inhabitants for his use the sum of two thousand pounds sterling. The royalist triumph, however, was but short-lived. It roused the Parliamentarians to great exertions to retrieve their losses; for Fairfax's army having been recruited, and the siege of Oxford raised, that distinguished commander was on his way to Leicester, with a view to its re-capture, when he encountered the King's forces near Naseby, and then ensued that celebrated battle, which had so great an eifect in deciding, the issue of the struggle. It was fought just a fortnight after the day on which Leicester was taken—on Saturday, the 14th of June. On the Tuesday following, the royalists surrendered their newly-gained prize to Fairfax, who was present before the walls with the whole of his army, and next day the garrison marched out of the town, with safe conduct to Lichfield; the officers being allowed to leave with their arms and horses.

In passing, it may be observed that it is alike the subject of tradition and inference that an event which led to John Bunyan's conversion—and the composition of his "Pilgrim's Progress," took place at the siege of Leicester. It is referred to by himself in the preface to his work entitled "Grace Abounding to the Chief of Sinners." It was his turn, it is supposed, to stand sentry one night on the line of defence, and his substitute fell by a bullet from the enemy. If this were the case, Bunyan would be a soldier in the Parliamentary army; and a young one, too, as he could not have been at the time more than sixteen years of age.

A state of insecurity was now inaugurated which interfered with all the accustomed habits of the people. Few men made their wills—for while many fell unprepared in the war, others felt they could not foresee what would become of their property after death For this reason, it was found that only ten wills were proved, and only twenty letters of administration granted, in the Archdeaconry of Leicester, in the year 1645; though, before the breaking out of the troubles, at least 152 wills were yearly proved, and 61 letters of administration yearly granted, in the same ecclesiastical district.

In the year 1647 there was a comparative lull in political affairs. Before January had closed, the Scotch had delivered Charles to the English Commissioners, who conducted him to Holdenby House, Northamptonshire. On his passage from the North to that place, on the evening of February 12, he lodged at the Angel Inn, in this town; leaving here for Holdenby next morning.

In the summer of 1648, Oliver Cromwell was at Northampton on his way to the North. His foot-soldiers, who were destitute of shoes and stockings, were ready at Leicester before him. The people of Northampton sent them 1500 shoes and stockings, which proved very serviceable. The Mayor and Aldermen waited upon Cromwell, and presented him with wine, biscuits, beer, and tobacco—for the Puritan general loved his pipe, which he doubtless smoked with the Mayor in the old Town Hall.

Towards the close of the year King Charles was apprehended at Newport, Isle of Wight, conveyed a prisoner to Hurst Castle, and taken thence to Windsor. In the month of January, in the following year (1649) he was tried in Westminster Hall, and condemned to die; and he was beheaded on the 30th. Among those who signed his death-warrant were Thomas Grey (of the Earl of Stamford's family), John Danvers, Peter Temple, and William Purefoy—all names well known at the time in this county.

THE COMMONWEALTH PERIOD. FROM A. D. 1649 TO A.D. 1660.

Chapter IX.

The decapitation of Charles was followed, in this and other towns, by the enactment of proceedings in every way extraordinary and unprecedented. In regard to religion, there was an entire overthrow of the authority of the Established Church; in political affairs, there was the substitution of a military oligarchy and republicanism in theory at least), in place of the monarchy. The Independents obtained for the period the mastery in this town, and elsewhere. Honest, but austere and gloomy, the Puritans suspended all popular recreations: horseracing, bear-bating, and cockfighting they held to be great enormities. All holidays were abolished. At Christmas, they frowned on the joyous celebrations of the season, and held Christmas-pies to be profane. The Maypole on the Green they also denounced as heathenish.

On the establishment of the Commonwealth, great freedom of religious opinion prevailed; when Presbyterians, Independents, Baptists, and others, for the first time in their history, enjoyed the untrammeled exercise of their worship in this and in other large places. Among those who availed themselves of the opportunity of promulgating their views here, was George Fox, the founder of the Society of Friends, who visited Leicester in the year 1648, and entered into a controversy with others in one of the "steeple-houses," which would seem to have been St. Martin's Church.

In order to show their contempt of the Church ordinance of infant baptism, the Puritans led asses to the fonts, and then went through the ceremony, thus ridiculing it in a manner the most offensive to the conscientious feelings of Churchmen. As might he expected, the partizans and opponents of infant baptism collected about the churches, and fighting was the consequence; the "liberty men" in general prevailing.

The greatest trial for all monarchists and moderate people came in February, 1650, when the Parliament passed the act for enforcing the Engagement, under the authority of which all public officers and soldiers were required to pledge themselves to be true and faithful to the Commonwealth without king or lords. In December, the Mayor received an order to deface all the arms and pictures of the late king in churches, chapels, and other public places. None of the parochial clergy but those who would renounce prelacy and the liturgy, were now suffered to retain their benefices. Even a townsman elected to serve in the office of chamberlain was fined, because he declined to act on the ground that his conscience would not allow him to subscribe the Engagement.

Early in the year 1652, the Mayor and Aldermen made an effort to provide for the Puritan parish ministers in Leicester; and the committee of Parliament ordered a certain sum to be paid out of the Prebend of St. Margaret's with that view; in addition to which, the local authorities petitioned that an act of parliament might be passed to levy what was virtually a *Compulsory Church Rate.* The Parliamentary Committee acceded to the request, and resolved on asking Lord Grey to prepare a bill for enabling the Mayor and Justices to levy a Church Rate, and to bring it before Parliament. Ministers of the Independent party were at the same time appointed to the parish churches, by the parishioners—or, at least, by those among them who were of that denomination.

The preponderance of the Independent party enabled them to eject from public positions all who would not take the Engagement, whether presbyterians or royalists. Mr. John Angel and Mr. John Price, two ministers of religion, were included in this proscriptive measure. The Council of State ordered them, in conformity with an act of parliament, to leave Leicester within fourteen days after the 5th of February, 1651, and to remove to a distance of ten miles from the town; nor were they to" officiate in any cure, in any garrison or market town, unless special permission were granted them to do so by the Council.

During the year 1653 Cromwell dissolved the Long Parliament: he entered the House of Commons with a file of musketeers, ordered the speaker to leave the chair, told his men to remove that "fool's bauble," the mace, ejected the members from the building, and then locked the doors and returned to

Whitehall. Although he was now virtually the holder of supreme power, he could not control the Press, there being in circulation printed "squibs" or lampoons satirising his person and government. A copy of one of these reached Leicester, and was openly sung by the pupils placed at a private school. It was laid before the Justices, who examined the persons who had copies in their possession, and forwarded one of them to the Council of State: but Cromwell's government took no notice of the affair. In the month of December Cromwell was made Protector.

Again, in 1654, Fox was in Leicester, having been apprehended by Parliamentary soldiers at Whetstone. He was forwarded to the Lord Protector Cromwell, in charge of Captain Drury, by order of Colonel Hacket, who was then stationed in Leicester. On being taken to Whitehall, Cromwell, after a friendly conversation, set the "Quaker" at liberty. Richard Farnshaw and John Whitehead, two of Fox's zealous disciples, were also imprisoned by the Mayor of Leicester. Both of them denounced his Worship in letters full of fury and invective.

A local circumstance worthy of passing mention was the issuing of "tokens" in 1655, for the first time, by tradesmen and innkeepers of Leicester. There was a deficiency of small change for payment of small articles, and therefore such persons were allowed to obtain and pass current coins, about the size of a farthing, bearing on one side the name of the utterer, and on the other some emblems of his trade, or the sign of an inn. The first of these seems to have been the token of Francis Elliott. Early in the year following, a proposition was made to the Corporation, by a Mr. Bewley, to lay down Waterworks, by means of which water would be conducted from the Castle-mill to the Cross. The scheme was to cost £400. It does not appear to have been successful.

An election of members took place on the 20th of August, 1656, when Thomas, Lord Grey, Sir Arthur Hesilrige, Mr. William Stanley, and Mr. Winstanley, were offered for the choice of the Corporation. A poll was taken

among them: the numbers were found to be, Hesilrige, 53; Stanley, 42; Grey, 22; Winstanley, 1. The last-named was evidently "put up " by a personal friend, without consultation with' any other parties. On the 17th of September the new Parliament met; but several members, having no tickets of approval from the council, were stopped at the door of the house. Sir Arthur Hesilrige was one of these; his colleague, Mr. Stanley, had a certificate, but was unwilling to remain in the absence of his friend. He was, however, persuaded to dp so. The Mayor wrote to Mr. Stanley, assuring him that they took Sir Arthur's exclusion from the house seriously "to heart. " It was in this Parliament that Mr. Christopher Packe proposed Oliver Cromwell should be elected King of England.

Cromwell was a second time proclaimed Lord Protector of the Commonwealth of England, Scotland, and Ireland, in Leicester, on the 15th July, 1657, in the presence of the Mayor, Aldermen, Recorder, and others. About a year afterwards he died at Whitehall.

Richard Cromwell succeeded his father in the Protectorate of England in September 1658. He was acknowledged by the Council, the army, the fleet, the great officers of the Commonwealth, the Counties, and the Corporations. Among the latter was numbered that of Leicester; the Mayor, Recorder, Aldermen, Ministers, Gentry, and Commonalty of this town addressing the new Protector on the 8th of October. To Mr. Winstanley, the Recorder, was entrusted the presentation of the address. On the 6th of November, the Recorder and two grave made-up Aldermen, proceeded to Whitehall, where his highness the Protector received them with a great deal of respect and courtesy; embracing them according to the custom of the period. The Recorder (who was known to Richard Cromwell) then made a short speech, and the address was read by his highness's secretary. The addressers promised cheerful and ready obedience to Richard, and they hoped that as his father Oliver had, as a designed instrument, helped them out of Egypt (thus comparing him to Moses) and had been called to Mount Nebo to die there, so he (Richard) would prove another Joshua, with his spirit redoubled, and might, by the efficacious conducting of the captain of the Lord's host, lead them into a more full possession of truth, righteousness, and peace, as their desired Canaan, which they trusted would be the happy result of his highness's government. Protector Richard humoured the spirit of the people of Leicester by replying to their address in the same strain, in which he continued half-an-hour, always alluding to this town as the "city of Leicester," as if his desire had been to have it a city; and desiring the Recorder to inform the people of Leicester that if they should have occasion to use him, he should be like the cloud which, having received the pure water from the crystal fountains, showers it down again upon the earth. Thus ended the affair; the Recorder, with a lawyer-like eye to business, when he sent a written account of it to the Mayor, advised the Corporation to avail themselves of the opportunity to procure an amendment of the town charter.

The brief protectorate of Richard Cromwell terminated on the 22nd of April, 1659, on which day Parliament waa dissolved by proclamation. In May he quitted Whitehall, when the government of the country fell into the hands of a portion of the Long Parliament.

At the commencement of the year 1660, General Monk crossed the Tweed with the army under his command, moving southwards. Meanwhile Scot and Robinson, the two Republican Commissioners, were sent from the Parliament, ostensibly to congratulate Monk on his military success and great service to the nation, but really to act as spies upon his movements, and to discourage the demand for a free parliament. On or about the 23rd of January, they went out of Leicester, and when six miles from the town met General Monk. His soldiers fired volleys of shot by way of greeting the commissioners; the bells rang from the towers of the village churches adjoining; and many of the county gentry left their mansions

to pay their respects to the general. He alighted from his horse to salute the commissioners, and took a seat in their coach with them as far as Leicester, where he supped with them in their quarters. Multitudes of people thronged into the town to see them and Monk. The Mayor and Aldermen entertained them at a banquet; but they did not unite in the demand for a free parliament, though they were pressed to do so by George Faunt, Esq., High Sheriff, and other gentlemen of the county, who followed the General to St. Alban's in order to present an address of that description. No sooner had General Monk declared himself favourable to a free parliament, on the 12th of February, than the public opinion drifted in the direction of reaction and royalty. Rejoicings were witnessed on every hand. The current of the national sentiment in favour of the restoration of the monarchy in the person of Charles the Second was irrestrainable.

THE REMAINDER OF THE STUART PERIOD. FROM A.D. 1660 TO A.D. 1714.
Chapter X.

In May, the King was solemnly proclaimed in London and Westminster, and on the 12th of that month in Leicester, at the High Cross, the Barrell Cross, and the Gainsborough. A large amount of money was expended on the day of the proclamation, in feasting the guests of the Mayor and the populace; and on the day of general thanksgiving this was repeated.

In order to strengthen themselves in the estimation of the government, the local authorities sought to obtain the patronage and services of Lord Loughborough—the Mr. Henry Hastings mentioned in a former chapter—then living in London, to whom they wrote to thank him for accompanying their messenger to Court, when they presented their gift to the King, and to express a hope that his lordship would "tread in the steps of his noble ancestors the Earls of Huntingdon in favouring them and their poor Corporation." They also reminded him of the observance of a custom which had been neglected during the Commonwealth—the administration of the

oath at the Castle, to the Mayor, requiring that functionary to maintain the liberties of the duchy of Lancaster. Lord Loughborough courteously acknowledged the letter, and appointed Mr. Walter Ruding to act in his behalf, when the oath was taken by Mr. Danett Abney, on his election to the Mayoralty in the year 1660.

Lord Loughborough, in a letter addressed to the Mayor early in 1661, states that he has been informed by Mr. Faunt and Mr. Orton of their forwardness to act on his Majesty's behalf, and for the country's security, and of " the good affections of the Corporation in general," in joining with the noblemen and gentry of the county, in preventing "the rising of some misled people, who, being not sensible of their present happiness under so good and gracious a king, seek the disturbance of that blessed peace which God has in great mercy granted this nation, with the eertainty of their own ruin." He desired the Mayor to return his thanks to the Magistrates and burghers of the town for their demonstrations of loyalty, which it would ever be his constant endeavour to reward. In his letter, in reply, the Mayor also gives an insight into the unsettled state of the inhabitants; as he says there had been meetings of the "fanatics" —the name his worship affixed to the subdued Roundheads—attended by others from the country. These assemblies took place in the houses of the party, the chiefs of whom had been arrested upon the first rumour of the recent troubles. The king's proclamation concerning the disaffected having been issued, the Mayor proceeds to say that they had not been seen to meet anywhere, though strict watch was kept upon their movements. Some individuals, too, were then in prison, for refusing to take the oath of allegiance, but they were described to be "inconsiderable persons."

At the assizes, in the two years following the Restoration, the calendars, which had been very light during the Commonwealth, became heavier; but some of the additional cases were either political offences, such as the utterance of seditious language, or offences against ecclesiastical law. In the latter instances, the offenders were chiefly Friends, or (as they were then generally designated) "Quakers"—a class of persons whom the Mayor and Justices treated as madmen: a "madman, taken in the Market-stead on suspicion of being a Quaker," being on one occasion imprisoned for two days.

George Fox came to Leicester again in 1662. Having met some of his disciples at Swannington, at a Friend's house, and being seated in the hall, "Lord" Beaumont of Coleorton entered, with a company of soldiers, and took him and the party into custody. They were sent to Leicester gaol. At the Sessions (probably those held at Michaelmas) there were about twenty Quakers put upon their trial for refusing to take the oaths of allegiance and supremacy; but the proceedings terminated in a virtual acquittal, as, when they were sent back to prison, and were all in their chamber again, the gaoler said, "Gentlemen, it is the Court's pleasure that you should all be set at liberty, except those that are in for tithes; and, you know, there are fees due to me; but I shall leave it to you to give me what you will." The prisoners were then all discharged.

In order effectually to purge the Corporations of all disaffected persons, the Parliament empowered Charles the Second to appoint commissioners for regulating those bodies, to whom was given authority to expel all those members who had been identified with the late government of the Protector and with the Nonconformists. The Commissioners appointed for Leicestershire ejected the friends of Liberal principles from the Leicester Corporation, for before the close of the year (1662) the names of Stanley, Ludlam, and Cradock, which had been associated in conspicuous connection with the proceedings of the Parliamentarians in this town, were erased from the list of those who composed the municipal body. It had been also enacted that all magistrates should disclaim the 'obligation of the Covenant, and make a declaration of the

illegality of taking up arms against the King on any pretext whatever. Mr. Winstanley, the Recorder, who had been allied with the Roundheads of Leicester in all the proceedings taken during the Commonwealth, consistently refused to conform to the new regulations, and (anticipating his expulsion from office) voluntarily resigned in favour of Robert Harding, Esq., whom he strongly recommended to the Corporation as his successor. But in September the Commissioners addressed an arbitrary letter to the Mayor and Aldermen, requiring them not to inter-meddle in the affair until *they* had done with the business. Emasculated as the municipal body had been by the royal commissioners, it had still a spark of spirit left; for, on their proposition being put to the meeting, twenty-two out of the twenty-four Aldermen voted against submission to the dictation of the Commissioners, and they at once proceeded to the choice of Mr. Harding as Recorder, and he held the office for some years subsequently. A new charter was granted by the King in the year 1665. The latter was chiefly noticeable on the ground of its requiring all municipal officers to take the oaths of "obedience" and "supremacy," and of its rendering the royal sanction necessary to the choice of the Recorder, Steward, and Town Clerk. The King's brother, the Duke of York, afterwards James the Second, also visited the town this year. In the month of July precautionary measures were taken to prevent the introduction of the Plague into Leicester. As it then prevailed in London to an unprecedented extent, it was feared the malady might visit this town. The course which had been followed here in 1625, was again in part resolved upon. Whether the plague did or did not visit the town is questionable; though its mortality was undoubtedly increased in the year referred to; for in St. Martin's parish it rose to 65, a number which had not been equalled except in the year 1610.

At the latter end of the year 1665, three townsmen who were elected to serve on the common council refused to renounce the Covenant, as required by

Act of Parliament, and to serve upon the Corporation. Their names were Edward Billers (haberdasher), William Warburton, and William Orton. Billers and Warburton were fined 100 marks each, and Orton 20—a large amount in each case— in order to escape irom serving upon the Council.

In the month of November 1666 an order of Common Hall was passed, forbidding any person from stamping, or causing to be stamped, any more halfpence or farthings; and all persons who had issued any were called upon to give security to the Mayor for exchanging these "tokens" for silver. They appear, notwithstanding, to have been in use after this date.

During the Commonwealth the postal communication between Leicester and London was maintained by employing a man to go the distance and return once a week. He was called a "foot-post." In 1667, a proclamation was forwarded to the Mayor of this town, setting forth that Lord Arlington had been appointed Postmaster-General, and prohibiting the secret and indirect conveyance of letters from place to place. His lordship about the same time chose John Pares deputy postmaster for Leicester, for six months. Letters were now stamped on the direction by the post-ofiice clerks.

In the year 1670 Parliament passed the Conventicle Act, of which the object was the suppression of Dissent, by means of the infliction of penalties upon the preachers and hearers of the various denominations, which it was intended to put down with "a high hand and an outstretched arm." In this Act every meeting-house was called a " Conventicle." The Dissenters, warned by this attempt to interfere with the rights of conscience, were on their guard, and probably evaded observation for some months; but in the month of February 1671 Thomas Ludlam, a constable, and John Veasey, and Thomas Laxton, churchwardens of all Saints', having received information of a " Conventicle" being held in a house in that parish (not improbably that in which Bunyan had lodged) went to the place, and there found several persons assembled. The constable and churchwardens ascertained the names of two of the men and eight of the women constituting the congregation, but heard neither preaching nor praying. At the ensuing Spring Assizes, the Mayor enquired of Judge Wyndham whether the meeting was a "Conventicle " according to the Act of Parliament. The Judge—evidently one of an enlightened and liberal judgment—said that it was not such a meeting; and that if the Mayor and Justices were to issue a warrant of distress against the defendants, an action might be brought against them by the latter to recover damages. This decision temporarily checked further vexatious proceedings against the Dissenters; and as in March, in the following year, the King published a declaration of indulgence, under which the penal laws against them were suspended, they soon felt relieved from the fear of persecution. The ministers of different denominations were, therefore, free to pursue their labours.

Amongst others who visited Leicester was John Bunyan. Of one of these visits a memorandum is preserved in the town records. He was in Leicester on Sunday, October 6, 1672, when he produced his license to teach as a congregational person, to Mr. Alexander Baker (the Mayor), Mr. Overing, Mr. Freeman, and Mr. Browne. His license authorized him to teach in the house of Josias Eoughead, in the town of Bedford, or in any other place, room, or house licensed by his Majesty.

The passing of the Test Act in the spring of 1673 bears evidence that the illiberal and bigoted principles of the Government had triumphed over all opposition. Under the operation of that Act, no Catholic or Dissenter could be a member of the Corporation or occupy the position of Chief Magistrate; as all officers, civil and military, were required by it to receive the sacrament according to the rites of the Church of England, and to make a declaration of disbelief in the doctrine of transubstantiation.

It was at this period the Stocking Manufacture began to be locally developed. Already there was a class of woolbuyers and wool-combers living in the town, who worked up yearly about 800 tods of wool, which they spun, and employed persons to knit by hand into stockings, and sold to the hosiers. In this way they kept at work about 2,000 poor people—men, women, and children—in Leicester and the adjacent villages. Some of these early manufacturers were freemen and others non-freemen. Their success had induced "divers freemen" to make the attempt to wrest the trade from them, by means of an order from the Common Hall, in order to obtain a monopoly of it for themselves. They made use of various pretexts to justify their selfish design; alleging that the free-traders did not give the spinners and weavers sufficient wages, that their work was slightly done, and the trade in this way injured. The latter, in self-defence, petitioned the Corporation to be let alone; arguing that if the freemen aimed at goodness of work they might now take the best "workfolks," give greater wages if they pleased, make better work, and "outsell" the petitioners, and nobody could hinder them in so doing. They made, further, the memorable observation that " it is not the curious making of a few stockings, but the general making of many, that is most for the public good; for that sets more people on work, as well children as others, and when the stockings are made up and sorted, there are amongst them some for all sorts of people, and the buyer is able to judge and give prices accordingly." The petition, which was presented to the Mayor, Aldermen, and Forty Eight appears to have answered its purpose; as no action followed inimical to the woolcombers. In the ensuing ten years the stocking frame was brought into Leicester; though in what way there is no clear evidence to demonstrate. As its introduction necessarily brought machinery into competition with manual labour, the tradition would appear to be based on truth which represents that the owner of the first frames (Nicholas Allsop) was under the necessity of working by night in a cellar, in order to escape observation by thé populace, whose violent hostility he feared to arouse.

Indications are not wanting that at this date the inhabitants of Leicester shared in the sentiments which elsewhere divided political parties. "Tumultuous petitioning" was the policy of the popular party; and there were "petitioners" and "abhorrers" (as the partizans of the country" and court were called) in this town. These names, however, were for the first time changed for those of Whigs and Tories, about the year 1680. The Privy Council was then watchful of the Corporations, and directed letters of enquiry to them in order to ascertain whether any persons had been admitted without taking the oaths of supremacy and for renouncing the Covenant. The court thus used its utmost endeavours to prevent any infusion of Liberalism or Dissent into the municipalities of the country. Several persons were charged with being present at a religious meeting or conventicle, and one with having permitted an assembly in his house, early in the year 1683: they were convicted before the borough justices of this so-called offence, for which they were fined When the constables went to collect the penalties on the goods of their offenders, they closed the doors of their houses, and resisted the entrance of the officers. A judge's opinion being taken on the question, whether the latter might break open the doors, it was decided in the affirmative.

In October 1684, the chief magistrate and his Tory coadjutors surrendered the town charter to the king, and they forwarded a petition to him, praying that their liberties and privileges might be re-granted, accompanied with such restrictions as his Majesty might consider necessary. Early in December the new charter was framed, guaranteeing the Corporation in the possession of all ancient rights and privileges, but rendering the election of all the officers and members of the Corporation subject to the king's approval, and liable to removal at any time he might think proper. Besides this, the number of the Common Council—the most popular portion of the municipal body, because always the most recently chosen from the townsmen—was reduced from 48 to 36.

Charles the Second did not long survive these measures. He died on the 2nd of February, 1685.

The Corporation presented an address to James the Second, on his accession, and celebrated his coronation; though there was no mention made in the *London Gazette* of their festivities, and they would seem to have been quite wanting in enthusiasm. His efforts to reintroduce Roman Catholicism, by proposing to grant religious liberty to certain classes of Dissenters, were generally seen through. In this town, the Corporation, composed of the nominees of the Court, chosen only by the direct permission of the Crown officers, retained still enough political and religious consistency to refuse concurrence in James's designs; since, in the month of October 1687, when an address to the King was proposed at a Common Hall, it was objected to by thirty-four votes against nineteen. He despatched his order to Leicester for the dismissal of several members of the Corporation, on the 9th of February, 1688. In their places James stated that he had thought fit to substitute others. No oaths except those pertaining to their offices were to be administered to any of these persons, whom the king and his advisers fancied would be made subservient to his will, and of whom some, at least, were Dissenters misled by the royal pretences of liberality. Within three months after this displacement of municipal functionaries, the king's declaration respecting liberty of conscience was ordered to be read in all churches and chapels. It was followed up in Leicester by an attempt to induce the Corporation to prepare and present a loyal address to the monarch, a copy of which was furnished by the Earl of Huntingdon, the partisan of the Court. When the entire Common Hall, composed of persons appointed under the king's own warrant, had assembled, only three persons voted in favour of the address, while the remainder met it with a direct negative!

In September, one of the measures James adopted was to restore to this and other towns their ancient charters and liberties; but even here, with characteristic vacillation and insincerity, he played a double part, for, on hearing that the fleet bringing the Prince of Orange to our shores was dispersed, he revoked some of the concessions he had made a short time before.

Happily for the nation, William landed at Torbay on the 5th of November. Three days after he was in Exeter with his soldiery; where an "Association" was formed by the gentlemen and noblemen who joined him, who thus pledged their lives and fortunes to support his pretensions. In December the "Association" was offered to the Corporation for its acceptance, and they, with few exceptions, signed the document, thus committing themselves to the cause of " William the Deliverer."

On the 23rd of December, James the Second left England for France, in a small ship, as Louis Philippe left France for England in 1848—a fugitive, never to return, but to find a grave in a foreign country.

Early in 1689 both Houses of Parliament recognised the Prince of Orange and his Consort Mary, as King and Queen of England; the regal power to be in the Prince alone. To the settlement of the Crown was annexed a Declaration of Rights, whioh introduced what may he called the Modern Epoch of our national and local history.

With the commencement of the eighteenth century, the town turned over a new leaf in its annals. Instead of famine, plague, civil war, poverty, religious persecution, and political oppression of which we read so much in previous ages, the story hereafter is of enlarged freedom, increasing prosperity, and comparative immunity from the ravages of epidemics.

William, Prince of Orange, and Mary, his Queen (the eldest daughter of the King who had just ahdicated), were crowned in April 1689. In Leicester it was resolved to celebrate the Coronation with every demonstration of rejoicing. At a meeting of the body held on the 11th, it was agreed that on that day they should dine at the Angel Inn, and that the costs should be paid by the Cor-

poration—all the gentlemen and " persons of good quality and fashion " to be entertained at the public expense. On the death of the Queen, a few years after, the friends of King James (who were commonly known as " Jacobites ") renewed their efforts to promote his restoration: a scheme of insurrection was framed, and a plan of assassinating the' King resolved on, by the desperate partizans of the exiled monarch. The failure of the former, and the detection of the latter, induced both Houses of Parliament to draw up an Association, binding themselves to assist each other in the support of the King and his Government, and to revenge any violence that should be committed on his person. In Leicester this Association was signed at a Common Hall, in January, 1696.

The decease of the exiled monarch, James II., took place at St. Germains in September 1701. Before the event he was visited by the French King, who declared that, in case of his death, he would own James's son as King of England; and accordingly, when James died, the pretended Prince of Wales was proclaimed King of England at St.

Germains, and treated as such at the Court of Versailles. All England was filled with indignation at Louis for thus presuming to declare who ought to be their Sovereign, and the City of London presented an address to the Lords Justices, expressing the deepest resentment at the French King's conduct; assuring William that they would at all times exert the utmost of their abilities for the preservation of his person and the defence of his just rights, in opposition to all invaders of his crown and dignity. Addresses of the same nature were sent up from all parts of the kingdom. At a Common Hall of the Corporation of this town, held on the 10th of October, it was ordered, *nemine contradicente,* that an address in similar terms should be forwarded to his Majesty.

William the Third died on the 8th of March, 1702. Anne, Princess of Denmark, ascended the throne as his successor. She was the sister of Queen Mary, William's wife, and of James Stuart, "the Pretender." She was immediately proclaimed in Leicester, when ale was distributed and bonfires blazed in the Market-place. At her coronation, the local rejoicings were still more general and hearty. In her speech to both houses, delivered on the 11th of March, she promised her subjects that there was nothing they could expect or desire from her which she would not be ready to do for the happiness and prosperity of England. The assurances made by her Majesty were considered to be so satisfactory that all the public bodies sent up addresses to her—among the others, the Corporation of Leicester, who resolved upon so doing at their meeting held on the 16th of March following the inaugural address. The successes of British arms in Spain, and under the Duke of Marlborough in the Netherlands and Brabant, were celebrated in Leicester in the usual demonstrative manner. In the upper room of the Gainsborough, the stout aldermen, with ruddy faces, their heads buried in huge wigs, sat with long pipes, amid «louds of tobacco-smoke, descanting upon the despatches which Mr. Mayor read out of the newspapers, and about which they grew more vainglorious the more rapidly the ale was circulated. Outside, the populace huzzaed round the bonfires, being allowed a share, proportionate to their station, in the same potations as those indulged in by their superiors.

The Conduit was taken down and rebuilt in 1709. The new edifice was built of brick, with stone quoins, in octagonal form, and was heavy in appearance. It merely served as a cover to a leaden cistern, and was standing in the remembrance of some among the readers of these chapters. In this reign brick buildings were very generally substituted for timber dwellings, owing to the discovery of clay in the locality.

On the first of August, 1714, "Good Queen Anne" died. She was the last Sovereign of the Stuart family. She reigned twelve years. By the Act of Settlement, passed in the year 1700., both Houses of Parliament resolved that the Princess Sophia, Duchess Dowager of Hanover, and the heirs of her body, being Protestants, should be declared the next in succession to the Crown of England, after William and Mary and the Princess Anne, and their descendants. As they died childless, George, the son of the Princess Sophia of Hanover, became the legal possessor of the Crown of Great Britain.

THE EARLIER H A.NOVERIAN PERIOD. FROM A.D. 1714 TO A.D. 1760.

Chapter XI. George the First succeeded to the Crown in 1714. His title was strictly elective. He was in Hanover when Queen Anns deceased, that being his home, where he lived very simply, like a German in all his habits. He was now in his fifty-fifth year.

On the third of August George was proclaimed in this town by the authorities, with the attendant rejoicings. The Mayor, John Pares, Esq. (evidently a Whig) ordered the Waits to play two entire days—a performance in addition to that of the drummers who roused the Market place with their discordant echoes. In Leicester, however, there were many who heard with secret pleasure of the Earl of Mar's rising in Aberdeenshire, where he proclaimed the Pretender by the name of James VIIL The populace (alluding to the rural occupations of the king's family, whom they considered to be German farmers) sang doggrel songs, of which only fragments have reached us. Thus they would hum such lines as these as they strolled through the streets:

We will give them hoe and spiittle,
And send them big and little,

To hoe their turnip lands again.

During September and October the rebellion made considerable progress; but on the 13th of November 1715 General Forster surrendered to General Willis, at Preston, in Lancashire, and the rising was virtually defeated, although the Earl of Mar fought the Duke of Argyle on the very same day at Dumblaine.

Leicester was not only too remote to witness the conflicts themselves but the proceedings attendant on them; though the town was made conscious, that events of serious importance were in progress, as the Chamberlains' accounts of the year suggest, several teams being hired to go to Loughborough to bring on the Scotch prisoners, where, no doubt, they were transferred to them in order to be passed on to the Metropolis. A body of soldiery was also quartered here in October;. for on the day of commemorating the Coronation (the 20th) the commissioned officers were invited to the Ordinary at Mr. Simon Martin's (the White Horse). In 1717 there were troops quartered in Leicester for some purpose, not now known; but on the king's return to England in January, after a visit to Hanover, twenty gallons of ale were allowed to each troup, when the Mayor and Aldermen had a demonstration on account of the event.

The most popular local festivity of the year was the Easter Hunting. Its character shows how little served to render Leicester men merry in the days of the last Stuarts and the first Georges. On Easter Monday, the Mayor and his Brethren, in their scarlet gowns, attended by their proper officers, in due form, went to Black Annis's Bower Close, where, if the day were fine, the young and the old, and persons of all denominations, assembled. The Spring was welcomed by all in harmony. The morning was passed in amusements of various kinds and athletic exercises. About noon a dead cat, sprinkled with aniseed water, was tied to the tail of a horse, and trailed over the fields in a zig-zag course for half an hour; after which, a pack of hounds were directed to the spot where the horse had begun its devious career. Here the dogs gave tongue in glorious concert. The people who had stationed themselves on the higher ground to watch the hounds following the scent, roared out rapturous applause. The horsemen dashed after the hounds, through foul passages and over fences, emulous to get the lead of their fellows. As the cat had been dragged to the Mayor's door, through the principal streets of the town, hounds and horsemen followed. The hunt being over, his Worship invited his friends to a "treat" at his house, and thus the day ended. The historian who had witnessed the Easter Hunting says of it: "It was a scene upon the whole of joy—the governing and the governed, in the habits of freedom enjoying together an innocent and recreating amusement, serving to unite them in bonds of mutual friendship, rather than to embitter their days with discord and disunion."

Some abuse seems to have crept into the observance of the holiday, in the reign of George the First; as at a Common Hall held in September, 1718, upon the motion of Mr. Mayor, it was ordered that "for the future at the Hunting Feast, which is yearly on Easter Monday, the Company of the Twenty Four in their formalities do attend Mr. Mayor into the field, if the weather permit, according to the ancient custom, and what entertainment shall he given that day shall be at the charge of the Mayor only, upon the forfeiture of £20 (the late additional salary)."

About the date of the events last recorded, Leicester was the scene of several tragedies in humble life, which have been briefly mentioned in the pages of a local historian. As no precise year is identified with them, they may be assumed to have occurred between 1720 and 1725. The first of these transactions was the murder of a wife by her husband. The unhappy pair lived in Thornton-lane. In the night, while his wife slept, the husband (who was a tailor) thrust a fine bodkin into her ear, and thus murdered her. He was hanged for the crime at the gallows which then stood near the Infirmary. A second sad deed of blood was committed by a young woman named Mary Hall. She had reared with tenderest care from infancy an orphan niece. From some unassigned motive, she cut the child's throat; and, with her hands yet dabbled in blood, and holding in one of them the knife which was the instrument she had employed, she presented herself to her father, avowing herself to be the doer of the murder. At the back of Johnson's Buildings in Southgato-street, near the Water House Pump, lived in a small house a man known by the cognomen "Bull Parker," which sufficiently indicates the popular estimate of his character. He had a quarrel with his wife;

and, listening to the horrid promptings of a brutal nature, he inflicted blows with au axe upon her while she was in bed—thus putting her out of existence. "When the horrid deed was completed, Parker's first impulse was to abscond, and with this view he set out early in the morning to leave the town in the quarter nearest to the country; but (as he declared) the devil stopped him on the West Bridge, whence he calmly proceeded to the Town Gaol, knocked up the Gaoler, and told him of the crime he had committed. The man was sentenced to die; and while on his way to the gallows, seated in the cart, instead of singing a religious hymn or preparing himself by solemn thought for the last moment, he sang the *refrain* of an old ballad:—

A light heart and a thin pair of breeches
Carry you through the world, my brave boys.

"With Parker was hanged poor Mary Hall at the same place—the gallows near the Infirmary.

After having been located for forty years in Leicester, the Hosiery Manufacture had become largely extended. In the Winter Season of one of the years above named, several warehouses were broken open, and goods taken away. The perpetrators of the robberies were discovered in a purely accidental manner. There was then living in the town a man whom his neighbours nicknamed "Tangle Harris." He was often employed to carry out frames to stocking-makers and to bring coals from the pits. One dark morning, about two o'clock, he was going by St. Mary's Church, on his way to the lanes or meadows where his horses used to feed, when he heard some person in the graveyard. Harris sprang forward and seized the man, meanwhile seeing a second man run away. Harris dragged his prisoner into the town, who proved to be either an apprentice or journeymen to a Mr. Carr, a hosier living in St. Nicholas's-street, near the Church. As great rewards had been offered for the detection of the robbers, and Harris thought he was in the right track, without loss of time he

went to Carr's house, after having given the captured man into custody. He contrived to effect an entrance and found Carr in bed; but his shoes standing by the bedstead were quite warm, as if only recently taken off. Carr was then apprehended. In the hope of saving his life, he confessed to the robberies. In vain, however; as at the ensuing Assizes both prisoners were convicted on clear circumstantial evidence, and were shortly after executed. It transpired, in the course of the trial, that when the man was captured, he and his master were employed in burying in the graveyard goods which they had that night stolen. Carr (who had previously had a fair reputation) was in the habit of taking the stockings to London for sale, and thus eluded detection.

The South Sea Company originated its scheme in the year 1720, and blew its "bubble" so successfully, by the promise of enormous dividends and other infamous arts, that the stock on which £100 was paid up was raised to the sum of £1,000. In consequence, the whole nation became stockjobbers, and people neglected their professions and employments in pursuit of chimeras. Before the close of the year, the Company collapsed; and in the commencement of 1721 Parliament interfered in the matter by enquiry and in other ways. At this time the Corporation of Leicester addressed the House of Commons on the subject, praying "that this Honourable House would proceed, with the spirit and justice they have begun, to disappoint every mischievous enterprise and avaricious design, and bring to condign punishment all who shall be found conspiring to enrich themselves by the undoing of their country." The country was at this period in a state of great political agitation, owing to the machinations of the Jacobites. Here, as in other towns, the authorities and the populace, being partizans of the Pretender, were strongly disaffected to the Government. In May, 1722, the king received full information of a conspiracy formed against him, and on the 10th of June there were disturbances in this town; of which we have no particulars, owing to the destruction of the papers of the Corporation relating to it; but the body felt it necessary to send a loyal address to the king in August, to preserve at least a show of fidelity; and in September the Town Clerk went to London with copies of the examinations of witnesses concerning the disturbances, in order to lay them before Lord Carteret, one of the Secretaries of State.

Although there were strong party feelings in existence, the habits of social intercourse were still kept up in town and county, at public balls and assemblies. The hours of opening such affairs were, however, very different from those observed in the latter part of the nineteenth century.

On the 28th of November a ball was held in the Castle.

Dining in the middle of the day, the fashionable people of the time could then attend at an hour at which now the same class has not even thought of dressing for dinner; as the card of notification here inserted indicates:

"A Bali
At the Castle in Leicester,
On the 28th day of November 1722.
Thomas Hodgson,
Master.
No admittance after 4 o'clock."

For reasons which will appear obvious, after what has been already stated, the Government this year stationed a regiment of dragoons in Leicester under Colonel Churchill; the evidence supplied to Lord Carteret by the Town Clerk having probably proved the existence in this town of a considerable number of sympathisers with the conspiracies of the Jacobite party. If the Corporation are not belied, their strong attachment to the cause of the Chevalier led them into partizan excesses which were notorious. They were accused (and it would seem not without reason) of open disaffection to King George, and of choosing members from among the lower orders of the people of the meanest character and abilities, contrary to the express letter of their charters; to the exclusion of persons attached to the reigning family, possessing good fortunes, and competent to the honourable fulfilment of municipal offices.

In June, George the First died, aged 67, after a reign of nearly thirteen years. He left a son, George Augustus (his successor), and a daughter, Sophia Dorothea, the Queen of Prussia.

George the Second was in the forty-fourth year of his age when he ascended the throne of England. In 1705 he had espoused the princess Wilhelmina Charlotte Caroline, daughter of the Marquis of Brandenburg Anspach; by whom he had two sons—Frederick Louis and William Augustus—and five daughters, one of whom married the King of Denmark.

Six days after the decease of George the First, at a Common Hall meeting, it was ordered that the new King be proclaimed in tlie customary style. An address of congratulation to his Majesty was afterwards sealed at a Common Hall, and ordered to be sent for presentation by one of the Borough Members. At this meeting, also, a portion of the Corporation took the oaths of allegiance and supremacy and abjuration. These, it may be presumed, were the thoroughly loyal; while those who refrained from taking the oaths may be suspected of Jacobitism. Exceptions to these remarks there may have been, of Corporators unable to attend owing to ill-health and other causes; but as a whole the absentees were doubtless disaffected to the reigning family. There were 33 of this class; 37 being the number of those who abjured the Pretender.

By the Charter of Elizabeth, the Corporation were empowered to make byelaws for regulating the ancient usages of the town, with respect to trades, offices, and businesses; ordaining such fines and penalties, in case of non-compliance, as they should think fit, so that they were not made contrary to the statutes. In the next reign (James I.) at a Common Hall, it was ordained that every non-freeman selling articles openly within the limits of the borough, excepting on market and fair-days, should forfeit 40s. for every month wherein he should offend. At a later date (about contemporaneously with the introduction of the stocking-frame into the town), efforts were made by non-freemen to establish their trades within the borough, contrary to ancient usage; and, therefore, in September, 1681, the Mayor and Aldermen made a byelaw, to the effect that if any person or persons, not being freemen, should at any time exercise their trades or callings, contrary to ancient ussge, he or they should forfeit 20s. to the Mayor, Bailiffs, and Burgesses of the Borough of Leicester, to be recovered by action of debt, bill, or plaint, in any of his Majesty's Courts of Record, or to be levied by distress. Tn this state the question remained for nearly fifty years; some new comer occasionally making the attempt to evade the regulation, as in 1718, when Job Stevenson, a tailor, refused to take up his freedom and endeavoured to follow his trade without so doing. He was sued by order of the Corporation, and thus prevented from carrying out his purpose. No other person appears to have repeated the experiment until twelve years after; Vincent Wing, Samuel Basford, and John Stubbs, glovers, having in the year 1730 attempted to set up in trade, without procuring their freedoms. They were sued forthwith; but Wing and Basford yielded, and took up their freedoms. Stubbs then stood out alone. He traded in open defiance of the Bye law. The Corporation doubtless thought that they had but to prosecute him to defeat him; but the issue was otherwise. They proceeded on the Byelaw of 1681, that is, they made him a debtor to them to the extent of the sum payable for taking up his freedom (£20). The case was at issue upon *Nil debet.* (" He owes nothing.") It was tried. The fact coming out in evidence that "foreigners" and non-freemen were permitted to use their trades and occupations upon market and fair days, as well as freemen, the plaintiffs were non-suited. Stubbs accordingly carried on his trade in defiance of the Corporation, and thus struck a fatal blow at the venerable monopoly. Stubbs' partially successful revolt against the Corporation was followed by imitators. The first was Bichard Glover, who attempted to sell goods in the borough without taking up his freedom. The authorities, instead of suing him (as they had done Stubbs) for the penalty attached to his violation of their regulation, committed him at once for refusing to pay the penalty. Glover brought an action against Mr. Mayor, Mr. Alderman Howkins, John Bellamy, and Samuel Shipley, for the steps they had taken in the matter. The Mayor found it necessary to take the advice of the Eecorder in the case; but with what result does not appear, though Mr. Farmer, the Town Solicitor, entered an appearance on behalf of the defendants. It is very probable the action was in some way compromised.

At the time under notice the river Soar was a small, narrow stream, its flow unchecked by locks or other artificial impediments, from its source near Leir in this county to its junction with the Trent. The thought at last occurred to some of the leading inhabitants (suggested, perhaps, by the steps taken at Derby some years before in regard to the Derwent) that the Soar might be made navigable. The Corporation took up the project. The scheme was vigorously prosecuted, but it was unsuccessful. When the Mayor went up to London about it, one of the opponents in Parliament politely said to his Worship, "Sir, do you choose to have it thrown out of the House at the first or second reading V

In the year 1738 a contested election took place in Leicester, which occasioned the manifestation of much bitter party feeling. The candidates were George Wright and James Wigley, Esqrs. , on the Tory or Jacobite interest, and Walter Ruding, Esq., of West Cotes, of the Whig or Hanoverian party. Bills were posted on the walls of a grossly treasonable nature, attributed by the Whigs to the Corporation party—the latter throwing hack the charge on their opponents. Both sides professed an anxiety to discover the authors of the papers. Among the Whigs the principal person was Mr. Norton, a solicitor, of high character, and he and his political friends sent an early account of the treasonable papers to the Government. The Whig candidate was defeated. After the

election, the Corporation having the local power in their own hands, insisted on Mr. Norton and his associates being taken hefore the Magistrates. When under examination, to the astonishment of the bystanders, Mr. Norton suddenly hecame speechless, and died without a groan—the excitement created by the unfounded allegation, and by his being placed in an ignominious position, having unquestionably caused the catastrophe. It happened on the first of February. In the Chamberlain's accounts the following entry was made relating to this matter:—

£ s. d. Paid the Expenses on the account of the several treasonable pipers stuck up in several parts of the town by the Whioqs, on the 1st day of February, 1737 1738 new style, highly reflecting upon his Majesty's person and Government, and the government of this Corporation, and defending our innocence against the malicious aspersions therein charged 42 11 7

At the Common Hall, held in March, it was ordered "That the Chamberlains do pay Mr. Mayor, and such persons as he employed, or shall employ, in going to London, or otherwise, the charges relating to the treasonable papers lately stuck up in several places of the town, and likewise the sum of JE100 offered as a reward to any person or persons who Rhould discover the author or authors thereof; so as such person be convicted of heing the author of such papers."

An event occurred a few months after, which must have sorely tried the patience of the Pretender's parti zans, who doubtless hoped sincerely the Hanoverian family would die out, and thus leave the way open for the restoration of the Stuarts—this event was the birth of a boy to the Prince of Wales, the son of George the Second.

When the news reached Leicester the church bells were set ringing, and bonfires were made in the Market-place; and on the Corporation meeting (June 23), nearly three weeks after, they rather tardily agreed to forward to George the Second an address of congratulation on the birth of the young prince. All, how-

ever, was formal; and the rejoicings were not on such an extensive scale as they were under similar circumstances when the sympathies of the Corporation were warmed by the event.

A controversy arose at this time between the Corporation and Mr. Leonard Piddocke, of Ashby-de-la-Zouch, as representative of the Earl of Huntingdon, concerning the appointment of a Bridewell-keeper. Late in the year 1739, a vacancy had been created in the office, owing to the decease of John Armston. A Court of Aldermen was held to elect his successor, when two candidates were proposed. The termination of the affair was, that Morris (the nominee of the Corporation) rem lined the Bridewellkeeper; the reason being probably this—as the Bridewellkeeper was the salaried servant of the Corporation, and the Gaoler's place was not worth having of itself, the Bailiff was glad to accept the Bridewell-keeper as Gaoler, as involving an arrangement less expensive to himself than the appointment of a second person as Gaoler.

One of the oldest suburban amusements of townsmen is bowling; a green for the purpose having been sometimes laid out at the public expense. In the neighbourhood of Leicester such a place was in existence early in the last century, and probably before that period; but mention is made in the Chamberlain's accounts of 1736-37 of £100 having been allowed to Mr. Newton and Mr. Howkins to finish the Bowlinggreen, and in the year 1740 the same persons had leave to remove the Green in the Horse Fair from the ground belonging to Mrs. Worthe, and to add to it as much ground as was necessary from the Corporation property. On or near the modern street known by the name of Bowling-green-street was the place thus allotted to the public for recreation.

In the year 1739 the third Earl of Stamford died, and was succeeded by Harry his son, the fourth earl. A visit of congratulation and respect was paid to this nobleman, on his succession, by the civic functionaries. It would thus seem that the house at Bradgate (now a ruin) was even then tenanted by the Grey family.

The Baces were held in St. Mary's Field for the first time in 1742, having hitherto been held in the Abbey Meadow, where the horses sometimes ran up to the knees in water. It was found that the alteration of the site to carry on the Baces, from the Abbey Meadow to St. Mary's Field, was either attended, or alleged to be attended, with injury to the tenants of the land; and therefore, at a Common Hall it was ordered that the farmers for the time being of the South Fields belonging to the Borough of Leicester, should be compensated for the damage they might sustain in consequence.

A quarrel arose in the summer of 1743, between the occupier of the Abbey Meadow and the freemen, which shows how encroachment has been attempted and resisted at all periods. The matter was brought before a Common Hall in August, at which this resolution was adopted: "Ordered, that if Mr. John Nedham or Francis Nedham, or any person whatsoever, do refuse to let the Freemen's horses or mares go into the Abbey Meadow (as has been used time out of mind), paying first, or tendering to the said John Nedham, or Francis Nedham, or such other person or persons concerned, fourpence for each horse or mare, to be tacked as usual— then such Freemen do turn in their horses and mares into the said Abbey Meadow untacked. And if the said John Nedham or Francis Nedham, or any person employed, do impound any horse or mare, horses or mares, belonging to any Freeman or Freemen, that such Freeman or Freemen do immediately after such impounding replevin their said horses or mares; the charge of which to be paid out of the town stock."

The ill-feeling created by the discovery of treasonable papers posted on the walls of the town was revived in 1744, and the Corporation evidently lay under the suspicion of the Government in relation to the affair; and were anxious (at least in appearance) to release themselves from it, by professing an anxiety to discover the authors of the papers. At their meeting (held February 22, in the mayoralty of Samuel Belton, Esq.) they came to the resolution to offer a reward of one hundred pounds for the discovery of the writing or publishing of a treasonable paper that was affixed to the window-shutter of John Brown's house, near the.North Gate. Nor did the authorities rest here; a message having been sent to both Houses of Parliament, informing them that preparations were being made in France to land the Pretender, public bodies like that in Leicester were bound either promptly to repudiate the supposition of sympathy with his cause, or to lie under the imputation of disaffection to their Sovereign. The Corporation of Leicester therefore adopted an address to the King, in which they said:—" We beg leave to assure your Majesty of our abhorrence of such an attempt against your Sacred Person and Government." Alluding to the treasonable placards, the Corporation said, "We will use our utmost Endeavours to discover and bring to Justice the Authors of the said Papers, and to render abortive any attempts that shall be made upon these Kingdoms, and to preserve the Protestant Succession in your Majesty's most Illustrious House, and to deliver down to Posterity our Religion and Liberties as we received them from our Ancestors."

It was natural that the Government and people of this country should be roused to hostility against the French King on his rendering help to the Pretender; but Prance took the initiative, declaring war against England on the 20th of March. On the last day of the month, George the Second declared war against France. The event was duly notified in this town—the grim ceremonial of the proclamation being intermingled with the grotesque, by the presence of the Halbert Men, armed in their helmets and breast-plates, who proceeded from the Town Hall to the High Cross, and then to the Coal-hill and to the Cornwall, at both which places the Declaration was read.

The country had been prepared by events for a repetition of the attempt to restore the Stuarts to the throne of England. As we have seen, the French King assisted Charles Edward (the son of the Chevalier), in a fresh enterprise to invade the island. On the 4th of September, 1745, the rebels took possession of Perth and there proclaimed the Pretender; and on the 16th of the same month he proclaimed his father King of Great Britain at the High Cross, Edinburgh, and himself Regent of his father's dominions. The battle of Preston-pans took place five days after; when Sir John Cope being defeated by the Highlanders, the rebels for the time became masters of Scotland, with the exception of a few fortresses. Preparations were now made all over England, by the loyal party, for the raising of soldiers to suppress the rebellion. In this town the Corporation did not contribute any money to the fund; but at their meeting on the 27th of September, they resolved on making application to William Wrighte. Esq., or any other gentleman whom the Mayor might select, to draw up an address to send to his Majesty, "upon account of the Rebellion in Scotland ;" and on the 2nd of October it was signed and sealed at a Common Hall meeting. In the crisis at which the country had arrived, the voluntary exertions of the people were sufficient to add 60,000 men to the King's forces; the Spitalfields manufacturers alone furnishing 3,000; but none were levied by the Corporation of Leicester, although they made very zealous professions of loyalty!

On the 15th of November the rebels entered Carlisle on their way southwards. On the 24th, at noon, they reached Lancaster. As there were now no daily newspapers, nor telegraphic wires, nor railroads, the people of this country could only obtain such casual information as rumour afforded, or as messengers brought of the movements of the Pretender and his Highlanders. But the inhabitants of Leicester, friendly to the Government, the Whigs and Dissenters, were not idle; the young men volunteered for service—some being drilled in the Castle-yard, and others in the burial-ground of the Great Meeting—then the principal Nonconformist place of worship. They do not appear, however, to have met with any encouragement from the Corporation, who were only anxious to ascertain the news; as their resolution, adopted at a Common Hall meeting on the 28th of November indicates: "Ordered that Mr. Mayor shall send out what Messengers he thinks proper to wait for, and send accounts of the motions of the Rebels at the charge of the Corporation." On the 28th the insurgents entered Manchester. Marshal Wade was now in pursuit of the Pretender from Newcastle, and the Duke of Cumberland had taken the command of the King's troops assembled in Staffordshire. He was at Lichfield on the day last-named. On the 1st of December the young Pretender entered Macclesfield with his main army, and on the 4th he reached Derby with about 7,000 followers.

The excitement in Leicester had now reached its climax. Reports had reached the town of the fierceness and barbarity of the Highlanders; descriptions of whose strange costume, unintelligible language, and wild manners, astonished and alarmed the peaceable townsmen. Moreover, it was reported that they outraged the women, and killed infants, whom, it was said, some of them ate like cannibals. The historian Throsby (a person having strong Jacobite predilections) ridicules the conduct of the townsmen, who, he says, when Charles Edward was at a distance, appeared in arms at mock-fights in the Castle-yard, but who, when his army reached Derby, deserted the parade, and sneaked away with the aged, the women, and the children, to seek asylums under the humble roofs of neighbouring villages. Of those who remained behind, some buried their valuable articles, money, and so forth, in the earth; while others, who wished well to the Pretender, either prepared food, meat baked and boiled, to set before his men on their arrival, or fervently prayed in secret for the success of the " old cause " and the army of the young Chevalier. The Mayor and a portion of the Corporation remained at home. Tradition relates that they were Jacobites, and that they had prepared an address breathing warm congratulation and

zealous loyalty with which to welcome the Pretender, whose arrival they awaited in the old GuildhalL

About the sixth of December, he was expected in Leicester. Scouts entered the town with breathless haste, and reports spread from mouth to mouth, in exclamations —" They are at Loughborough!" "They are at Eothley!" "They are at Belgrave!" The place became empty. Shop-keepers unused to warfare, volunteers unorganized, and people terrified by the prospect of indiscriminate slaughter, fled in all directions. In a day or two after, intelligence was brought of the retreat of the rebels from Derby; and then the address to the Pretender (known doubtless to the Mayor, and Mr. Herrick, the Town Clerk) was smuggled away, and the townspeople returned to their shops and houses, to be jeered at by the Jacobites who had remained behind in safety to welcome their fellow-rebels. On the 16th of April, 1746, the rebels were entirely defeated at Culloden—-an event followed by outrages and butcheries, committed by the order of the Duke of Cumberland, which the historian blushes to record—committed upon men, women, and children alike. It trust have been with ill-concealed chagrin and mortification that the Jacobites of the Corporation adopted a congratulatory address on the 16th of May. The victory at Culloden was celebrated by displays of fireworks and illuminations—especially by the lighting up of the old Elizabethan High Cross with candles. It was ordered that the ninth of October be kept as a day of Thanksgiving according to his Majesty's Proclamation, and that both Companies should attend Mr. Mayor to Church in their gowns on the occasion. On that day, accordingly, the Aldermen and Councillors met at the Town Hall, at ten o'clock in the morning, and then heard a sermon at Church; afterwards returning to the Hall, and proceeding thence to the Three Crowns, where an Ordinary was prepared for their refreshment.

The building called the "Gainsborough" seems now to have become either inconvenient or inadequate to the requirements of the period. How long it

had been standing it is impossible to say; but we know that part of it had served as a place of confinement early in the sixteenth century, when it was used for purposes connected with the administration of justice. It stood on the south side of the Market-place, and was a two-storey building, of which the upper part was devoted to public business. There were shoemaker's shops below, and a balcony with piazza at the end nearest the Cornwall, with a dungeon beneath the level adjoining. At the beginning of the year 1748, the Corporation ordered that the structure be taken down, and a new one erected, according to the plan produced by Mr. Mayor at a Common Hall. The edifice was erected; but at what exact cost it is impossible to say, as the items are not defined in the Chamberlains' accounts. Mr. John Westley, however, received £200; which, representing five per cent, on the total—the allowance above specified — makes the outlay £4,000. Instead of being called the new Gainsborough, the structure was known as the "Exchange," and it existed until November, 1850, when it was removed, and the Market House built on a site nearly adjacent.

In May the King had left England for Hanover; and after the completion in October of the treaty of Aix-la-Chapelle, returned to England on the 23rd of November. It was in relation to these events that the Corporation agreed to and sealed an address which concluded with the expression of a wish for his Majesty's long reign, and the possession of the throne by his posterity to the latest generations.

On previous pages the strenuous resistance of Job Stevenson, a tailor, to the restrictive regulations of the Corporation, in respect to the exclusion of non-freemen from setting up trades in the borough; the partially successful effort of Stubbs, a glover, in the same direction; and the similar attempt of Richard Glover to throw off the local shackles, have been described. Between that time, and the date at which these annals have arrived, the Corporation unwisely raised the fee, or admission to freedom, from £20 to £30. Early in the year 1741 a suit was commenced, which had a long continuance and a determinate issue; the local authorities instructing the Town Solicitor forthwith to sue George Green *alias* Smith (above-named) for following the trade of a watchmaker in this borough, not being a freeman of the Corporation. At the commencement of the year 1742, also, other persons were ordered to be sued on the same account, namely, Robert Phipps, Edward Jennings, Richard Cheney, and Daniel Wood; but their cases drop out of sight, and all the attention of the townsmen was absorbed in Green's case alone. The cause was heard, and was decided against the Corporation. They were, in fact, non-suited. In September they had the disagreeable duty of paying the costs to perform. They were chafed greatly at the result; so much so as in December to threaten a renewal of action; but. this was an impotent menace.

In this way was brought to a conclusion a struggle which, in various forms, had been carried on for several generations. Its result was the entire overthrow of the old system, and thenceforward any tradesman might settle in this borough without being subject to the heavy payment before required by the Corporation. Publicans were still subject to the regulation, but none besides. It may, then, be considered only just to rank George Green, *alias* Smith, the watchmaker, among the "unnamed demigods" of this locality.

One of the last acts of the Corporation in the year 1749 was to order a petition to be presented to the House of Commons for obtaining an Act of Parliament for " enlightening and cleansing the streets, and for keeping a regular and able watch, and for repairing and keeping in good order the public pumps and wells within this borough." Previous to this date even oil-lamps were unknown, and the public thoroughfares were therefore left in complete darkness in winter—the inhabitants having recourse to lanterns to to guide them to their homes or their neighbours on the dark evenings. A smaller measure of improvement was also successful—the

erection of a new Assembly Rooms, at the Hay Market, where Mr. John Bass raised a building in which the players and those who gave concerts might find greater accommodation than in the old Town Hall.

The period was one of turnpike amelioration. In January, 1752, the Corporation petitioned the House of Commons in favour of an Act of Parliament to make a turnpike road from Leicester to Ashby-de-la-Zouch, and they advanced the money out of the town stock for the

L purpose, and for obtaining the Act, and the other charges relating thereto; the money to be repaid by the Road Commissioners. In December, 1753, they petitioned Parliament for a similar Act to make a road from Hinckley to Leicester, thence to Uppingham, and thence to Stamford, and for the insertion of a clause for amending the Leicester and Ashby Turnpike Act, at the joint expense of the Corporation and of the Gentlemen and Inhabitants of Rutland; if the latter would consent to the proposal. A grant of £63 was made in January, 1754, towards the charge of obtaining an Act for the repairing of the road from this town through Uppingham to Wansford, in the county of Northampton. Again, in February it was ordered that £100 be paid to Mr. Thomas Halford, solicitor for the Corporation, towards the charges of obtaining an Act of Parliament for making a turnpike road from this borough to the town of Narborough, in this county, and from this borough to the city of Coventry and other places. And also, towards obtaining a clause to be added thereto, for amending the Act passed in the previous Session of Parliament for making the Ashby turnpike road. The sum required was to be paid by the Chamberlains out of the town stock, and repaid out of the first money raised under the operation of the Act.

It must have already occurred to the reader that in the course of the two first Georges' reigns the place was rapidly emerging from the dulness and slowness of the small market-town to a state more important and improving. Its population had doubled in fifty years, having been at the commencement of the

century only about 4,500, and being now estimated at more than 9,000. It had established a kind of fire brigade, erected a new exchange and new assembly rooms, attempted to procure a lighting and watching act, and was promoting the formation of turnpike roads: it next encouraged Mr. John Gregory to commence a weekly newspaper. On May 12, 1753, lie accordingly issued No. 1 of the *Leicester Journal,* containing just four advertisements, and price only twopence. The paper consisted of four small pages, filled with news taken from the London Journals and very meagre paragraphs concerning local affairs, and presenting nothing in the shape of a leading article: it was, however, an average sample of the early provincial newspaper.

In 1754, all the turmoil of a contested election was witnessed in the Borough. It took place in a period of unusual local excitement, the Corporation and the freemen being arrayed in bitter antagonism to each other, in consequence of the attempted enclosure of the South Fields; yet the raking up of the embers of the old political strife between Jacobite and Hanoverian was, if possible, more productive of violent feeling than the freemen's movement.

At a Common Hall, held March 19, 1752, these conclusions had been arrived at:—" Ordered at this Hall that the South Fields belonging to this Corporation be not let out in farms, as usual, and that Mr. Mayor and five or more of the Commissioners for the time being agree with Mr. Comyns, or his agents, for the purchase of so much of the land, and of such of the tithes of the said fields as belong to the said Mr. Comyns. Ordered, likewise, at this Hall, that when the said South Fields are laid down for grass ground that the commoners may turn in their cattle according to the usual stint on the first day of September in each year. Ordered, that this Corporation defend such person or persons as shall be molested or sued for enclosing all or any part of the said South Fields, in case such enclosure be made according to the directions of the Corporation. Ordered, that no part of the South Fields shall be ploughed or converted into tillage after Michaelmas which shall be in the year 1755."

In December, the Commissioners for Letting the Town Lands, contrary to the tenor of the above resolutions, gave leases to Mr. Alderman Ayre, Mr. Alderman Phipps, and S Mr. Oliver, of certain parts of the South Fields for twentyone years. It was anticipated that means would be taken by the poorer freemen to resist the proposed enclosing of the South Fields, and therefore the Corporation ordered that Mr. Mayor should cause a sufficient number of proper persons to be ready on the Wednesday in the second week of December to set out the boundaries of the fields in question.

All through the following year 1753 the discontent among the freemen fermented, until in September it manifested itself in open outbreaks. The malcontents assembled in the town and South Fields and created riots on a considerable scale; to such an extent that the Corporation resolved on taking counsel's opinion how to proceed against the rioters, who had pulled down the house of Samuel Hall, the shepherd, and all the fences recently raised by the lessees. The next step was to order prosecutions to be carried on against the offenders; but on more mature consideration the Corporation (November 2) modified their course of proceeding, by offering them the option of affording satisfaction to the prosecutors for the injury inflicted, and of giving bail to appear at the ensuing Assizes.

The reason of this alteration of policy in regard to the rioters is not at first sight obvious; but when we learn something of contemporary events, the state of affairs becomes more intelligible. It seems a borough election was impending. On the very same day, and probably at the same meeting at which the modified resolution relative to the rioters was adopted, the Corporation (as we learn from the *Leicester Journal*) met to support the interests of Messrs. Wigley and Wrighte, the retiring members, who offered themselves for re-election, and who were Tories and Jacobites. It would

therefore be inexpedient to press forward unpopular prosecutions at such a juncture. A month afterwards (December 8) Messrs. Wrighte and Wigley, in an address to the electors, expressed their intention to defend the rights and privileges of the freemen in the dispute existing between them and the Corporation relative to the South Fields. Meaawhile, the Whig party was active, and James Winstanley, Esq., its leading local representative, was invited by some of the freemen to meet them at the Lion and Dolphin; the meeting being called by advertisement, in which the advertisers expressed their determination to cut down the fences in future.

The election took place in April, 1754. On the 13th, the mobs on both sides—for the Corporation had one and the Whigs had another—had fights in the streets, accompanied by bloodshed, and all the front windows of the Three Crowns and the Lion and Lamb Inns were broken during the disturbances. The polling began on the 19th, and ended on the 23rd in the defeat of Major Mitford, the Whig candidate. When the election was over the Corporation altered their tone concerning the riotous freemen, by ordering proceedings to be taken against the parties who had pulled down the shepherd's house and the fences made in the South Fields. All this tended only to inflame the resentment of the freemen—a feeling which was raised to the highest pitch in September by an arbitrary resolution passed at a Common Hall meeting by a small majority. It was as follows:—-" Ordered that Eardley Willmott, Esq., be applyed to by the Sollicitor of this Corporation to prepare the form of an order *for the excluding of such of the Freemen of this Borough as this Corporation shall think proper from turning any Cows, Horses or other Cattle in the South Fields meadows belonging to this Corporation."*

A paragraph having appeared in the *Evening Advertiser* —a London paper conducted on the Whig side of the question—reflecting on the proceedings of the Pretender's partizans in Leicester, during the election, an advertisement

was published in reply in the *Leicester Journal,* to which the names of the Mayor, the Kecorder, and four of the magistrates were appended. The statements in the *Advertiser* were that on the Monday morning before December 4, some of the mob there cried, *"no Hanoverian King," " Prince Charles for ever;"* and that while he, who gave such account, was writing it, he heard the following lines sung with daring insolence:—

"As I was going to the Blue Bell,
I saw Major Mitford going to hell j
I up with my foot and kicked him in,
And bid him make room for his Hanoverian King.

And further, the writer added, with a sneer, " That it was impossible but the magistrates themselves must, repeatedly, have heard those insolent and rebellious cries; and yet, such was their zeal for his Majesty, that no notice was taken of it."

The Mayor, Recorder, and Justices answered that they severally declared, and were ready, upon their corporal oaths, to swear, That neither on the said Monday morning, or at any other time before, or since, they, or any of them, ever heard such cry or song, as in the said paper was inserted, or any part thereof, or any other indecent expressions, either concerning his Majesty, or his ministers, in any of the streets of the said borough or elsewhere: nor had they, or any of them, had information of any such rebellious cries, or songs, brought before them, or any of them.

The *Evening Advertiser,* in commenting upon this advertisement, asks the magistrates to be a little more explicit: "As, for example, is there any distinction betwixt swearing and taking a corporal oath *1* Is treason or sedition never *audible* but when Justice Lee, Justice Wright, Justice Marten, Justice Simpson, Justice Denshire, and Justice Chapman, are together? Otherwise, how can their worships offer, *each* of them, to make oath, that neither *they nor any other,* ever heard, &c. Who do they mean by 'his majesty':—the king of Spain, Annamaboe, or any colour of the cards? What do their worships comprehend under the term 'indecent' in their political vocabulary *l* When these gentlemen in their great wisdom and *loyalty,* have Hatched with their Heads—(to use their own language, full and unequivocal explanations of the above difficulties, we shall do ourselves the honour to make our proper acknowledgments for the favour that will thereby be done the public, and the *loyalty* of the Borough of Leicester by our means. "

Various handbills and placards appear to have been freely circulated in opposition to and defence of the Magistrates. One issued by the Jacobites retorts upon the Hanoverians that they are still "disposed to adhere to their stratagem of contriving and executing wicked devices and charging them upon their neighbours, agreeable to their notorious dark scheme in 1737." The quarrel only died out by degrees; so that it was not until George the Third ascended the throne that Jacobitism ceased to exist to any formidable extent in Leicester.

During the year the irritation of the freemen exceeded endurance. They assembled in the town on the first Monday in September, 1755, and proceeded thence to the South Fields, where they took up and destroyed all the posts and rails separating the closes into which they had been divided. For a fortnight, the fires composed of the posts and rails were kept continually blazing. It was felt by the freemen that a tyrannical Corporation was trying to rob them of their birthright privileges, and they became reckless of the damage they did while gratifying their determination to resist and to punish their oppressors. The authorities were for the moment paralyzed. On the 10th of the month they met in Common Hall, and resolved on taking counsel's opinion how to proceed against the insurgent freemen, and appointed a committee of twenty-four to enforce whatever proceedings might be resolved upon. At the same meeting they ordered that £41 be paid to Mr. Ayre, £247 to Mr. Phipps, and £223 to Mr. Oliver, for the damages by them respectively sustained in consequence of the proceeding just related.

In January, 1756, a committee was appointed by the Corporation to enquire into and direct what fences were necessary to be made, and at whose expense, in the South Fields: and also to determine what further opinions were necessary to be taken concerning the said fields; Mr. Mayor to call the committee together when it was desirable. The feeling of popular indignation continued in existence unabated until April, when mobs destroyed the windows in the houses of every member of the Corporation, and the town was reduced to an appearance of desolation— many houses having no doors, windows, or windowshutters left by the rioters. A case was drawn up, narrating the riotous proceedings which had occurred in the South Fields, and explaining the terms of the leases and the claims of the freemen, which was laid before Thomas Caldecott, Esq., barrister-at-law, and which he fully answered. It is inferrable from the opinions of Mr. Caldecott, that he thought the freemen were warranted in removing the fences made by the lessees, as their rights had been encroached upon by them; but he recommended that new leases should be drawn up reserving to the Mayor, Bailiffs, and Burgesses the liberty of permitting such and so many freemen residing within the said Borough, *as they might think fit,* to turn each of them two mares and geldings, and two cows each, into the meadows at certain periods specified; this proviso enabling the lessees to bring actions against freemen who turned in without the permission of the Mayor, Bailiffs, and Burgesses. It will have been seen throughout that the Corporation assumed a right to select such among the freemen as they pleased upon whom to confer the privilege of pasturage; while it was the ancient, undoubted, and unalterable birthright of *every* freeman to turn horses or cattle into the South Fields. The Corporation had, strictly speaking, neither the authority to give nor withhold the "liberty" of pasturage: their assumption in so doing was purely an act of innovation and usurpation. They, however, acted on the advice of Mr. Caldecott at a Common

Hall meeting, held on the 2nd of February, 1757. They ordered that "the present tenants of the South Fields, on surrendering their present leases, shall have new ones granted for twenty-one years from Michaelmas last j" "that all the three fields be laid down for grass ground;" "that the freemen have liberty to turn in cattle according to Mr. Caldecott's opinion;" and "that the freemen shall turn in to the fields either on the 1st day of September or on the 12th, to take their cattle out again on the 2nd day of February or the 13th, which the Corporation shall think most proper." These resolutions were in the main carried out; and as the freemen were not further hindered in their enjoyment of their common right (for no attempt seems to have been made to exclude any of their number from it), the quarrel ceased, and the excitement gradually subsided.

Early in the year 1756, the friendly relations between England and France were disturbed. On the 23rd of March, the king sent a message to Parliament informing them of the intention of the French to invade either England or Ireland, and on May 18 the declaration of war was published. Before the war was commenced, Count Beuville, and thirty other French officers, had been made prisoners and were sent to Leicester. Most of them were men of high rank of the *ancien regime,* and they were feted by the principal inhabitants, by whom they were much esteemed for their polite and agreeable manners. They were received in all public assemblies with high consideration and a courteous welcome; and, as they expended about £9,000 during their stay in Leicester, it was of benefit to a large portion of the inhabitants.

In March, the Mayor and Corporation took proceedings to help in the prosecution of the war. Colonel Montagu's regiment was then quartered in the town; so in order to encourage recruiting they ordered the Mayor to pay 25s. to such able-bodied men among the inhabitants as should be approved of as fit persons to serve his Majesty in that regiment, who might enlist. They also gave the same bounty to naval volunteers. The

Corporation further manifested their desire to serve the king, by adopting an address to his Majesty on the 21st day of April, saying therein they would cheerfully submit to whatever his Majesty and the Parliament might think necessary to strengthen his hands, that he might long reign over a free and obedient people. In May the Corporation ordered a "treat" to be given at the Three Crowns to the High Sheriff of the County, to Colonel Montagu, and to the rest of the officers quartered in the town—to drink the king's good health and success to his arms; the expense to be paid by the Chamberlains out of the public purse.

A great scarcity of corn was experienced in the second half of the year. The effects of the dearness of price induced the Corporation here to pass the following resolution (Dec 23): "In order to prevent the ill consequences of any unlawful combination amongst the bakers within this Borough, and that the town may be supplied with bread in this time of scarcity and dearness of corn, It is ordered that such of the country bakers as Mr. Mayor and the Justices shall think fit may have the liberty of bringing their bread and selling the same within this Borough, without being molested, until the 1st day of May next, provided they keep the assize in weight and goodness, and observe all other regulations relating thereto, according to the laws and statutes of this realm in sucJi case made and provided." In February (1757) the Corporation passed an order for laying out thirty pounds in bread, for the use of the poor of the several parishes in the borough, at ten pounds a week, the same to be disposed of in such manner as Mr. Mayor should think fit. During the year, wheat was sold in the market at 9s. per strike, and in consequence of the high price the people became tumultuous. In Leicester, they forced the corn from the inns into the market, but offered no injury to any person. At Mountsorrel the mob destroyed a bolting-mill, and then went on to Sileby and Loughborough, where they also destroyed bolting-mills. In other parts of the country similar disturbances occurred.

The war against France had been maintained up to the end of the year, apparently with considerable success, and therefore the municipal body of this borough came to the conclusion to forward an address to his Majesty George the Second, in which they remarked on the victories of his Majesty's arms by sea and land, and declared their willingness to bear the heavy burdens of the war with pleasure, as the only means of preserving their religion, liberties, and trade.

The son of George the Second (known as Frederick, Prince of Wales) being dead, his son George was the heir apparent to the throne. At this time he was approaching his majority. He was a good-natured, affable, agreeable prince; well acquainted with the language, habits, and institutions of the country—not (like his grandfather, the king) a German in interests and prejudices. On the 4th of June 1759, he came of age. The people of Leicester celebrated the event with all honour, and with the usual demonstrations of public delight.

In September, there were great rejoicings in the town upon the receipt of important news of the reduction of Ticonderoga, Crown Point, and Niagara, and the destruction of the French Fleet. The bells were rung, bonfires were lighted, and illuminations were general; but they were scarcely sufficiently demonstrative to express the popular exultation, which was unbounded.

The period was, however, one of considerable anxiety, owing to the continuance of the war with France. The press-gangs were out, and in June the Parliament was informed of the preparations in progress in the French ports for an invasion of England. The topic uppermost in all minds was consequently the necessity of taking measures for national defence. In November the Corporation resolved on opening a subscription in the town forthwith, for the support of the Government. On the 23rd they held a special Hall meeting to make arrangements for the promotion of the object, and adopted a series of resolutions in the style now customary. A week after the date of the meeting when these resolutions were adopted, another Common Hall meeting was held, at which the Corporation manifested their high opinion of William Pitt, the premier and leader of the House of Commons, by voting to him the Freedom of the Borough. On the same occasion, an address to the King was agreed to.

A spirited appeal to the patriotism of the inhabitants was made in an address, to which a response was given by a subscription amounting to £314 5s., of whish £226 16s. was paid to fifty-four men enlisted by the Committee.

An explanation of the state of the town in reference to its Water Supply at this date is furnished in an arrangement for the keeping in repair of the public pumps. Originally a number of draw-wells were dis tributed throughout the town, in every parish and ward, and persons called Well Peeves were annually appointed to look after them; the inhabitants fetching the water they required from these wells daily. The Well Reeves assessed upon the householders what they required to cover the expenses of keeping the wells in proper order. The Mayor and Alderman, finding that pumps would be more useful than open wells, directed them to be placed over the wells; and in this way Cank Pump, another in Redcross-square, with others elsewhere, were erected. An assessment was directed to be made to meet the disbursements, but several of the householders refused to pay their proportionable share of the charges. In November, 1759, the Mayor and Alderman, at the request of the Common Council, ordered an annual election to be made of two Pump Reeves, whom they empowered to raise such a levy as they required; on the basis of the land-tax; defaulters to be proceeded against in the same way as persons were who refused to pay the poor-rate.

The winter of 1759 was rendered unusually gay in Leicester by the arrival of the Suffolk Militia, who were stationed here for some months. "With them came the Duchess of Hamilton (the wife of Colonel Nassau), Lady Ann Hamilton (her daughter), Lady Barker, and other ladies of distinction. The theatre was then constituted of a part of the building at the Eastgates, erected by Mr. Bass, and was under the management of Messrs. Durravan; the performances taking place on Mondays, Wednesdays, and Fridays. The visit of the Suffolk Militia to the town gave a stimulus, not only to the amusements, but to the public and private hospitality of the inhabitants. At a Common Hall, held on the 8th day of February, it was ordered "That Mr. Mayor give such a feast to the Duke of Grafton and the Suffolk Militia officers now in the town as he shall think proper." The Duke of Grafton was the Lord-Lieutenant of Suffolk, and a brigadier-general, and on Monday, the 11th of February, reviewed the Suffolk Militia in the neighbourhood of this town, when an immense concourse of people was drawn together by the spectacle. In the evening, Messrs. Durravan's company performed, by desire of the Misses "Wright, the "Conscious Lovers." The theatre in the Eastgates was crowded by a distinguished and fashionable audience, including the Duchess of Hamilton. On the day after, the Mayor and Aldermen paid their compliments to his Grace the Duke of Grafton, the Hon. Colonel Nassau, and the other officers of the Suffolk Militia, inviting them to a cold collation at the New Exchange. The members of the Corporation attended in their gowns, and the night was spent in mirth and conviviality. The feast was the costliest ever given, up to this date, by the body corporate, "and," says Throsby, "one of the most inebriating. Mr. Mayor, at night, was assisted by the duke down stairs; and the duke soon after by the town servants; there not being a soul left in the room capable of affording help to enfeebled limbs: Field Officers and Aldermen, Captains and Common Council, were perfectly at rest—all were levelled with the mighty power of wine."

While all this enjoyment at the theatre and revelling at the banquet was the order of the day in Leicester, there was a prisoner lying in the County Gaol, then standing in Blue Boar Lane, whose name and whose ultimate end were no-

torious to the nation. The captive was taken to his place of confinement on the 21st of January, and lay there in the custody of Lambert, the gaoler, till the very day on which the Suffolk Militia was reviewed, when he was removed to the Tower. The *Leicester Journal* shrank from even naming the prisoner, whose family had been identified for centuries with our county, and whose crime was murder. While the nobles and ladies who have been mentioned were night after night laughing merrily at the sallies of Messrs. Durravan's comedians, there lay incarcerated in the County Gaol, a building not very far distant, Lawrence, Earl Ferrers, bis hands stained with the blood of his steward, and only a few months left to him before meeting an ignominious death at Tyburn.

In March, this year, a Stage Coach commenced running between London and Nottingham, passing through Market

Harborough, Leicester, and Loughborough, which performed the journey, "if God permitted," in two days. The proprietors (Richard Needham and Company) would not be accountable for any plate, jewels, writings, watches, and rings, unless entered and paid for as such; the highwaymen who then infested the heaths frequently stopping coaches and stripping passengers of their valuables.

On the 25th of October George the Second died at Kensington Palace, in his 77th year, after a reign of more than thirty-three years' duration.

THE LATER HANOVERIAN PERIOD. PROM A.D. 1760 TO A.D. 1837.

Chapter XII

The news of the king's death was scarcely known in Leicester before his grandson was proclaimed. On the day of proclamation all the church bells were rung, halberdmen attended the authorities to the places of proclamation, and a bonfire was burnt in the Market-place; but the burial of George the Second prevented further rejoicings for the time, and on the day when he was interred in Westminster Abbey (the 11th of November) the great bell in every

church in Leicester was tolled from seven to ten in the evening. On the same day, however, the Corporation adopted an Address of Congratulation to the young monarch on his accession.

In this document no Jacobite reserves concerning the king's rightful succession are conveyed or understood. It contains the clearest and fullest possible recognition of his right to the throne and to his prerogatives, which are said to be "legally derived" from his "royal progenitors."-George's declaration had done much to cement the popular feeling in his favour, while the entire failure of all the enterprizes of the Chevalier, and his son, Charles Edward, had rendered the cause of the Stuarts utterly and for ever hopeless. The Jacohites died off one by one; and all thought of the Young Pretender ceased except among a few sentimental spinsters, and old convivial companions, who, when in their cups and with closed doors, toasted "Charley over the water." George gave the climax to his popularity on his accession by the speech which he delivered on opening Parliament on the 18th of November. "Born and educated in this country," said his majesty, "I glory in the name of Briton." He also referred to the flourishing state of the kingdom, the successes of the war, and the extinction of internal dissensions; and he declared the ends of the war to be the support of the Protestant interest, the independence of the national allies, and a safe and honourable peace.

Some local events excite in us a thrilling interest from the horrible circumstances attendant on them: of these, a murder, which took place in Leicester in January, 1761, is an example. Early on Thursday morning, the 29th of that month, a travelling pedlar named Edward Brown, was found dead in a chamber in a common lodging-house, kept by widow Johnson, of Church-gate, situate nearly opposite Butt Close-lane. The deceased was found with his throat cut, and three wounds in his left breast, one of the latter reaching to his heart. A coroner's inquest was held on the body the same day, at which various persons were examined as to what they knew of the matter. The lodging-house keeper said that the deceased, with two other persons, a man and his wife, had come to her house the previous day, and asked to be provided with the use of one room, in which they might all be lodged. They were then shown into a room, in which they seated themselves. They afterwards passed the evening very merrily. Next morning, however, when widow Johnson went down stairs to the street door, she missed the key. She returned upstairs to inquire for it; and, on reaching the stair-head, she found the body of the deceased, covered with blood, on the floor. The jury brought in a verdict of " Wilful murder by persons unknown." The two companions of the deceased having fled, they were pursued to Kettering, in Northamptonshire, where they were capoured on the evening of Thursday. They confessed their guilt, and were committed to Northampton Gaol, by Mr. Hill, of Howell, on the Friday. At the ensuing Assizes, on March 13, the prisoners were placed on their trial for the murder, under the names of Thomas and Elizabeth Castledine; though the husband's name was Thomas Cherry. He was a native of Ramsey, Huntingdonshire. The husband at once pleaded guilty—the wife not guilty; but as she confessed to the murder on her first apprehension, the pair were sentenced to be hanged on the Monday following, that is, on the fourth day after the trial. In order to strike terror in the popular mind, the authorities ordered the gallows to be erected on the open space in the Butt Close, opposite to the house in which the deed had been committed. On the morning of the execution, at nine o'clock, the culprits were put into the cart, with the executioner, and conveyed to the gallows. Here they prayed very devoutly for some time, being aided by a clergyman. They then rose from their knees, and kissed each other affectionately. The wife said to her husband, "Now, my dear, am I guilty or not guilty 1" He replied, "My dear, you are not guilty." The hangman then, on his knees, asked forgiveness of each separately, and proceeded to fulfil his ap-

pointed task. The ropes being fixed, and the caps pulled over their faces, the cart was drawn away from beneath the wretched couple, and they were left to suffer the agonies of a wretched death. When taken down, the bodies were handed over to the surgeons for dissection.

On the 17th and 18th of May, 1762, the Warwickshire militia marched into Leicester. In the week following, the Leicestershire militia was quartered in Harborough, Lutterworth, and Hinckley. When the King's birthday was celebrated, on the 4th of June, the Warwickshire militia, commanded by Major Sir Koger Newdegate, Bart., were drawn up in the Market Place, colours flying, and then fired three volleys in honour of the day. There were constant movements of military in this locality in June. In its second week, the first division of the Lancashire militia, commanded by their colonel, Lord Strange, arrived here on their march for the camp at Winchester. The second division, under Lieutenant Colonel Townley, followed the day after. The men were noticed as "straight, handsome fellows." On Saturday, June 12, the first division of General Holmes's regiment arrived here on their route to Sandy Heath, and on Monday, the 14th, the second division. Although they had marched three hundred miles (from Scotland), they came from Nottingham in one day, and went hence to Northampton the next day. They were mostly Scotchmen. On the 19th the Rtijtal Cheshire militia marched into this place, on their return to their own county; the day after, the Warwickshire regiment left here for Worcester; and on the 28th, the Leicestershire marched into the place from the markettowns already named.

All the warm wishes of the local authorities, expressed in their loyal congratulations to George the Third and his Queen on their marriage, were gratified on the 12th of August by the birth of a prince, who afterwards succeeded to the throne as George the Fourth. When the news reached Leicester, the inhabitants testified their delight by ringing the bells all day; and in the evening the

principal people met at the Exchange, at the invitation of the Mayor, and were there entertained with plentiful supplies of wine and ale, in which they drank many healths to the royal family, and the young prince, amid loud huzzas.— The Corporation addressed the King in reference to the auspicious event. In one part of their address they said: "Great as our joy is, on this important occasion, it is still heightened by the late Glorious Success of your Majesty's Arms. We reflect, with inexpressible pleasure, that at the very time when your Majesty and your People were blest with an heir apparent to your Throne, one of your Enemies strongest fortresses and most valuable possessions was submitting itself to your Majesties Government; and as it graciously pleased the Divine Providence to join together these great Events, we humbly beg leave to join them likewise in our Dutiful Congratulations."

The Leicestershire militia was disembodied in December; the Duke of Rutland announcing the fact under his hand and seal, on the 18th of the month, and this being accompanied by a letter from the War Office, expressive of his Majesty's great satisfaction with their seasonable and meritorious service.

It was towards the close of an early day in June 1763 that a post-chaise was seen hurrying towards Leicester, the passengers within being a man and woman. The chaise was pursued by horsemen, who proved to be from Warwickshire, and who, having succeeded in overtaking the fugitives, immediately returned with them the way they had arrived. So severe had been the chase that the horse of one of the pursuers fell dead from, exhaustion, and was left near the Dane Hills. The curiosity of the whole town was, of course, roused by the circumstance. After the lapse of a week, news came from Coventry of a robbery at the Castle Inn, in that city, on the fair day, committed by two well-dressed men and two women, who, having been shown into an upstairs room, in which stood a bureau containing a considerable sum of money, broke open the bureau, and took therefrom cash and plate to a large amount. Evidence was soon forthcoming to show that these persons constituted a portion of a formidable band of dangerous and desperate confederates known as "The Toys," whose deeds had rendered them a terror to the inhabitants of Cumberland, Westmoreland, and Northumberland. Alderman Hewitt, of Coventry, came over to Leicester, and was the cause of seven other members of the gang being taken into custody in this town on the morning of Sunday, June 12. Six of them were sent to Coventry in two post-chaises under strong escort, one man was committed to our town gaol, and one man and one woman were admitted to bail.

Two years before the date of these events a good-looking, gentlemanly young man, visited Leicester, and stopped at the Bell Hotel.. He paid attentions to the landlord's daughter, which proved agreeable, and were followed by an offer of marriage. His conduct appearing unexceptionable, the girl's father permitted her to marry the stranger. Some time after, the landlord died; upon the occurrence of which event, Mr. Douglas (for such was the name he bore), succeeded to the business of the Bell Hotel. When he assumed this position, he increased the favourable impression he had made, by a zealous observance of religious duty, by punctuality and honesty in his dealings with his neighbours, and by abstaining from fraud even under circumstances in which he was sheltered from suspicion. He was, besides, a most affectionate husband, a tender parent, and remarkably kind to his wife's poor relations. John Douglas was, in fact, in the estimation of the whole town of Leicester, a really good citizen.

But it happened, to the surprize of everybody, that among other disclosures made by the prisoners in Coventry Gaol, was this one—that this man had been transported from Rochester for stealing a silver tankard in the year 1757, and had escaped from transportation. He was therefore apprehended without ceremony, and immured in the prison of the county of Leicester, then standing in Blue Boar Lane. Evidence

was accumulated against him, and accordingly he was put on his trial at the Leicestershire Assizes, held at the Castle, on Saturday, July 30 j the issue being life or death. He was dressed in a white broad-cloth coat, trimmed with black, and a black silk waistcoat. His comparative youth (for he was scarcely thirty), and his affecting behaviour on his trial, moved the court to compassion, and brought tears on the cheeks of even those who were ordinarily indifferent spectators. William Marsden, clerk to Sir John Fielding (the celebrated London magistrate), swore to the identity of Douglas. Judge Mansfield sentenced him to be hanged by the neck until he was dead, and might God have mercy on his soul!

A reprieve for one month was granted. A memorial, praying that the extreme penalty of the law might not be enforced, was handed round for signature in Leicester. To it were appended the names of the Mayor, Justices, most of the Aldermen and Common Councilmen, and upwards of 150 gentlemen and principal tradesmen in Leicester, and it was laid before George the Third by the Earl of Egremont. Though hopes had been entertained that he would be spared, Douglas was executed on the gallows near this town on the day appointed, leaving his wife a widow and his offspring fatherless, for the offence of returning from transportation before the term of his banishment had expired. Such was the aspect of justice to the grandfathers of our grandfathers one hundred years ago!

Four of the offenders above-named—Margaret Clarke, William Ogden, Margaret Brown, and John Philips—were capitally convicted at Coventry on August 1, and were executed at Whitley Common on August 10.

Up to this period, no banking establishment had been carried on in Leicester. The commercial concerns of the locality were managed in a very primitive manner by one or two of the principal tradesmen, who received deposits and who undertook to make payments in London for their customers. But, at the close of the year, what may be called

a "bank" was commenced in the town, which was thus made known to the public in the *Leicester Journal* of December 31: "We are credibly informed that Mr. Joseph Bunney and Mr. Thomas Pares, both of this place, propose taking upon their notes, payable to bearer, any sum that shall be offered to 'em, and will allow £2 per cent, per annum for every sum amounting to X25 and upwards, from the end of thirty days after the time of its being advanced."—"With the families of Pares and of Paget the business of banking has been thus identified in Leicester for four or five generations in the former case and three in the latter.

The readers of these pages who remember the great change effected in locomotion by the transition from coach travelling to railway communication, and the impression of great speed experienced by those who, having gone from Leicester to London in the "Telegraph," the "Defiance," or the "Rapid," in twelve or fourteen hours, were whirled in three or four from this place to the Metropolis, may conceive what were the feelings of the good people of Leicester, when, in 1764, having previously been shaken that distance in a day and a night, they were promised to be carried it in a "Flying Machine" in one day! The enterprising persons who paralyzed the public with the bewildering proposal thus advertised themselves in the *Leicester Journal*: "Leicester. "Flying Machine; "In One Day; "To Carry Four Passengers: "Begins Monday, April 9th, and will continue to set out from the Cranes Inn in Leicester; Monday, Wednesday, and Friday mornings, at Two o'clock precisely; and gets to the Ram Inn, Smithfield, London, the same night; sets out from the Eam Inn, Smithfield, every Tuesday, Thursday, and Saturday mornings, at Two o'clock precisely, and gets to Leicester the same night; each Passenger to pay £1 5s., and so in proportion to any part of the said Road; Children in Lap and Outsides at half-price.

"Perform'd if God permit by
"Samuel Oliver, of Leicester;
"Thomas Stoakes, of Dunstable."
Let the reader imagine the task of ris-

ing at two o'clock on a raw spring morning to set out on a journey for London, and being rocked along all day until midnight in the Flying Machine, and then reaching the dimly-lighted streets; and then compare the wearying journey with the present mode of travelling—and be thankful.

Shortly after this arrangement had been begun, a company, consisting of Messrs. Stoakes (Dunstable), Oliver (Leicester), Howe (Derby), Tenant (Manchester), Richardson (Leeds), and Glanvil (Sheffield), was formed to run from Nottingham, Derby, and Leicester, in one day, *six* days a week, and to make the return journeys as often. The machine was advertised to be on steel springs.

The "march of intellect" began in Leicester about this date, an "inimitable piece of art," called the " Microcosm," being introduced to the wondering gaze of the inhabitants at the " New Exchange" in October. It consisted of Architecture, Sculpture, Painting, Music, and Astronomy, with a vast variety of moving figures. At the same time, the "learned and ingenious Dr. Griffis," delivered lectures on Natural and Experimental Philosophy, in the Town Hall, amid universal applause; exciting the admiration of all visitors, and entirely answering "all the just expectations of the curious."

As the winter approached, the high price of food with the depression of trade rendered the condition of the working-classes extremely deplorable, and excited the compassion of their wealthy neighbours. Collections were made by the several parishes, and several private donations were also given away; a committee being appointed to superintend the proper distribution of the money subscribed. The distress continued throughout the winter. So high was the price of grain that the Corporation of Leicester and Nottingham petitioned the House of Commons to take into consideration the fact, and devise some means of speedy relief. In Leicester, it was alleged, wheat was sold for 58s. per quarter, and the poorer housekeepers must have perished of starva-

tion had not the more opulent inhabitants assisted them by donations.

On May 27,1765, the militia of this county, commanded by the Hon. Colonel Grey, were clothed, armed, and embodied, in order to be exercised for twenty-eight days, pursuant to act of parliament. On the 4th of June (the king's birth-day) they were drawn up in the Market-place, and fired three volleys in honour of the day. It was observed of them by the *Journal* that " though principally composed of young lads taken from the plough and the loom, who had never seen any service, they made amazing progress in learning the use of arms."

The popular sports of this date were more varied, perhaps, than at present. The *Leicester Journal* of September 7 announces, for example, that "all persons who take delight in the manly and noble exercises of single sticks and wrestling are desired to take notice that at the Cross Keys at Desford, in the county of Leicester, on Friday, the 27th of this instant September, will be given the Annual Prizes of a gold-laced hat for the best gamester at single sticks, and a pair of buck-skin breeches for the best champion at wrestling." Strangers who might wish to make trial of their manhood and dexterity were promised fair play on the occasion.

Early in the year 1766 Dr. Watts, of Medbourn, a physician, commenced his benevolent advocacy of the foundation of the Leicester Infirmary. In the columns of the *Leicester Journal* he made frequent appeals to the affluent on behalf of his proposal; pointing out the examples of Winchester, Exeter, and Northampton, as worthy of imitation. In that paper of May 10, he showed how the poor would have the benefit of ventilation, and cleanliness, in a well-constructed and well-drained Infirmary, and in subsequent numbers answered the objections of opponents—for he had to encounter such; no good scheme being ever without bitter enemies. On the 22nd of July, the public were informed by advertisement, that proposals having been laid before the High Sheriff (Charles James Packe, Esq.), and the

Grand Jury of the County, at the Assizes, for the establishment of a Public Infirmary, and the sum of £2,000 having been subscribed for the purpose, they called a meeting of the Nobility, Gentry, Clergy, and Freeholders of the County, to consider the ways and means of expeditiously carrying out the plan, to be held at the Three Cranes, on September 11, at ten o'clock in the forenoon. At this assembly, a resolution was unanimously adopted in favour of the proposal, and the meeting was adjourned to October 8, at twelve in the forenoon.

In the month of September, mobs of people assembled at Hinckley and Shilton, and stopped waggons laden with cheese, which they took, and distributed among themselves. These provision riots (for such they proved to be) were occasioned by the scarcity then prevalent, and the high prices by which it was necessarily accompanied. On last day of the month, Mr. Pridmore, a cheese factor, of Market Harborough, having lodged a considerable quantity of cheese at a warehouse at the Bell, in Humberstone Gate, contrary to the advice of the magistrates, was imprudent enough (considering the state of public feeling) to attempt to remove a part of it before the fair. A waggon was accordingly loaded with it and sent off; but at the end of Humberstone Gate, leading out of the town, it was stopped by several women who seized the fore horse by the head, while others mounted the waggon, and taking the cheese out of it gave it away among the crowd, before the local authorities had any knowledge of the proceedings. A riot ensued, and a party of soldiers was called out to disperse the multitude. When several prisoners had been taken, a determined attempt was made to break into the prison where they were confined, and it was only the presence of the military guard which prevented the success of the rioters. The threat of being fired on at last had its effect on stopping their proceedings. The state of affairs at Cavendish Bridge was more fearful than at Leicester; an armed conflict taking place between the guard set to keep a warehouse, who discharged grape and small shot, and the mob, who returned the fire with muskets or fowling-pieces. The mob at Donington had a stand-up fight with thirty farmers mounted on horse-back, assisted by footmen; and, assailing them in front and flank at the same time, drove their antagonists to the bridge, and there routed them altogether.

On October 8, the meeting of the gentlemen friendly to the establishment of the Infirmary was held at the Three Cranes; when Sir Thomas Cave, Bart., was called to the chair. On this occasion certain preliminary resolutions were adopted, with a view to the immediate promotion of the success of the new undertaking.

The successor to Mr. Chambers in the Mayoralty this year was Mr. Fisher, who was duly chosen Mayor on St. Matthew's Day (Sept. 21); though not without a spirited opposition to his nomination, as the minority against his appointment was only eleven below the majority Mr. Fisher was one of the few remaining Jacobites, who were always ready to manifest their aversion to the reigning dynasty when occasion offered. It was the invariable custom of the newly-elected Mayor, previous to his election, to proceed (in accordance with the requirements of the charter of James the First) to the Castle, on the Monday after Martinmas Day, there to take an oath before the Steward of the Duchy of Lancaster, to perform well and faithfully all and every ancient custom, and so forth, according to the best of his knowledge. When Mr. Mayor and his attendants arrived at a certain place within the precincts of the Castle, the bearer of the great mace lowered it from its upright position, in token of acknowledgement of the superior authority of the representatives of the ancient feudal earls, within their own stronghold. This ceremony was purposely omitted when Mayor Fisher attended at the Castle Gateway, the town servant refusing to "slope the mace," as it was designated. The Constable of the Castle, or his deputy, therefore refused admittance to the civic functionary, and he was excluded from the building. After

that date, the Mayor went in private to the Castle to comply with the terms of the ancient charter.

On the 4th of January, 1767, the Bishop of Lincoln addressed a letter to the clergy of this county, strongly urging them to support the proposed Infirmary; and on the 21st of February appeared a list of subscriptions in the *Leicester Journal,* which may be regarded as in part a response to the episcopal appeal. It may interest the descendants of the original subscribers to read the names of their ancestors on the following roll of donors:—

The Legacy of Mrs. Keck'a Will £500 0 0

Sir John Palmer, Bart 300 0 0
Anthony JameB Keck, Esq. 300 0 0
Shuckburgh Ashby, Esq 300 0 0
John Darker, Esq 300 0 0
Charles Jennens, Esq. Gopsall 100 0 0
Charles James Pache, Esq 100 0 0
William Pochin, Esq 100 0 0
Joseph Cradock, Esq 100 0 0
Sir George Robinson, Bart 100 0 0
Samuel Phillips, Esq 50 0 0
The Rev. Dr. Bentley 50 0 0
Mrs. D. Ashby of Quenby 50 0 0
Thomas Peach, Esq 30 0 0
Thomas Boothby, Esq 20 0 0
E. W. Hartopp, Esq., by Mr. Boothby 20 0 0
Mrs. Ann Wigley, by Mr. Boothby 20 0 0
Mr. Sanderson 20 0 0
Thomas Babington, Esq 10 10 0
Mrs. Babington 10 10 0
Rev. Mr. Gamble of Ashby 10 10 0
David Wells, Gent 5 5 0
William Burleton, Esq 5 5 0
Mr. John Grew 5 5 0
John Westley, Gent 5 5 0
Harley Vaughan, Esq 5 6 0
Mrs. Elizabeth Bewicke..., 5 5 0

In July, a "Dissenting Clergyman," whose name was not made public, paid £22 2s. 6d. into the hands of Mr. Ald. Phipps, as a donation to the Infirmary. On the 17th of September, a general meeting of the subscribers was held, at which it was unanimously agreed to carry the benevolent work into execution, and in the issue of the *Journal* following

the meeting, builders willing to tender for the erection of a County Infirmary in a plain, strong manner, for a sum not exceeding £1,500 were invited to send in plans and estimates, either to Mr. Thomas Pares or Mr. Aid. Phipps. At a meeting held on October 7 the plan was submitted for consideration, when it was agreed to purchase the Chapel Close for the erection thereon of the building designed. The site was spoken of as " a dry and airy piece of ground, situate at the south end of the town, upon the London-road leading for Wellingborough." On the 4th of December the purchase-money was paid to Mr. Walker, the owner of the ground, and immediate measures were resolved upon by the subscribers.

It will have been perceived already by the reader, that Leicester had, by this time, become on a small scale and with a smaller population, essentially what it is, in its social and institutional aspects, in the present day and generation. The inhabitants did not yet number more than 10,000 or 11,000.

The local circumstance in the year following (1768) most notable was the visit of a royal personage to the town, in the month of September. We learn that the King of Denmark made a progress through this country at that date. He went to Burleigh House, the seat of the Earl of Exeter, and on the same day dined with the Duke and Duchess of Ancaster, at Grimsthorpe, where a magnificent entertainment was provided for his majesty. On Saturday, September 2, he lay at Derby. On Sunday morning, about nine o'clock, the king arrived in Leicester. At that hour a carriage drove up to the door of the Three Cranes Inn, in Gallowtree-gate, and a traveller stepped out of it into the principal parlour of the establishment. Walking to the window, the stranger threw up the sash, showed himself, and bowed with affability and condescension to the people assembled. He was about the middle size; he had light hair and a fair complexion. He was dressed in a light drab coat and blue waistcoat, edged with silver; wearing on his breast a star and the ensign of the Order of the Elephant.

This was the King of Denmark, the unworthy husband of George the Third's youngest sister. Part of the Regiment of Horse Guards Blue were drawn out opposite the Three Cranes, to receive his majesty, who called to the officer on guard, and conversed familiarly with him for several minutes. A numerous suite accompanied the king, who were brought to the town in thirteen post-chaises and upon saddle horses. Shortly after nine, the whole *cortege* left the inn for Market Harborough.

In the course of the year, the Infirmary buildings were making progress to completion. On the 23rd of September Mr. Wyatt's plan for the erection was approved of at a meeting of the subscribers, and the superintendence of the works assigned to Mr. Henderson—orders being given for carrying the plan into execution as soon as the materials could be brought together. At a general meeting of the Infirmary Committee, held on the 18th of October, it was agreed at the ensuing meeting to lay out the ground for the intended building; Mr. Henderson, the undertaker of the work, being directed to attend for that purpose. Oa November 1, the gentlemen of the Committee accordingly set out the ground, as agreed upon; and Mr. Henderson placed himself under obligations to complete the structure before May Day, 1770.

As yet the people of Leicester walked in darkness through their streets in the winter evenings, only lighted by hand-lanterns when they happened to go from home to public amusements or to visit their neighbours. In the beginning of December, the inhabitants of Gallowtree-gate had the spirit to raise a private subscription for erecting oil-lamps, at regular distances, to light up that street on the dark nights.

It will illustrate the perils which the people of this town formerly incurred in coach-travelling if we mention an incident that occurred to the "Leicester Fly," at this date. On one of the last days in March, 1769, the cumbrous vehicle had reached Holloway, when a single highwayman rode up to it, ordered the driver to stop, and demanded the passengers' money. Thrusting the muzzle of his pistol into the window, he pointed it at the breast of one of the two gentleman inside. This person happened to be a naval officer, and therefore was less alarmed than an ordinary passenger would be: he therefore turned aside the barrel, the contents of which were not discharged, as the pistol flashed in the pan. The officer immediately fired on his assailant, and the other gentleman imitated his example. The highwayman was evidently wounded, as he rode off groaning, and fell from his horse. The body could not be found, though the horse was taken. Two fellows, supposed to be confederates, were also apprehended and taken to Highgate.

In June, the Infirmary buildings were reported to be in a state of forwardness; and on the 21st of July, at the General Meeting of the Subscribers (Sir Thomas Cave, Bart., in the chair,) £500 was paid down to the builder on account (agreeable to the contract), on his raising the first floor. The gentlemen went down to view the building, and suggested several improvements and additions, which were effected.

The year concluded with another effort to light the streets by subscription, like that begun by the inhabitants of Gallowtree-gate; the residents of Belgrave-gate imitating the example of their neighbours. The lamps were lighted for the first time on the evening of December 15.

The Infirmary ought to have been opened in May, 1770, in pursuance of the arrangement made with the contractor; but, instead of being ready for use at the time promised, the event was delayed until July. On the 10th of May, a general meeting of the subscribers was held (Sir George Bobinson, Bart., in the chair), when it was resolved immediately to form a Committee, to consider the most proper means to be adopted for carrying out the objects of the Institution, and preparing for the reception of the patients with all possible expedition. The company went down in a body to visit the building, which was highly approved, and gave general satisfaction; much to the credit of Mr. Wyatt, the architect, and Mr. Henderson, the builder. Perfect unanimity was witnessed at the meeting; the sole desire being evident on every side to promote the success of so useful and beneficial an institution.

A meeting of the subscribers to the Infirmary was convened for Friday, the 5th of July, to make rules for the conduct of the institution, to fix the date for the reception of patients, and to define the privileges of subscribers. Before the day of meeting, Dr. Vaughan, then the principal physician in Leicester, had been requested to draw up the regulations, which he did accordingly. On the occasion, the thanks of the assembly were conveyed to him by Sir Thomas Cave, the chairman, for the care and trouble he had taken in the task; and a similar vote was also passed to the Rev. Dr. Watts, in acknowledgment of the benefit accruing from his original plan and proposal of the establishment; he was also elected a Governor. The Duke of Montague was elected President, and the Earls of Huntingdon, Denbigh, and Stamford, and Viscount Wentworth, Vice-Presidents of the charity.

The tradition has been preserved of John Bunyan having lodged in a house still standing in St. Nicholas Street, nearly opposite the Church of that parish. Another of the great religious reformers of a past age also took Leicester in his circuit of propagandism this year, and is said to have been lodged in the same building. He was short in stature, dressed in a black garb, and long white locks flowed over his shoulders. To an earnest and intelligent countenance, an aquilline nose imparted force and dignity of expression. The person here described was John Wesley. On Tuesday evening, the last day in July, this remarkable person presented himself to a large assemblage in the Castle-yard, for the first time in Leicester. The rain falling heavily before he finished his discourse, he postponed the conclusion of it until the following morning, at five o'clock, at the meeting-house in Mill-stone-lane—then the place of assembly used by his followers.

At last, on the 11th of September,

the Infirmary was opened for the reception of patients. The day was made one of great ceremony. About half-past ten in the forenoon, the Governors waited on the Bishop of Lincoln at the Three Cranes, and theie formed a procession to St. Martin's Church. Upon their entrance a grand overture was played, and in the course of the service several selections from the Messiah were performed. The Bishop preached a sermon from Mark, c. I, v. 34; and the Coronation Anthem, sung by the choir of St. Margaret's, concluded the musical portion of the service. The Bishop, attended by the Governors, then walked down to the Infirmary, which they opened with due solemnity; afterwards returning to an ordinary at the Three Cranes—the ladies dining at the Three Crowns. In the evening, a Grand Concert was performed in the Haymarket Assembly Room, which was under the management of Joseph Cradock, Esq., of Gumley, and the Bev. Mr. Jenner; the performers having been engaged, and the music-books lent for the occasion, by Mr. Garrick. Mr. Fishfr played the violin, Mr. Fischer the hautboy, and Mr. Vernon and Mr. Bartheleman sang the songs. The collection at the church doors amounted to £139 12s. 4d., the admission tickets to £94 2s 6d., and the concert tickets to £98 10s.; the whole sum thus realised being £332 4s. 1Od. The annual subscriptions now amounted to £440, which was exclusive of the interest of the capital stock of £600 in the funds. In the treasurer's hands there was the sum of £672 12s., to which the £332 above-mentioned would be added.

It has been already noticed how by the voluntary efforts of the inhabitants, the lighting of the streets by oil lamps commenced in this town. The example of the residents of Gallowtree-gate was followed by those living in Belgrave-gate; and in August, this year, it was still more extensively imitated in different quarters, so that it was attempted to light up generally in time for the occurrence of the races. When, therefore, the country cousins of, the townspeople poured into the place on the 19th of

N

September, their curiosity was gratified by seeing the new arrangements; and as the ladies and gentlemen who attended the ball in the Assembly Rooms, Hay-market, passed along the streets in sedan-chairs, or carriages, to that building, they were lighted by the glimmer of the oil-lamps in the principal thoroughfares.

Already had the staple trade its troubles—the framework knitters being full of complaints of ill-usage; averring that they laboured under greater hardships than any other set of manufacturers in the kingdom. They alleged that their wages had some time before been reduced twopence in the shilling. They stated that about one stockingmaker in four could get 9s. a week by close work; out of which sum he was obliged to deduct 9d. a week frame-rent, 9d. a week for seaming, and 3d. a week for needles. In the winter, fire and candles might justly be calculated at 9d. a week in addition; so that the nett earnings of one of the better hands in the summer season was 7s. 3d.— in the winter, 6s. 6d. weekly. With this small sum they had house rent and lodgings to pay, and provisions to purchase for themselves and families, at a period when the coarsest bread was nearly 2d. per pound, and butcher's meat in proportion. The deputies from the workpeople laid their case before the hosiers; and they were then so humble that they said they were sensible of "the impropriety of interfering with matters of government," in regard to the laws regulating the prices of provisions—*that* must proceed from their employers. The hosiers held a meeting at the Three Cranes, at which they resolved on an answer to the framework knitters. In this document they remind the men that in many branches of the manufacture their prices had been advanced on an average 10 per cent.; and they urge that as the great demand for Leicester goods came from foreign markets, it was the united opinion of the trade that if the price of goods sent abroad, were to be increased, all would experience the injury resulting therefrom; they must be careful not to be undersold by the many rivals they

had in their branch of commerce; as they would be were prices raised. With regard to the cost of provisions, they admitted it must affect the workpeople, and they wished it was in their power to remove the grievance, and they said they would make it a subject of their particular attention.

It rarely happens that a drama is enacted in a provincial town, the composition of a resident, or author of local connection; but such was the case in the year 1772, in Leicester—"Zobeide," a tragedy by Joseph Cradock, Esq., being presented on the boards of the Theatre in the Haymarket. The principal performers were Mr. and Mrs. Whitfield, Mr. Robertson, Mr. Kelly, Mr. Maddocks, and Mr. Cooke. Mrs. Monk impersonated Zobeide.

On the 18th of June, the Quarterly Board Meeting of the Infirmary was held, when the Governors attended in large numbers. Lord Wentworth was called to the chair. The thanks of the meeting were voted to Joseph Cradock, Esq., of Gumley, and to the Rev. Mr. Jenner, for the essential service the hospital had received from their conduct in directing the musical performance at the opening of the institution. Sir John Palmer. Bart., and the Rev. Robert Burnaby were requested to assume the management of the next musical meeting, to take place in September. The institution was now clearly in working order. On Thursday, September 24, the anniversary meeting of the opening was celebrated with every demonstration of pleasure and distinction. The Governors met at the Assembly Room, Coal HilL and thence walked in order to St. Margaret's Church, where the Hon. and Rev. Dr. Noel (by request) preached a sermon from the first epistle of Peter, chapter 4, verse 10, "As every man hath received of the gift, even so minister one to another, as good stewards of the manifold grace of God." The Rev. Mr. Haines read the service, during which certain songs and choruses from the "Messiah" were performed. In the evening a grand concert was given at the Assembly Room.

The year 1773 was long remembered,

among the working classes especially, as one in which the spirit of framebreaking very widely prevailed. It seems that an ingenious mechanic from Scotland had constructed a stocking frame, which he had offered for sale to several of the hosiers, who were soliciting a patent for the invention. It was commonly believed amongst the workpeople that one man, by means of the new frame, could do as much work as sixty men with one of the old kind, and consequently, that the value of labour, already wretchedly remunerated, would be still further depreciated. It had been set up on the premises of Messrs. Simpson and Goode, and was known to be there by the populace. Crowds of country workmen entered the town from all sides on the morning of Monday, March 12, assembling in the Market-place, for the express purpose of violently taking possession of and destroying the new machine. One of the manufacturers addressed the multitude, assuring them that their ideas respecting its probable operation in making their labour useless, were wholly untrue, and that he would permit any number of them to examine it, and see it worked, and if it were found to possess any property tending to injure the stocking-maker he would freely give it up, to be broken to pieces. For a short time, the mob was pacified by this appeal, and the frame was ordered immediately to be taken to the Exchange and there set up, in order that all who chose might examine its construction. However, before it was made quite ready for working, the ringleaders forced themselves into the building, seized upon the frame, removed it into the Market-place, carried it round the town in triumph, and then pulled it to pieces, and threw them among the disorderly multitude. On their return into the Market-place, the hosiers met the rioters, and then adjourned to the Exchange; where they promised the frame-breakers that they would neither seek to obtain any patents for any newly-invented stocking-frame, nor cause to be made any such machine as might occasion any reduction in the number of workmen-then employed;

but, on the contrary, would do all they could to prevent the realization of such a result. This assurance being signed, the stocking-makers dispersed quietly, without offering any insult to any person. It is worthy of notice that not only did the unenlightened workpeople resist the procuring of patents for the working of the new frame, but that some of the hosiers themselves joined in the unreasoning opposition to the invention.

Early in 1774 so much of extreme Puritan feeling prevailed in Leicester, that a local association was in existence with the avowed purpose of enforcing the laws against dramatic entertainments. Mr. Chamberlain, the manager of the Theatre, an inhabitant of the town, pleading the distressed condition of his company, obtained their forbearance, on condition of playing only for six weeks after January 15. In the ensuing February, performances by Mr. and Mra. Siddons were announced; the "Queen of Tragedy" being now only an obscure provincial actress, in her nineteenth year, having yet to pass through an ordeal of eight years of unappreciated toil in her profession before her great powers became recognized in the Metropolis. The coincidence may be noted that in this year, in which Mrs. Siddons made her appearance in the town, John Wesley paid it a second visit—probably less than a month after the actress's departure. Wesley preached in the "Tabernacle" in Millstone-lane, to a crowded congregation, on Thursday, March 24, and on the following morning, at five o'clock, he again addressed a numerous audience.

Up to this time, the four old town gates, erected in the Middle Ages, were still standing. The thought probably occurred to Mr. Drake, the Mayor—an auctioneer—that a public improvement and a litte private business might at the same time be effected; and he therefore proposed the entire removal of the ancient fabrics. In pursuance of his recommendation, doubtless, an advertisement was inserted in the *Leicester Journal,* stating that on the 28th of March, the building materials of the four gates would be sold by auction at Mr. James

Bishop's, the Three Crowns Hotel, Leicester. The East, "West, North, and South Gates, were to be sold in four lots, to be removed at the buyer's expense. The order of Common Hall for taking down the four gates of this town, we are assured, was complied with at his particular motion, and had been executed under his immediate inspection. The East Gate had already been cleared away, and a commodious passage opened, which, when completed, we are told, would measure 54 feet wide, and the West Gate was then in course of removal.

One improvement often leads to another, and thus we are led to infer that the removal of the Town Gates suggested the alteration of the custom of holding the Beast Market near the East Gates, to the holding of it in Horsefair-street, between the Three Crowns Hotel and the top of the street. Mr. Mayor's direction, publicly made known, was found sufficient to carry the measure, without recourse to private Act of Parliament or any foreign aid whatever.

In September the Infirmary Anniversary was celebrated with unusual *eclat,* by musical performances in St. Martin's Church and the Castle. Never was such an assemblage seen before in Leicester; all that was distinguished in rank, brilliant in fashion, and fascinating in beauty, being represented in the New Assembly Rooms, the Church, and the Castle. There was the popular young Marquis of Granby, in his twenty-first year, his heart probably still free, and not a few beauties anxious to captivate the future lord of Belvoir. Among the company also was Mr. Banks, with Omai, prince of Otaheite, who had been brought to this country by Capt. Cook, the celebrated circumnavigator. The black man, Omai, attired in his strange costume, attracted the notice of everybody; and particularly of a boy, or child, four years of age, with rosy cheeks, bright teeth, wavy hair, and animated countenance—the son of one of the musicians, then in the orchestra, and who, in after-life, remembered the scene and wrote an account of it and of himself. The child was William Gardiner, afterwards the author of *Music and Friends.*

In April, 1770, the war had began between Great Britain and the Colonies of North America. In June, the battle of Bunker's Hill was fought. As the year advanced the inhabitants of the large towns held meetings to address the King, deprecating the American Rebellion. In Leicester, the Corporation adopted an address, urging him to take such measures with the insurgents as would convince them that the " sword is not borne in vain," and assuring his Majesty of their best assistance at all times. Early in December, at a meeting of the Corporation, a proposal was made by the Mayor, and unanimously agreed to, in favour of opening a subscription "towards the relief of the soldiers who are, or may be, in his Majesty's service in America, and for succouring the distressed Widows and Orphans of those brave men who have fallen or may fall in defending the Constitutional Government of the country. " The Corporation headed the subscription with a contribution of fifty guineas. It should not be omitted in connection with this subject, that appeals were made to the friends of a peaceable settlement of the American struggle, and of the concession to the colonists of their claims, with a view to the restoration of harmony between them and Great Britain.

Hitherto no coach communication existed between Leicester and Manchester. In the *Journal,* of August 24, 1776, first appears an announcement by Messrs. Barlow, Kendall, and Co., of their '' Manchester and London New Diligence," which set out every morning at four o'clock (Sunday excepted), from the Blossoms Inn, Lawrence-lane, London, and fiom the Lower Swan Inn, Market-street Lane, Manchester, for the Swan-with-Two-Necks in Leicester, where it lay each night, arriving in London and Manchester the next evening. From Leicester the Diligence ran through Welford to Northampton. The proprietors would not undertake to be accountable for money, plate, or any other valuable article, unless entered and paid for accordingly—a precaution-

ary notice which the constant occurrence of highway robberies at this period seems to have rendered necessary.

The only other event of this year which we notice, was the observance of a Day of Solemn Fast and Humiliation, for imploiing the blessing of the Divine Majesty on the British arms by sea and land. The churches were crowded, and all ranks of people evinced the feeling which the importance and solemnity of the occasion were said to demand: the dissenters of all denominations uniting in the observance of the Fast Day, by paying religious-regard to it in the same devout way as Churchmen.

We pass over a year unimportant in local events to record a movement made by the Framework Knitters, in 1778, to better their condition. This was an attempt to obtain an Act for the regulation of their business. They presented a petition to Parliament, praying that leave might be given to bring in a Bill, to settle and regulate the wages of persons employed in the art or business of Framework Knitters, in such manner as to the House should seem meet. The petition was referred to a committee, to report upon the subject. The Hosiers were inimical to the proposed measure. In the month of March, a meeting of the Framework Knitters was held at the great room in the Bath Garden, to organize the workmen, with a view to the agitation of their case; and in April the Committee of the Associated Company resolved that General Meetings of the Fraternity should be held at Leicester, Sheepshead, Hinckley, Narborough, Wigston, Ullesthorpe, Syston, and Mountsorrel, at which Mr Hallam was announced as the person who was to give a full account of the proceedings adopted relative to some new regulations in a Charter to be obtained by the Framework Knitters to prevent frauds and abuses, and to limit the number of apprentices to be taken by members of the fraternity. We infer that the workmen were partially successful in their movement; since in October the Committee invited their Brethren of the Town and County to be present in Leicester, on the 10th of that month, as Mr.

Reynolds, clerk to the Worshipful Company of Framework Knitters, was to sit on that day, in order to admit Brethren Framework Knitters to their freedom, under the sanction of the Royal Charter. The Committee exhorted all interested in the manufacture to attend, hoping they would consider the regulation of the trade by law and rule to be as necessary as it was for the State to be so regulated.

In May, the feelings of the townspeople were stirred, and their woist passions roused, by an event well calculated to do so—the alleged murder of a townsman by a foreigner. The year before, a Frenchman named Soules, an officer and prisoner of war on parole, came to the town, announcing himself to be a teacher of his native language and fencing. He frequented the billiard room at the Lion and Dolphin Inn, Market-place. Here he met Mr. James Fenton, with whom he played, losing a few shillings which he was unable to pay on the spot. An altercation here ensued between the two men. Soules, conceiving himself to be grossly insulted by Fenton, challenged Fenton to fight him either with the sword or the pistol, or otherwise apologize for his conduct. Fenton refused to do either, and shortly after, in order to avoid the rencontre, fled to the house of his mother, who was landlady of the Green Dragon Inn. Thither Soules pursued him, and in so doing came in contact with John, the brother of James Fenton, the offender, who directly seized Soules, and blows passed between them. While John Fenton was grappling with Soules, the latter drew a pistol and shot Fenton through the neck; the wounded man instantly dropping to the ground. His assailant escaped without his hat, his face bespattered with blood; the cry of "murder" being raised by the people who followed him into the Market-place and through the streets. He ran to the Three Crowns, and sought refuge in a closet in one of the garrets, whence he was taken by the constables; after which, the same evening, he was committed to gaol by the Mayor. The bullet had entered the back of the head and passed out at the lower part of the chin of the unfortunate Fenton, and thus made a mortal wound, under which he languished till Sunday evening, when he died.

Soules was tried at the Summer Assizes, in the Guildhall, on the charge of murder. The proceedings occupied six hours; the jury at the close bringing in their verdict of guilty. But the evidence on the record, together with the verdict, having been laid before the Court of Queen's Bench—while its decision was that Soulds had been guilty of murder, a special messenger appeared at the same time with the King's pardon. When the body of John Fenton was laid in the grave, near the south doorway of St. Martin's Church, a stone, recording his decease, and indignantly protesting against the injustice of the verdict (the inscription being written by Charles Rozzell, the local poet), was raised over the place of sepulture. The gravestone is still in existence. Soules left the town, and it was once thought fell beneath the guillotine during the Reign of Terror in Paris; but in 1802—twenty-four years after the date of his trial—the late Mr. William Gardiner encountered him on board ship, on his (Soules') return to France, when Napoleon was Consul.

An agitation among the Framework-er-knitters, to procure legislative interference in their manufacture, absorbed the attention of the working classes in the year 1779. By virtue of a royal charter, a "Court of Assistants" was established, to which the stockingmakers were summoned, to be admitted to their freedoms; the Court holding its sitting at the White Hart, Coal Hill, in the month of April. The workmen complained of the existence of frauds, abuses, and the exaction of frame-rents. On the 5th of May, leave was asked to bring in a bill into the House of Commons, to redress the grievances complained of, but it was rejected, and disturbances took place in consequence, at Nottingham, where the riot act was read. In Leicester, a disposition to create a tumult was manifested on Monday evening, June 14, chiefly by strangers to the place; though no necessity was found to call upon either constables or soldiers to interfere for the preservation of the peace.

The Leicestershire Militia (which had returned from Liverpool under the command of Lieut.-Colonel Pochin the previous December) marched to Bristol in May, where they were stationed till August 21, when they were ordered off to Plymouth; and, while there, were joined by their colonel, the Duke of Rutland. They broke up their camp in December.

A number of French prisoners who had been brought from Tavistock in Devonshire remained in this town about six months, and produced agreeable impressions upon the inhabitants by their light hearted and amiable manners. They behaved well, and were very civilly treated. On the third of February they left here for Dover; singing and dancing on departing from this place. They were free from boasting, temperate and even plain in living, and paid the debts they had contracted while here resident.

The Leicestershire Militia were encamped at Plymouth in June, 1780, and volunteers from this district had offered themselves to serve in the army; and much need had the country of their services, for England was now at war with France, Spain, and America, sixteen Russian men-of-war lying in the Channel, with numerous transports to convey stores to our enemies. The Militia returned home in November, 1781, from Roborrow Downs in Devonshire, after an absence of two years and nearly six months. Crowds met them near the Dane Hills, where the companies halted for the last time before entering the town.

Towards the close of the year, Mr. and Mrs Kemble and Miss Kemble made their appearance on the boards of the Theatre, in the Haymarket, when the former played John Moody in the "Provoked Husband," the second lady taking the part of "Lady Wronghead," and the last impersonating Lady Townley. They performed here on a few occasions in December and the January following.

The Earl of Shelbourne having communicated to the Lord Lieutenant a plan for strengthening the hands of the Government, by raising volunteers in the different towns of the country, a meeting was held in the Castle in 1782, to consider the proposal, when Sir Thomas Fowke read a plan lo the assembly; but after some discussion, it was negatived.

At the close of the year, the first movement for a Reform of the Parliamentary System of this country, was begun in Yorkshire; certain preparatory resolutions having been adopted by gentlemen of that county, which were forwarded by the Rev. C. Wyvill to the Corporation of Leicester. The Yorkshire Reformers proposed to introduce a bill into Parliament for the abolition of fifty of the most obnoxious boroughs, but enabling the electors resident therein to vote as freeholders in the counties; to repeal the Septennial Act; and to admit proprietors of copyhold lands, with fine certain, of the yearly value of 40s., to vote for county members. The Corporation of Leicester, having received the propositions, and deliberated upon them, resolved on a strenuous opposition to them, and expressed their opinion of the tendency of all committees and associations, other than Parliamentary ones, intended to alter the Constitution, as calculated "to create at least anarchy and confusion." Consistently with their views, early in the following year, when the Eeform movement again came under the formal condemnation of the Corporation, at a Common Hall, held on January the 17th, they resolved unanimously that the Constitution of the country stood " unparalleled in excellence, owing to the equilibrium which it preserved throughout its grand component parts," and that an alteration might destroy the balance, and therefore confuse, if not overturn, the whole. The Corporation further deprecated the agitation of such a measure as unseasonable, as well as unnecessary and impracticable; as the Government was then braving a world in arms, and its undivided attention was required to secure a peace at once safe and honourable. The authorities accordingly agreed to send instructions to the Hon. Booth Grey and Mr. Darker, the Borough Members, strenuously to oppose "any alterations" which might be attempted to be made "in the present Representation of the People in Parliament."

The Militia (which in the year preceding had been stationed at Hull) left Scarborough for Leicester in February, 1783, marching in three divisions. Their route lay by York, Tadcaster, Doncaster, Worksop, Mansfield, Nottingham, and Loughborough, and they were fourteen days on the road. The *corps* was disembodied in the third week in March.

Great rejoicings took place on Monday, August 10, to celebrate the event of the Prince of Wales (afterward George IV.) attaining his majority. The morning was ushered in by the ringing of bells, and a grand entertainment was provided by the Mayor. In the evening a large bonfire was made in the Market-place, and several hogsheads of ale given to the populace. Earl Ferrers also invited the Corporation to an entertainment at Staunton Harold, and sent half a buck, a brace of carp, a pike", with pines, melons, and so forth, as a present to the authorities! On Monday, October 5, Peace was proclaimed at the usual places in the town; but not a member of thd Corporation, not a single inhabitant, attended-the ceremony; not a bell rang in any 01 the church-towers, not a bonfire blazed, not a festive dinner was anywhere given, to rejoice over the return of peace; for it was one which was considered humiliating to the nation!

At the commencement of the year 1784 the country was in a state of great political excitement, owing to the proceedings of the "Coalition Ministry" in supporting a measure of which the object was to destroy the privileges of the Eastt India Company, and whose policy had occasioned his dismissal. The Corporation of this town used their influence to sustain the cause of the Company and the Tory party, and with this, view adopted an address to the King, at a Common Hall, held on the 19th of January, expressing their utmost satisfaction that his Majesty had been pleased to dismiss from his councils men who had attempted to enforce such arbitrary measures. The inhabitants of the town also held a separate meeting at

the Exchange, when a similar address to the King was resolved on unanimously. In March the Corporation presented Mr. Pitt with the freedom of the borough. The great statesman acknowledged the honour, for which he expressed his warmest thanks in a letter to the Town Clerk (Mr. John Heyrick.)

The winter was bitterly severe, the rivers being frozen all over the country. The Soar was so thoroughly set with ice, that a masquerade was held upon it, near the Vauxhall Gardens, on Monday, February 2, 1785. when Harlequin, Columbine, Pantaloon, and Clown, were represented, and thousands of spectators assembled upon the hanks and West Bridge to witness the performances, Another aspect of the season was its effect upon the condition of the poor, who were in great distress, and who were relieved by means of a public subscription. More than £400 was raised, which was applied in disposing of bread at half price, and retailing coals at 4d. per hundred.

Although the Tory Coiporation of this town set its face against the movement in favour of Parliamentary Reform, its authority was not absolute; as the friends to political progress in Leicester and neighbourhood proved, by forming themselves into a society, in the month of September, for the purpose of asserting their principles: They designated their society the " Revolution Club;" in reference to that great epoch in the annals of our country which is identified with the abdication and flight of the last of the Stuarts, and the accession of William, Prince of Orange, by whom the Bill of Eights was granted, and in whose reign the principles of popular freedom and the rights of conscience were recognized. Clement Winstanley, Esq., was appointed the President. It was established for the purpose of "uniting the independent interest of the town and county of Leicester; preserving the freedom of election: and maintaining the other rights and franchises of the burgesses and others; and supporting and defending them against any oppression or invasion they might suffer from the undue exertions of mis-

placed power, or the venal influence of the enemies to freedom." A yearly meeting was appointed to be kept every 4th of November. Fortnightly meetings were also held, the place of meeting being the Lion and Lamb Inn, On the 4th of November, this year, general meetings of the members were held at that house and at the Bear and Swan Inn, at which Mr. Winstanley presided. Two hundred and forty members dined together, and liberal subscriptions were entered into on the occasion.

Hitherto, no mail coaches had commenced running from Leicester northward—those which were in use were merely stage coaches. When new mails were first put on the roads, towards the close of the year, their arrival in the town stirred up all the curious and those who were fond of sight-seeing. As the new carriages rattled along the streets at a great speed, the discharge of fire-arms announced their approach, the coachmen and guards wearing the royal livery of scarlet and gold, and having blunderbusses thrown over their shoulders, with pistols thrust into their belts. Crowds collected round the vehicles, admiring them and being fully impressed with the arms richly emblazoned on the panels, and viewing with considerable reverence the King's gaudily-attired servants. The mail from London arrived at the post-office about nine o'clock in the morning, and the mails from Leeds and Manchester about six in the evening.

Ninety years ago, the inhabitants of Leicester had no suburban walks, other than the ill paved or miry roads, or the footpaths to the neighbouring villages; the Corporation therefore resolved on providing a public promenade. For this purpose, at a Common Hall, it was unanimously determined to set apart a piece of ground, ten yards wide, from the north end of St. Mary's field next to the town to the gnte opposite the turnpike leading for London. The whole extent was announced to be more than a mile, and was intended to be planted on each side with elms. The first part of the walk was designed to be a vista, seen from the Recorder's Garden, and continuing to the corner of the fields opposite the windmill. The Corporation also allowed the gravel to be got from its pits to cover the walk. As the probable cost of its formation was estimated at £250, a public subscription was commenced to raise the amount. Before the close of the year 1785, the " New Walk" or "Queen's Walk" (as. it was at first called) was opened to the enjoyment of the public.

Persevering efforts were now made to establish canal communication between Leicester and other places. In June, a meeting of inhabitants was held in the Exchange, when £13,500 was subscribed towards the proposed navigation from Leicester to the Trent. Some delay was occasioned by the neglect of the appointed surveyor; but it was resolved, should he report favourably of the scheme, to call a meeting of the proprietors of land interested in it, and, with their consent, to make an application to Parliament for a bill. In September a general meeting of the subscribers was held at the Castle; Lords Rawdon and Ferrers opposing the scheme. The Earl of Denbigh was in part friendly to it, and spoke with more candour than the other peers, who declared their intention of opposing the bill in Parliament. One fact remained unanswered at the meeting, namely, that 2d. per hundred, upon an average, would be saved in the purchase of coals consumed in the town and neighbouring country; exclusive of the great saving to the public in all other heavy goods. Another meeting was held at the Castle in October (the High Sheriff in the chair), at which a petition to Parliament in favour of the bill was adopted unanimously. In November, a third meeting was held at the Castle— Gerard Noel Edwards, Esq., in the chair—and a resolution agreed to without dissent, to forward a petition to Parliament for a General Navigation from Coleorton to Loughborough and thence to Leicester.

The "Revolution Club" held its annual dinner in November at the Lion and Lamb, White Lion, and Bear and Swan Inns, over which Sir John Danvers, Bart., presided. Three hundred members dined on the occasion. Among the toasts drunk were these: "The Immortal o

Memory of William the Third," "The Cause of Civil Liberty throughout the World," "His Grace the Duke of Rutland and other absent Members." An Ode, specially written by Charles Rozzell, the laureate of the Club, was recited amid the applause of the company.

Early in May, 1786, the Leicester and Loughborough Navigation Bill was introduced into the House of Commons, when it was lost by a majority of nine.

Up to this date, no Sunday Schools, either in connection with churches or chapels, were in existence in Leicester. The children of the poor were therefore left untaught on the only day when instruction could be imparted to them in respect of religious matters. The principal mover in the establishment of the system was H. Coleman, Esq., who was chairman of a meeting the inhabitants held on June 14, in the Exchange, when several resolutions were adopted, of which this was the principal:—" That the general plan of this Institution be upon the same liberal principles with those of the Society established in London for the support and encouragement of Sunday Schools; and that this charity shall extend to the children of the poor of every denomination." Churchmen and Dissenters cooperated in the work of extending the system, which from that day to the present has been sustained without intermission, and with increased usefulness. On. Sunday, the 23rd of July, eleven schools were opened, and the children were conducted twice in the day to their respective places of worship. A subscription list, ultimately amounting to £133 9s., was commenced, to raise funds for defraying the necessary expenses incurred in the outset of the proceeding.

The spirit of brutality existing among the people at this period indicates the great necessity of the educational movement described in the previous paragraph. Prizefighting at this time was a frequent practice; Mendoza being now in all the questionable glory of his reputation. A very notable pugilistic display took place on the 22nd of May, 1787, between Loydall, the celebrated Whitwick collier, and Dore, of this town, which was witnessed by more than five thousand persons. After bruising each other for eighty minutes, the collier by one furious blow struck the Leicester champion to the ground, entirely disabled. The rough chivalry of the victor induced him, when Dore was on crutches for a fortnight after the battle, to give him a shilling out of his scanty earnings, and to affirm with an oath, "Thou shalt never want coals while I live."

The "Revolution Club" held two meetings this year, one on June 14, when Edward Dawson, Esq., took the chair, and another on the 5th of November. On the second occasion, the stewards were Sir W. C. Farrell Skeffington, Bart., and Walter Ruding, Esq. The annual dinner took place at the Lion and Lamb, Bear and Swan, and White Swan Inns. Upwards of five hundred persons dined together, and several hogsheads of ale were distributed to the populace. But the recent decease of the Duke of Rutland—one of the Club's chief patrons—depressed the convivial spirit of the members, an effect which was thus alluded to in Rozzell's *Revolution Ode:*—

"How shall the Muse of Freedom tune her Song,
Now Belvoir's Tow'rs are all with Cjpress hung?"

In October Howard, the Philanthropist, visited the town. While here, he inspected the borough prison, with which he found great fault, describing it as unwholesome and unsafe;. and he severely condemned the custom of allowing the keeper to sell ale. He next visited the County Bridewell, which he highly commended for its neatness and cleanliness. In like manner he complimented the keeper of the County Gaol upon its cleanliness, and suggested alterations to be made by the justices. He afterwards visited the Infirmary, with the management of which he found great fault, particularly with the situation of the Asylum, and pointed out seme amendments that he considered necessary. In the las instance, Mr. Howard's visit was productive of immediate attention to the matters complained of, the governors calling in Mr. Johnson, architect, to their assistance, and ordering various changes to he effected in the ventilation and drainage, and limewashing to he done and other improvements made, which were adopted at their meeting held on the 12th of November.

On Monday, October 15, the Militia assembled for the first time under the Act of Parliament passed a short time previously. The regiment was stated to be the best ever before raised; not one of the new men being above twentyone years of age. Their clothing was said to be good, and the band equal to any in the service. The Duke of Rutland was Colonel; George Pochin, Esq., LieutenantColonel; and — Cheselden, Esq., the Major.

Up to the year 1785 the process of spinning worsted for the Leicester trade was of a purely domestic character, but at this date Mr. Joseph Brookhouse conceived that worsted might be spun by machinery. He was assisted with capital by Mr. Joseph Whetstone, of Northgate-street, and Mr. Coltman, of Shambles-lane. The two latter gentlemen had already formed large connections—the one as a spinner, and the other as a manufacturer of hosiery. The business was carried on in Northgate-street, upon the premises of Mr. Whetstone. The same dread of the injurious effects of machinery upon their labour which the Framework-knitters had shown some years before, extended to the worsted spinners in connection with the application of Mr. Brookhouse's invention to their manufacture. In consequence they became greatly incensed against the new firm, and vowed they would destroy the machinery recently brought into requisition. On the night of Saturday, December 1, after having been openly requested to assemble at the White Lion and Red Lion Inns, a mob of drunken and infuriated people, some furnished with missiles of various kinds, proceeded to Mr. Whetstone's premises, which they at once attacked; being resisted by the occupier of the house and his family

with discharges from fire-arms. The mob, however, succeeded in obtaining possession of the lower storey; sacking the premises, and destroying everything which fell in their way. Mr. Whetstone was lowered by a rope from a back window, and thus escaped their violence. The mob also went to Mr. Coltman's, and the houses of several personal friends of Mr. Whetstone, where similar outrages were committed. Not content with the damage they had done in the town, the party, a day or two after, visited Market Harborough, where they found a spinning machine, which they burnt in the Market Place. Subsequently, hearing that another machine was being worked at Melton, they went there, but found they had been misled; the suspected owner assuring them he not only had no machine but never intended to have one. The result of the mad movement was that worsted spinning was driven from Leicester for more than twenty years. The manufacture was carried on in large factories at Bromsgrove, Warwick, Bedworth, Arnold, Bristol, Kettering, Nottingham, and elsewhere; the inhabitants of Leicester meanwhile losing all the commercial and other advantages which would have accrued therefrom, had it remained here during that interval.

About this period the agitation for the overthrow of the negro-slavery system was initiated in this locality. A subscription had been commenced in promotion of an application to Parliament for abolishing the slave trade, which was liberally encouraged, and a meeting was held at the Castle, on the 7th of February, 1788, when Joseph Oradock, Esq., was called to the chair, and resolutions condemnatory of the slave trade, and calling for the adoption of remedies, were unanimously accepted. The petition received about five hundred signatures. The clergy of the county also met, with the Archdeacon at their head, and adopted an anti-slavery petition.

About this date the formation of an Agricultural Society for the county, under the presidency of Lord Rawdon was announced. Among the subscribers were Lords Huntingdon, Harborough,

Winchelsea, Gainsborough, and Bawdon, and Sir John Palmer, Colonel Hastings, and Messrs. Abney, Bakewell, Buckley, Burgess, B. Carver, R. Cresswell, John Cave Brown,. Joshua Grundy, T. Paget, W. Pochin, T. Pares, T. Pares, jun., C. Winstanley, Dr. Kirkland, Bev. W. Gresley, and others. The first meeting was held on April 2, on which occasion subscriptions were entered into of one guinea each, and Mr. Mansfield's bank was appointed to be the place for payment.

This year the Bevolution Club made an unusual demonstration, which they called a "Jubilee," to celebrate the hundredth anniversary of the memorable landing of William, Prince of Orange, "who preserved the liberties of this country, and secured a free constitution to every Briton." At the dinner (held at the Lion and Lamb, White Swan, and Bear and Swan Inns) 672 persons feasted. Colonel Pochin read a resolution on the occasion, adopted by the Committee, "that it is the opinion of this meeting that this town is improperly represented in Parliament," and informed the meeting that a gentleman, a member of the club, would offer himself as a candidate on the occasion of the occurrence of a vacancy in the representation—an announcement received with an outburst of applause. A spirited ode, written by Charles Bozzell, was recited at the dinner. A kind of counter-demonstration to the Jubilee, it may be assumed, was the Mayor's Feast, held in November, when Henry Watchorn, Esq. , gave a grand entertainment, served up in two courses. The king had by this time become afflicted with symptoms of insanity, which occasioned this toast to be given from the chair: "A speedy re-establishment of the health of our beloved Sovereign." When "God save the King" was sung, every voice joined in the strain, and re-echoed the prayer with energetic feeling.

The Jacobites had now become Tories, and Pitt was their idol. In Leicester, they began in the y.ear 1789 (through their leaders on the Corporation), by resolving that the thanks of that body be given to the Right Hon.

William Pitt, Chancellor of the Exchequer, and to the Borough and County Members, for their support of "the important right of the Lords and Commons of this Realm to provide the means of supplying the defect of the personal exercise of the Royal authority, arising from his Majesty's indisposition." The Tories wished to confer the Eoyal authority on the Prince Eegent, while the Whigs were desirous of postponing the measure, in the hope of the king's early recovery. In April, however, George had so far recovered that addresses were forwarded to him and his Queen, congratulating them on the King's restoration to health.

While the townsmen of Leicester were speculating about street alterations, or conversing only about the militia muster or the last freemason's dinner, events of surpassing interest were transpiring across the Channel. In July, forty thousand people of Paris rose in arms, and a day or two after captured the Bastille, beheading its governor and the Archbishop of Paris, and carrying their heads on poles through the thoroughfares; the House of Representatives thereupon declaring itself the National Assembly, and the Revolution being fully inaugurated. The startling news of these proceedings reached this town but slowly; yet the Conservatives of Leicester soon bestirred themselves in the formation of a "Constitutional Society," whose beacon light was Mr. Pitt. They held a first meeting late in October, and a second on the 9th of November. At the latter they adopted a number of resolutions, their object being obviously to counteract the efforts of the Revolution Club, who, not deterred by the appearance of affairs in France, held their customary anniversary meeting on Wednesday, November 4; the stewards being E. C. Hartopp, Esq., and Lieut.-Colonel Packe. In addition, many gentlemen of the county and town were present, with upwards of five hundred freemen of the borough. William Pochin, Esq. (one of the members of the county) and Robert Abney, Esq., of Lindley, were unanimously chosen stewards for the year ensuing.

At the close of 1789, a meeting of importance, marking the position assumed by the Dissenters of this district, was held at the Lion and Lamb Inn, to consider what measures were proper to be pursued to procure the repeal of the Corporation and Test Acts, and other penal statutes in matters of religion. The different town congregations requested that every congregation in the county would appoint a delegate or delegates to attend with their ministers on the business. Accordingly, on the 20th of November, a large number of ministers and delegates met at the place appointed, and put Dr. Thomas Arnold in the chair. They adopted twelve resolutions, of which the main purpose has been suggested.

In the year 1790, the unparalleled political agitation prevalent throughout the country manifested itself, in this locality, in the movements of the two antagonistic political parties. The Conservatives held frequent meetings of the Constitutional Society, and the Liberals (who designated themselves "The Independent Interest") dined together to celebrate the National Thanksgiving Day for his Majesty's recovery; upwards of fifteen hundred persons sitting down to the feast, including many of the leading gentlemen of the town and county. The Revolution Club also re-organised itself, and celebrated its anniversary on the 4th of November. At an earlier period of the year the Dissenters held a general meeting in the town, attended by Dissenting Deputies of the three denominations resident in Derby, Nottingham, Lincoln, Warwick, Worcester, Shrewsbury, and Stafford. The groundwork of their position was thus expressed in one of their resolutions: "That all subjects of the State, conducting themselves in an equally peaceable manner, are equally entitled, not only to protection in the possession of their peaceable rights, but also to any civil honours or emoluments, which are accessible to other subjects, without any regard to their religious opinions or practices." The holding of this meeting created a warm political controversy; the Corporation at a Common Hall dep-

recating the admission of Dissenters into civil offices, on the ground of its giving them perpetual opportunities of injuring the state, "by applying the powers with which they would be entrusted for the support of their own party"!

The establishment of Sunday Schools having proved to be of advantage, they were carried on for five years; but in the year 1791 the zeal of their promoters began to relax, and therefore an effort was needed to maintain them in a state of efficiency, and the original advocates of the system were exhorted not to desert the cause. At a meeting of the Special Committee of Subscribers, held in St. Martin's Vestry, on the 28th of April, resolutions were passed embodying this appeal, as the expenditure incurred had exceeded the income.

A matter of more general interest than any other to the townspeople, was the passing of the bill for canalizing the Soar from Leicester to Loughborough. It received the the Royal assent on Friday, May 13. The measure had been long and anxiously desired by the public. On the 1st of June, a meeting of the proprietors of the Navigation was held at the Three Crowns, to consider on the proper methods of facilitating the plan. Several resolutions having that ohject in view were passed, and contracts for the works were advertised for in the *Journal*.

A few years before this date, a stranger named Richard Phillips became an inhabitant of Leicester, announcing himself as a teacher of mathematics and the other sciences. He subsequently became a bookseller, carrying on his business at the corner of Gallowtree Gate and Humberstone Gate, where he opened a pamphlet-room, in which the works of Paine and others, advocating the principles of the French Eepublicans, were provided for perusal. In this year (1791) a "Church and King" mob burned down Dr. Priestley's old and new Meetinghouses at Birmingham, with several houses of leading Liberals, and destroyed the valuable philosophical apparatus, books, and manuscripts of that learned and distinguished divine. Mr. Phillips's exertions were not merely of a political nature, one of his special efforts being the origination of a Literary Society, which was instituted for the purpose of establishing a Permanent Library. The date of its foundation was July 1, 1789.

The agitation for the abolition of the Slave Trade was continued in this town in the year 1792 by the holding of a meeting of the inhabitants on the 1st of February, at which an address was delivered by Thomas Babington, Esq.; but it is remarkable that at this time the arrangements for the relief of the destitute in Leicester were so inadequate that it was found necessary to apply to Parliament for an act to furnish the inhabitants with power to erect a House of Industry, wherein the necessitous poor of the several parishes might be employed, relieved, and maintained.

The decease of Charles Eozzell, the local poet and politician, occurred this year. At twelve years of age, unassisted by a master, he commenced the study of the Latin language; becoming acquainted with Horace and Virgil in a few years. His *forte* lay in satire, his favourite author being Churchill, in whose style he modelled his compositions.

The excitement created by events in France grew in every succeeding month this and the following year. The various societies and clubs having forwarded addresses of congratulation to the French National Assembly, on its success, the king issued a proclamation for the suppression of seditious publications at home, and of seditious correspondence with people abroad. In Paris, Louis the Sixteenth was besieged in the Tuileries, his Swiss Guards being slain in his defence, and his family afterwards incarcerated in the Temple. Eed Republicanism was now in the ascendant, the streets of Paris witnessing the murder of twelve hundred persons. One effect produced on the public mind was the withdrawal of many persons from the Liberal standard, and the alienation of English Reformers generally from the cause of the French Revolution. At an assembly of the inhabitants, held in the Town Hall, on December 17, at

which persons of all parties attended, resolutions were adopted expressing their firm determination to support the Constitution of Great Britain, and their sincere and steady attachment to the King's person and family. Only a few Reformers declined to sail with the stream of re-action; among whom were Mr. George Bown and Mr. Richard Phillips, who, in the early part of the year, had began a Liberal journal, called the *Leicester Herald.*

At this period of universal panic, in regard to political affairs, when almost every body raised the cry of "mad dog" against those who still adhered to Liberal principles, in spite of the deeds by which they had been caricatured and disgraced in France, even the Licensed Victuallers of Leicester joined in the demonstration against the so-called "Jacobins." They had a meeting at which they resolved they would suffer no person or persons to hold any society in their respective houses, or to make use of any expressions which would have a tendency to subvert or disturb the Government, without giving immediate notice to the Mayor or other magistrates. Meanwhile, the "Constitutional Society" had held a meeting on the last day of the year 1792, at which it lifted up its voice in opposition to the storm raised by the Tory nobility, gentry, and clergy throughout the district, in indiscriminate denunciation of all Reformers. An advertisement was published signed by Clement Winstanley, William Pochin, Charles James Packe, Henry Coleman, jun., John Simpson, William Bentley, and Thomas Buxton, Esqrs., and others who had been known as Whigs before the outbreak of the French Revolution, but who had taken fright at the excesses committed by the "Rouges" of Paris, and had united with the Tories in adopting resolutions in condemnation of seditious assembles and publications. This advertisement "the Constitutional Society," in a manifesto signed by Mr. George Bown, the secretary, replied to, by declaring "its concurrence in the sentiments of the Duke of Richmond on the subject of Parliamentary Reform, and its warm ap-

proval of Mr. Pox's manly and independent political conduct, adding that the society assented to the resolutions lately passed at the Town Hall, but regarded all such meetings as mere manoeuvres of place-men and courtiers." A reply from the Committee of the Association for promoting the King's proclamation was provoked by these observations, the society being called by it "a factious club," whose object was declared to be to render the unwary disaffected to the Government, and discontented with the necessary measures it might adopt. The Government now took proceedings of a persecuting character against the leading Liberals. It may be here interposed that the sentence to death, and execution, of Louis the Sixteenth in the month of January, 1793, spread a thrill of horror throughout all England. A war with France was therefore hotly demanded. In the month of March, in accordance with a requisition from the County Grand Jury, the High Sheriff convened a meeting of the nobility, clergy, freeholders, and others, of which the understood object was to swell the outcry for an armed conflict with the French Revolutionists. When the High Sheriff announced the meeting for the 9th of April, four Whig gentlemen—John Simpson, Charles James Packe, Clement Winstanley, and Walter Euding—declared their disapprobation of the proceeding and their opinion of the non-necessity of the meeting. It was held however, Lord Ferreis moving an address to the King in approval of the war, which was seconded by Sir Charles Cave and carried, there being only two dissentients present. The day after this meeting, Mr. Richard Phillips was placed on his trial at the Town Hall for selling a publication called the "Jockey Club," and two of the works of Thomas Paine. In spite of all his protests and statements in extenuation of his conduct, the defendant was sentenced by the Recorder to eighteen months' imprisonment in the Borough Gaol. The revolting deeds of the *sans-culottes* of Paris, with the decapitation of the French King, operated so strongly on the minds of the local Liberals, as to prevent any meetings of the Revolution Club afterwards. Occasionally an ardent spirit (like Mr. George Bown) defied public opinion, and did not hesitate to proclaim himself an admirer of most of the deeds of the National Assembly and the Convention. But the moderate Reformers for the time sank their differences, and united with the Tories in testifying at public assemblies their attachment to the Constitution, and their hatred of the Red Republic. When, therefore, Mr. Mansfield, the Mayor, gave his feast in November, at his venison dinner, followed by a rich and varied dessert, Earl Ferrers sat down with Viscount Wentworth, Sir Charles Cave with William Pochin, Esq., John Peach Hungerford, Esq., with Charles James Packe, Esq., and John Simpson, Esq., with William Herrick, Esq., and other Whig and Toryesquires, to drink loyal and constitutional toasts amid repeated bursts of applause.

It may be noted that this year the Leicestershire Militia, commanded by Colonel Pochin, marched from Leicester to Norwich, where in June the four companies took part in the celebration of the King's birthday, and much praise was accorded to them for their steady and military appearance.

The attention of the people of Leicester was somewhat diverted from the political frenzy in which it had become absorbed by the progress being made in canal communication between Loughborough, Melton, and other places, and Leicester. In February 1794 two boats arrived at their respective wharves in Leicester, laden with merchandize from Gainsborough. Each returned with cargoes of wool consigned to merchants in that town. But on an expectation of invasion by the French the young men of all classes in Leicester were called on to enrol themselves-in a public book, as ready to serve in the defence-of the country on the landing of the enemy. A large sum was also subscribed by the county magnates for the augmentation of the militia. At a meeting in April, presided over by Earl Ferrers, it was resolved that a number of men be added to each company, and that not fewer

than one hundred be formed into cavalry. As a consequence growing out of this movement, a special meeting took place, under the auspices of Penn Assheton Curzon, Esq., M.P., for promoting the formation of the Leicestershire Volunteer Yeomanry, to consist of six troops, each containing not fewer than fifty men, officers included.

While, however, the Tory party was urging on the war with France with unrestrained vehemence and passion, the Reformers were advocating peaceful measures. Thia drew down upon them the rage of their political opponents, who insisted that they were friendly to the introduction of all the horrors of the sanguinary party across the Channel into this country. There was now living in Leicester Mr. Harley Vaughan, a son of the Venerable Serjeant Vaughan, a godson of the fourth Earl of Oxford, and an accomplished young gentleman. He was a second master of the Free Grammar School. He was associated with Mr. Richard Phillips, Mr. Paget (surgeon), Mr. "William Gardiner, and other young Reformers of that period. One day he was seen reading a hand-bill, which he had received from a coachman, the purpose of which was to summon a meeting in favour of Peace and Reform at Manchester. This he gave to a person who was then a supporter of the Tory Corporation, who passed it on to the local authorities. At the Quarter Sessions in April they arraigned Mr. Vaughan on a charge of distributing seditious papers; tending to inflame the minds of the people and render them dissatisfied with the Government. Mr. Vaughan was found guilty, and sentenced by the the Recorder to three months' imprisonment in the Borough Gaol. On his release, brooding over his wrongs, and the persecution to which he had been subjected, he walked into the fields between Leicester and Belgrave, until he reached a pool of water, when, tying his legs together, he threw himself in and was drowned. About a month afterwards, Mr. George Bown was also arrested and incarcerated on a charge of pursuing seditious practices. The prejudice of the local authorities against all

Reformers was such as to betray them into even ludicrous excesses. It is related that when the "Adelphi Society," composed of the gentlemen whom we have mentioned as the associates of Mr. Harley Vaughan, erected above the roof of the room in which they met a high pole in the form of a spear, to draw the electric fluid downwards, the Corporation forwarded an intimation to the society that its meetings had a dangerous character. Rumours were also current of the "Jacobins" having met by hundreds in different parts of the towu, having assembled by the side of Stocking Wood to learn the use of arms, and having applied to a gunsmith in Leicester to furnish them with a large number of stands of arms. Meanwhile, Mr. Pitt moved and carried in the Commons the Suspension of the Habeas Corpus Act; by virtue of which any suspected person could be arrested and imprisoned without ceremony. On the King's birthday the Corporation and its supporters made enthusiastic demonstrations of loyalty.

During the remainder of the year the townsmen were mad with volunteering. The newly-raised Cavalry met on the Race-Ground for the first time, and the Leicester Volunteer Infantry mustered more than one hundred men in the Market Place in September.

It must be added, in connection with this year, that a proposal having been made at several meetings of the graziers, farmers, butchers, and others, for the establishment of an additional number of fairs for fat and lean cattle and sheep, in Leicester, the Corporation was asked to give its sanction to the measure. The days named were Jan. 4, June 1, August 1, Sept. 13, and Nov. 2, and on them the Common Hall agreed the additional fairs should be held—the cattle to stand in Millstone-lane, the sheep in the usual places.

The year 1795 was long remembered by the poor of this district in consequence of the great distress created by the high price and deficient supply of wheat; starvation having been very generally experienced. On two Saturdays in succession not a sample of wheat was exhibited in Leicester market, and on the third eight pounds per quarter was asked for the article. While this state of things continued the famished multitude, irritated against everything and everybody, thronged the streets, and on one occasion came in contact with the Leicester Volunteer Infantry. The tumultuous feeling extended to Barrow-on-Soar on the 6th of August. A waggon laden with corn was stopped there, and conveyed to the church by the populace, who refused to give up the corn. The Eev. Thomas Burnaby proceeded with the Leicester Troop of Cavalry to the scene of disorder, where the Biot Act was read. It was proposed to leave eight quarters of the grain and take away the remainder; but no sooner did the escort move on with the waggon, than they were assailed with brickbats, and shots were fired at them from the adjoining houses. The Cavalry then made a stand, and discharged their carbines at their assailants; eleven persons falling in consequence—three dead and eight dangerously wounded. The waggon was brought on to Leicester by the Cavalry, with two prisoners. A profound sensation was created by this event, which was always popularly known afterwards as the " Barrow Butchery."

So great a change had taken place in the supply of grain in the following year, that the Committee appointed for the purpose of administering relief to the poor, owing to an unexpected abundance and the reduction in prices had left on its hands such an excessive quantity of breadcorn and flour, that it had to sustain a loss of about two thousand pounds—a loss which the county left the town to sustain wholly unaided.

A place for public amusement much frequented during the middle of the last century, known as the " Vauxhall," ceased to be resorted to in the year 1797; being then sold by auction for a commercial purpose.

In the month of April, this year, the Reformers of Leicester exerted themselves, much to the disgust of their political opponents, to procure signatures to a petition to the King, condemning the conduct of his Ministers, and urging

their immediate dismissal, as the only means of p saving the Constitution and restoring peace to Europe. Within a month or so after the date of this movement, the King concluded a Treaty of Peace with the French Republic.

In this year, also, the career of a once notorious highwayman and footpad, a terror to the district, was brought to a close. George Davenport was convicted at the Assizes held in August of having stopped a country butcher on the high road, for the purpose of robbing him of his money. From his own confessions, Davenport had been a highwayman for eighteen years, and had deserted from different regiments forty times. The unfortunate man was executed at the gallows on the Red Hill, near to Birstall; to which he was driven in a postchaise, accompanied by his brother. One peculiarity attending his execution was that he was allowed to draw over bis clothes the shroud in which his body was about to be buried, intending thus to cheat the hangman out of his perquisite, which was considered to be all that was found or placed "outside the shroud" of the criminal, on his being taken down from "the fatal tree."

The news of Admiral Duncan's great victory over the Dutch Fleet, on the 11th of October, was received in Leicester with every demonstration of popular rejoicing. An entertainment was provided at the Three Crowns, attended by the principal persons of the locality, and in the evening the whole town was illuminated. The Leicester Infantry paraded the principal streets with their band, firing *feu-de-joies* at intervals.

The year 1798 was in various respects eventful; an invasion by the French under Napoleon Buonaparte having been threatened, subscriptions for the support of the war were made in Leicester on an unprecedented scale. A general meeting of the inhabitants, convened by the magistrates, was held in May, at which the establishment of an armed association for the preservation of the peace in Leicester, and within five miles of the town, was resolved upon, a committee being appointed to carry out its decisions. At this time arrests

were made of certain Liberals, who were supposed to be allies of the French Republicans. For the first time, they were this year called "Radical Reformers." In the month of September, the Leicestershire Militia, to the number of 1,000 volunteered to serve in Ireland for the suppression of the Rebellion in that country. The Duke of Rutland, then in his twentieth year, joined his regiment as Colonel. At this exciting period, the news of Nelson's great victory off the mouth of the Nile, spread like a flame of living fire over the land; warming the people into a fever of defiance and hatred of their neighbours across the Channel, and imparting to them an exultant feeling, probably never before experienced.

In the quiet country towns of England, enjoying the security afforded by an insular position, and a powerful Government, nothing noticeable happened in the year 1799. The news of foreign battles between the Russians, French, and Germans, in Italy and Switzerland, frequently reached this town; but within its precincts the flow of life was even and regular. For the first time after the Reformation, a chapel for Roman Catholic worship was erected here, in the neighbourhood of Causeway Lane, and opened for public worship on October 13, the Rev. H. Chappel being the appointed priest.

In the last year of the century, a physician named Alexander, residing at Stoneygate, was slopped by four footpads, on the road to Leicester, and robbed of his watch and some silver. Four privates in a regiment of light dragoons, then quartered in the town, were apprehended on the charge of being concerned in the robbery. Three of them were liberated—the fourth, James Murray, being committed to gaol to take his trial. He was tried at the Summer Assizes, convicted, and sentenced to be hanged on Wednesday, August 20th. Having disarmed the vigilance of the turnkeys, on the Saturday morning previous to the day on which his execution was fixed to take place, he succeeded in ascending to the roof of the building, in descending into the yard of a house outside the prison, and in escaping thence, while carrying his fetters, into the country. He fled through the fields to Peckleton, where he was soon surrounded by a crowd of villagers, who struck off his chains, gave him food, provided him with a change of dress and money, and speeded him on his flight from the gallows. He was never heard of again.

A great scarcity of bread and corn having existed in the year 1799, continued during the last year of the century. Wheat was now selling at five pounds the quarter. On the first Saturday in September, a riot occurred in the Market-place, which might have been attended with serious consequences, had not the Eiot Act been promptly read, and a party of Dragoons been on the spot for its suppression. A meeting of noblemen and gentlemen, the Duke of Eutland being in the chair, was held shortly after, to take into consideration means of alleviating the then existing distress, and resolutions were passed for that object.

The last matter in connection with the year under notice, is the erection by a proprietary of the Assembly Rooms in Hotel-street. It appears £3,300 was required, to complete the building; some difficulty having been found in raising the necessary amount. Loans of one hundred pounds each were advanced by the Duke of Rutland, the Earl of Stamford, Lord Rancliffe, Sir J. Palmer, Sir E. C Hartopp, and J. P. Hungerford, G, A. L. Keck, C. Winstanley, E. Dawson, S. Smith, C. J. Packe. T. Paget, J. King, E. Stephens, J. Mansfield, J. Willows, E. Harrison, junr., J. Johnson, T. Miller, J. E. Carter, T. B. Buxton, and David Harris, Esquires. The Assembly Rooms were opened in time for the Race Ball in September.

The Nineteenth Century offers in its advancement a striking contrast to its predecessors. In a hundred years the population had nearly quadrupled. The census returns of 1801 showed a total of 16,953. It was destined to be still more rapidly augmented by the establishment of new branches of industry in the locality. Before this epoch, the Hosiery Manufacture had remained little altered from the date of Nicholas Allsop, merely minor improvements in detail, in the construction of the frame, having been effected. Now, however, instead of stockings alone, plain and ornamental, other articles were produced; such as worsted cravats or comforters, gloves, muffatees, children's boots, and net braces. To this new kind of manufacture the name "Fancy Hosiery" was given. It was begun by Mr. William Kelly (son of Mr. William Kelly, hosier), who took into partnership his brother, Samuel, and carried on business upon premises in Belgrave Gate, and subsequently upon others near the Bow Bridge. The example of Mr. Kelly was soon followed by others—chiefly by the late Mr. Richard Harris, the founder of the firm known as "Richard Harris and Sons." Afterwards, also, the firm of William and John Dunmore succeeded in establishing an extensive business in the same line.

The religious thought of the community was now largely influenced by the Rev. Thomas Robinson, vicar of St. Mary's, who, as a teacher of "Evangelical" tenets, was earnest in an age of indifferentism. His labours were followed in the same direction by those of the Rev. Robert Hall, Baptist Minister, the pastor of the congregation assembling in Harvey Lane Chapel, whose distinguished reputation as a pulpit orator and a writer on religious subjects is recognized in the history of contemporary literature. It was not until the year 1810 that a newspaper was permanently established in the town for the maintenance of Liberal principles; the first number of the *Leicester Chronicle* having appeared in that year.

An industrial insurrection, which existed among the working population of North Leicestershire and Nottinghamshire, and spread terror throughout those districts, prevailed for some years; the intention of its promoters being to prevent the employment of machinery in connection with the hosiery and lace manufactures. The conviction and execution of James Towle was followed by the discovery of the other persons engaged in the movement; his disclosures having enabled the magistrates to bring to justice the leading conspirators, six of whom were hanged at the new drop in this town on April 17, 1317.

The proclamation of George the Fourth in Leicester was celebrated in the style of the previous century - oxen being roasted whole, and the old Conduit being filled with ale, for the gratification of the populace. About the same period the oil-lamps, which had hitherto lighted the streets, were superseded by the use of gas. In a population of 30,125, in the year 1821, this invention had become a necessity.

In this History it is not considered appropriate to allude to matters of a party political nature. The election of 1826, however, stands out as an event of more than usual interest. It was a great trial of strength between the Corporation, then strongly combined in support of high Conservative principles, and the Liberals. It took place in June; Sir Charles Abney Hastings and Otway Cave, Esq., being the candidates of the former, and William Evans, Esq., and Thomas Denman, Esq. (afterwards Lord Denman), of the latter party. The poll was kept open for ten days. At last, enraged by the unfair conduct (as they alleged) of the town authorities, the populace destroyed the polling-booth in the Market-place, and attacked the old Exchange. The Eiot Act was read by the Mayor, and the constables in vain endeavoured to put down the disturbance; which was not quelled until a party of Life Guards rode into the Market-place, and terrified the rioters so completely that they fled in all directions. In the year 1831 the population had become 38,904. The demand for manufacturing labour had greatly extended after the introduction of the Fancy Hosiery business, and the discovery of coal in the district around Swannington had conduced to the rapid development of steam-power machinery. The connection of Leicester with Swannington was effected in 1832 by the opening of a railroad—the third of the kind formed in this country.

William the Fourth, popularly designated the "Sailor King," having succeeded his brother, George the Fourth, within two years after his accession the Reform Bill received the royal assent. One of the early legislative fruits of this measure was the appointment of a commission to enquire into the state of the old Municipal Corporations in England and Wales. In the year 1833, Messrs. Whitcombe and Cockburn visited Leicester, as Commissioners of Enquiry, and carried on their labours at the Castle; when they called before them the Town Clerk (Mr. Burbage) and other witnesses, in opposition to and on behalf of the Corporation.

The reader will have noticed the attempt made by Mr. Phillips in 1791 to establish a Literary and Philosophical Society. This shortly fell to the ground in a period when every endeavour to promote progress in any shape was viewed with suspicion and dislike; but in an epoch of reform the project had a chance of success. When, therefore, in the year 1835, it was proposed at a meeting of a few friends to literary and philosophical pursuits, held in June, at the room of the Medical Library, the Rev. Charles Berry in the chair, to form a Society, the resolution was adopted. The opening address was read by Dr. Shaw, the acting Chairman, on the 7th of September; Mr. Alfred Paget was the Honorary Secretary.

In the course of the same year the Act was passed for the Reform of the Municipalities of this country. In this town, the old system prevailed which had been in operation substantially from the reign of Elizabeth; the Corporation being self-elected, and consequently irresponsible to the townspeople, who were ruled and taxed without their consent being sought or permitted. On the 26th of December, 1835, however, the burgesses, for the first time under the new law, chose the members of the Town Council. Thomas Paget, Esq., of Humberstone, was appointed the first Mayor under the new regime, and Mr. Samuel Stone (recently deceased) the Town Clerk. By the introduction of this Act a complete transfer of the municipal authority from the Conservative to the Liberal party was secured. Under the reformed system of town government the

burgesses have uniformly elected their representatives on the Town Council; that body has published a yearly statement of accounts; and local improvements of various kinds have been accomplished. One of the earliest acts of the New Corporation was the institution of a Police Force, consisting of fifty men, under the superintendence of Mr. Frederick Goodyer, who came down from the Metropolis, upon the recommendation of the Home Office, in the month of January, 1836. Another Liberal journal, the *Leicestershire Mercury,* commenced its existence on July 9, in the first year of the rule of the new municipal body.

The reign of William the Fourth terminating with his decease on June 20, 1837, he was succeeded by his niece, the Princess Victoria, the daughter of the Duke of Kent.

233 FROM A.D. 1837 TO A.D. 1876. Chapter XIII.

The accession of Queen Victoria to the throne of the United Kingdoms was an event hailed with universal rejoicings, and in no provincial town with more genuine demonstrations of loyalty than in Leicester. In her reign, the town has continued to make rapid strides in commercial prosperity and social improvement. Railway communication between Leicester and Derby was commenced in 1840: and the year after, the population numbered 50,806. The *Leicester Advertiser* issued its first number on January 1, 1842, as a neutral journal. The trade and manufacture, and public confidence in financial operations, received a great shock through the stoppage of payment by Messrs. Clarke, Mitchell, Philips, and Smith's bank, in the year 1843. But a discovery which proved of incalculable value in enriching some of the inhabitants, and in finding profitable employment for others, was now brought into use: there was living in Highcross-street a manufacturer, in a moderate way of business, named Brampton, who invented an improved fastener for gloves, by inserting strips of sheet Indiarubber in the cuffs of the gloves he made. He communicated the invention to the late Mr. Caleb Bedells, who,

about the year 1843, gave it a new application, by weaving a web which was used in the making of boots, and thus began what is now known as the Elastic Web Manufacture. Other enterprising manufacturers took up the idea, especially Mr. Archibald Turner, and subsequently Messrs. Hodges and Sons, and numerous improvements were the result, which cannot be here specified. Nearly coincident with the introduction of the Municipal Reform Act into operation in Leicester, was the establishment of the New Poor Law system, by the formation of the town into a Union for the administration ol the details of the measure within its limits. In the spring of 1838 the Union Workhouse had been erected. In the years 1847 and 1848 the inhabitants passed through a period of adversity and suffering which had not been precedented for generations before. For some time the reward of labour had been low and employment uncertain. In May of the former year, it was recorded that one person out of every four in the population had become dependent on his neighbours for daily subsistence. In the winter following, the distress reached its widest and most fearful prevalence; so that in the quarter ending Lady Day 1848, the number of persons relieved was 19,109 in a population estimated to be not exceeding 57,000; the expenditure for the year having been £32,000.

It was not until 1849 a Chamber of Commerce was added to our local institutions, its first meeting being held in that year, in which also the Cemetery was opened, the Town Museum formally transferred to the inhabitants by the Literary and Philosophical Society, and the Leicestershire Fine Arts' Society held an exhibition.

Other depressions of the local branches of trade occurred, at irregular intervals, in subsequent years; but, fortunately, not to so disastrous an extent as in 1847-8. There can be no doubt that the condition of the more provident of the industrial classes was much ameliorated, and that many of them were enabled to tide over those calamitous times, by the operations of that excellent institution—the Leicester Savings' Bank—in which they had laid something by "for a rainy day." A number of philanthropic gentlemen of the town and county, at whose head was the late Duke of Rutland (who filled the office of President up to his decease), availing themselves of the provisions of a then recent Act of Parliament (by which they were enabled to guarantee a certain rate of interest, with Government security, for all moneys deposited in their hands), founded this institution in the year 1817. Beginning in a very humble way, its business was for some years carried on by permission of the Mayor, in the Magistrates' Room at the Old Exchange, and at later periods in hired rooms over two or three different shops in the Market-place. At the end of the first year £7,926 14s. had been received from 419 depositors, whilst only £307 1s. 4d. had been withdrawn. Three years later the deposits had increased to £17,219, and for several years the capital continued to accumulate and the number of depositors to increase. At length, however, this state of prosperity came to an end. During the fearful commercial panic of 1847 and 1848, before described, and for some time previously and subsequently, the savings of former years were drawn upon to a considerable extent—the withdrawals during the five years ending November 20, 1850, having been £10,000 in excess of the deposits.

The Queen and Prince Albert passed through Leicester in 1850. Every year since then some event or incident of interest to the public has transpired; and consequently the summarizing of them in this account becomes little better than a catalogue, or the recital of condensed annals— many particulars of secondary consequence being altogether overlooked. By the opening of the railway from Leicester to Hitchin, and so to London *via* Bedford, in the year 1857, increased facilities for intercourse with the Metropolis were secured; the route by Rugby having been already available. In the same year the *Leicester Guardian* (Conservative) was commenced by Mr. T. B. Cleveland. In

1858, the publication of the *South Midland Free Press* was removed from Kettering to Leicester.

About this period a new department of industrial enterprize found a place in this town for its extension. Like other changes, it came almost unobserved into operation. In or about the year 1851, soon after the completion of the Syston and Peterborough Railway, a number of shoemakers living between Leicester and Stamford, who had been accustomed to make heavy articles for the railway labourers on the line, were suddenly thrown out of employment. A well-known firm from Northampton, having Government orders for the description of goods described, opened a warehouse in Cank-street, in this town, and gave out materials to be made up into boots and shoes. The arrangement succeeded, and for some time the demand and supply continued. On the invention of rivetting, instead of sewing the soles to the upper leather, being applied, and machinery being introduced, at Northampton (where the trade was being prosecuted), the workmen resisted the innovations by striking against their employers. Mr. Crick then entered into the manufacture in Highcrossstreet, under the improved circumstances, and the result was its extraordinary development, and the creation of a large class of manufacturers and workpeople, which has imparted a marvellous impetus to local prosperity. When the Census year 1861 arrived, several leading houses had established themselves, and the population, which was ten years before 60,642, had become 68,186.

About the same date as that given for the commencement of the Shoe Manufacture may be assigned as that in which a trade of secondary importance was established in Leicester: we mean the Hat Making. It was introduced by Mr. Thomas Webster more than twenty years since, and was commenced in the county several years previously, having found employment for between 300 and 400 persons for a considerable part of that time. The felt-hat bodies were made by the firm of Thos. Webster and Co., first in Lancashire, where a branch was

kept for the manufacture, but afterwards brought to Leicester. Twelve years ago the firm introduced patent machinery of singular construction, and have now at work all the great improvements that have been invented for the manufacture of felt hats, by which the quality is improved and the quantity increased.

The amount invested for depositors with Government by the Savings' Bank up to 1850 was £76,275; and the business of the Institution made no further progress until after the resignation, in 1856, of the secretary, Mr. William Cooke, who had held that office since 1817. In the former year it had been resolved to purchase a site and to erect offices for carrying on the business, and the result was the Savings' Bank in Gallowtree-gate, lately vacated, which, it was then thought, would afford every facility for all future operations of the Institution. From that time, under the zealous management of the new secretary, Mr. Malin, and the greater facilities offered to depositors by the new rules adopted by the Committee, an uninterrupted flow of prosperity set in, so that by the end of 1861 the number of depositors had risen, after 1856, from 2,545 to 6,209. and the deposits from £77,972 to £130,066. Six months later, on the resignation of Mr. Malin, the present secretary, Mr. Kelly, was appointed. Sometime previously (17th May, 1861), the new " Post Office Savings' Banks Act" had been passed, and not long afterwards a branch Bank was established in connection with the Post Office in this town, followed gradually by many others throughout the county. In each succeeding year the business of the old Savings' Bank has regularly progressed, so that on the 20th May, 1874, the number of accounts had risen from 6,209 to 9,960, and the accounts invested with Government from £130,066 to £219,648. Owing to this rapid extension of the business, and the offices in Gallow tree-gate having for several years past become quite inadequate to the requirements, the Institution has been removed lately to the new and handsome Bank in St. Martin's and the Grey Friars, erected in the domestic Gothic

Style. In addition to the beneficial operations of the Savings' Bank, the numerous Sick Clubs and Friendly Societies connected with the various Orders of Odd Fellows, Foresters, Druids, &c., must not be forgotten, as having during such periods of commercial disaster afforded great assistance to the working classes in times of illness and distress, and thus relieved the pressure which would have otherwise fallen upon the rates. There are 163 Friendly Societies and 125 Charitable or Provident Societies (for the distribution of clothing, blankets, coals, &c., among the members), which have accounts with the Savings' Bank with an aggregate amount of nearly £25,000. The Penny Savings' Bank, held at the Town Hall, on Saturday evenings, has also proved of great use in promoting provident habits among the juvenile population.

Among the street improvements effected by the *New* Corporation must be noticed the removal of the East Gates obstruction. A block of buildings had long stood in this locality, consisting of a shop and houses on the west, with a weighing machine; above which was the room formerly resorted to for assemblies and theatrical representations, at the eastern end of the pile. The machine was used by the frequenters of the Hay Market; while in the reign of the second George, and during the earlier part of that of the third George, the great actors and actresses of the day figured on the stage (as already related) to the great admiration of the aristocracy and gentry of the neighbourhood. In the year 1862 the East Gates buildings were removed, and a Clock Tower was erected near the site six years after. In the month of October 1864, the *Leicester Chronicle and Leicestershire Mercury* were united under the proprietorship of Mr. Jas. Thompson. A great change was resolved on by the Town Council in 1865, in the proposed removal of the Cattle Market from the neighbourhood of Bowling-green-street to that of the Welford-road, and the erection of public slaughter-houses in connection with it at the expiration of five years. The advantages already afforded by railway

communication were added to, on the opening of the South Leicestershire Railway from Leicester to Hinckley in 1864, and by the opening of the Midland Railway from Bedford to London, for passenger traffic, in 1868. In the year following this, the Borough Lunatic Asylum near Humberstone was completed, and Dr. Finch appointed its superintendent.

Among the political movements distinguishing the eighth decade of this century was the election in January 1871 of a School Board, preparatory to the carrying out of the provisions of the Elementary Act in this town. The first Board (chosen under the operation of the minority clause) was composed of about equal numbers of the Church of England and Nonconformist, the Conservative and Liberal, sections of the community. The population this year amounted to 95,914. Compared with the return for the year 1861, it showed an unprecedented augmentation. Of the eighteen large towns in this country selected by the Registrar General for comparison in his returns relative to the public mortality, Leicester stood at the head of the column in reference to the increase in the population; for while at Bradford the decimal rate of progress between 1861 and 1871 had been 37.3, in Leicester it was 40.0; at Nottingham it was but 16.0—at Birmingham 16.1. The numbers in this town bounded from 68,186 in 1861 to 95,220 in 1871. In this year a School of Art" began its operations on premises in Bowling-green-street, with Mr. Wilmot Pilsbury as its master, and it has since been carried on successfully; there having been 251 pupils under instruction last year (1875).

The relative local proportion of Churchmen and Dissenters was indicated with general accuracy by a return made in the *Nonconformist* paper in November 6, 1872. In the statistics therein supplied, the figures relative to religious accommodation were as follows:—Churches of the Established Church, 15, with 13,178 sittings; Chapels of Nonconformists, 38, with 24,909 sittings; showing an increase in

twenty years of 7 edifices in connection with the Church of England, with 4,350 sittings; and 21 Dissenting Chapels, with 8,722 sittings. In April 1872 the new Cattle Market was opened by the Mayor and the Corporation, and about the middle of the year the *Daily Post* issued its first number in Leicester.

During the few last years, the principal events requiring mention in this summary are the origination of the Leeds Company scheme for laying down tramways in the Borough, to which the Town Council gave its sanction in January 1873; the introduction of the scheme for the establishment of the Wigston Hospital Schools, the first Board of Governors having been appointed in that year; and the Erection of the new Municipal Buildings in Horse-fair-street. These are in the style called "Queen Anne." Owing to the unprecedented downfall of rain in the year 1875 the lower parts of the town were repeatedly inundated; some of the streets on the western side being two ieet or more under water. In consequence, certain measures taken by the Town Council, for the lowering of the bed of the canal and river, were pressed forward with greater expedition than previously. During the year ending November the amount received from depositors in the Savings' Bank had increased to 11,165; having been at the same date, the year before, 10,234. The balances due to depositors had, in the same interval, risen from £227,873 to £252,567.

The increased number of the population is estimated to have brought up the total, at the commencement of the year 1876, to quite 112,000; and, with the development of the various local manufactures, the future prosperity of Leicester may, in every respect, prove equal to the sanguine expectations of its zealous friends. What the position of the town may be socially and financially in 1900, should the advancement of the mass of the population in Education and Temperance be correspondent with that of its commercial and financial progress, it would be difficult to conjecture; but that the sum of human happiness will be incalculably augmented cannot be fairly denied. Compared with the pages of the history written of the sixteenth and seventeenth centuries, it will be as a day of happy sunlight after a night of troubled dreams.

INDEX

s